The Organization of the Expert Society

It is often claimed that we live in an expert society—a society where more and more individuals take expert roles in increasingly narrow fields. In contrast to more traditional experts, most of these *new* experts lack generally accepted mechanisms for the certification and legitimation of their expertise. This book focuses on these new as well as established experts and the efforts undertaken to secure and legitimate their expertise. We view these efforts as organizing attempts and study them on four different levels—the society, the market, the organization and the individual.

Based on empirical studies on these four levels of analysis, *The Organization of the Expert Society* makes the argument that current organizing initiatives in the expert society are based in an objectifying view of expertise that risks concealing and downplaying key aspects of expertise. Well-intended organizing initiatives in the expert society thus run the risk of promoting ignorance rather than securing expertise.

The book focuses on a current, general and global phenomenon: the rise and organization of an expert society. *The Organization of the Expert Society* will be key reading for scholars, academics and policy makers in the management fields of organizational theory, management consulting, organizations and society, critical management studies, as well as the disciplines of sociology, political science and social anthropology.

Staffan Furusten is an Associate Professor at the Department of Management and Organization at the Stockholm School of Economics (SSE), and the director of the Stockholm Centre for Organization Research (SCORE), an interdisciplinary research center run jointly by SSE and Stockholm University, Sweden.

Andreas Werr is a Professor at the Stockholm School of Economics (SSE) and Head of its Department of Management and Organization. He is also Head of the Center for HRM and Knowledge work at the SSE institute for Research, Sweden.

Routledge Studies in Management, Organizations and Society

This series presents innovative work grounded in new realities, addressing issues crucial to an understanding of the contemporary world. This is the world of organized societies where boundaries between formal and informal, public and private, local and global organizations have been displaced or have vanished, along with other nineteenth century dichotomies and oppositions. Management, apart from becoming a specialized profession for a growing number of people, is an everyday activity for most members of modern societies.

Similarly, at the level of enquiry, culture and technology, and literature and economics, can no longer be conceived as isolated intellectual fields; conventional canons and established mainstreams are contested. **Management, Organizations and Society** addresses these contemporary dynamics of transformation in a manner that transcends disciplinary boundaries, with books that will appeal to researchers, student and practitioners alike.

Recent titles in this series include

The Organization of
the Expert Society

Edited by
Staffan Furusten and Andreas Werr

Routledge
Taylor & Francis Group

NEW YORK AND LONDON

First published 2016
by Routledge
711 Third Avenue, New York, NY 10017

and by Routledge
2 Park Square, Milton Park, Abingdon, Oxon OX14 4RN

First issued in paperback 2018

Routledge is an imprint of the Taylor & Francis Group, an informa business

Library of Congress Cataloging in Publication Data
A catalog record for this book has been requested

ISBN 13: 978-1-138-34068-8 (pbk)
ISBN 13: 978-1-138-94795-5 (hbk)

Typeset in Sabon
by Apex CoVantage, LLC

Contents

Contributors

Susanna Alexius is a Researcher at SCORE (Stockholm Centre for Organization Research) at the Stockholm University and the Stockholm School of Economics, where she also took her PhD. Her research interests include modern management ideals and forms of control and how different kinds of organizations relate to the conditions, ideas and demands the environment puts on then. Recent studies concern issues related to value conflicts, responsibility and morality in markets as well as hybridity, corporate governance and the social meaning of money.

Jesper Blomberg is an Associate Professor at the Department of Management and Organization at the Stockholm School of Economics, where he also took his PhD. His research has focused on the organization of projects and project management tools and methods and, during the past ten years, the financial market, investment banking, its experts, organization and risk management. Recent publications include *Markets, Marketing Shares: Experts in Investment Banking* (Palgrave-Macmillan, 2012 together with Hans Kjellberg and Karin Winroth).

Pernilla Bolander is an Associate Professor at the Department of Management and Organization at the Stockholm School of Economics, where she also took her PhD. Her research interests focus on HR processes are put into practice in organizations. More specifically, recent research projects have investigated how different HR processes describe, assess, categorize and quantify individual employees. In her earlier research, she has studied employee selection and competence mapping initiatives and now focuses on Talent Management.

Staffan Furusten is an Associate Professor at the Department of Management and Organization, Stockholm School of Economics (SSE), and the Director of the Stockholm Centre for Organization Research (SCORE), an interdisciplinary research center run jointly by SSE and Stockholm University. He holds a PhD from Uppsala University and has published widely on the production and dissemination of management ideas and on management consultants. Other research interests include the transnational organization of knowledge and markets in the intersection between the public sector, the industry and the civil society and governance and management in different organizational forms.

Ingalill Holmberg is Professor in Business Administration at the Department of Management and Organization, Stockholm School of Economics (SSE). She is also Head and Research Director of the Centre for Advanced Studies in Leadership (CASL) at SSE. She holds a PhD from SSE. Her main research interest is leadership ideals and leadership as practice in organizations with global reach. Recent projects focus on responsible leadership, leadership and management in professional organizations, everyday leadership and self-branding among students. She holds editorial positions in several academic journals and has frequently been awarded for journal articles and books.

Savita Kumra is an Associate Professor at Middlesex University in Dubai. Savita combines this with a Visiting Fellowship at Cranfield School of Management and an International Research Fellowship at the Said Business School, University of Oxford. Savita has published two books in the areas of gender in organizations and diversity management, as well as a number of academic and practitioner journal articles. Savita's key research interests focus on diversity, the gendered nature of the career development process in the professional services and the importance of developing and deploying key career enhancement strategies—e.g., impression management, networking and building and leveraging social capital.

Lovisa Näslund is a Researcher at the Stockholm Centre for Organizational Research and an Assistant Professor at Stockholm Business School, Stockholm University. She earned her PhD at the Stockholm School of Economics with the dissertation "The Leap of Faith. Creating Trust on Professional Service Markets". In her ongoing research, she has continued studying trust, with a focus on dynamics of trust and distrust, and system trust in theater, the food industry and violent conflict.

Patrik Nilsson is the Director of Stics (Stockholm Institute of Communication Science) and a Researcher at the Centre for Media and Economic Psychology at the SSE Institute for Research (SIR). He holds a PhD in business administration with a focus on marketing and market communication from Umeå University. His research focuses on the conditions under which market communication is perceived by consumers. In a current project, he focuses on consumers' complaint behaviors and the strategies and activities of organizations dealing with complaints.

Frida Pemer is an Assistant Professor at the Department of Management and Organization at the Stockholm School of Economics, where she also earned her PhD. Her dissertation focused on how management-consulting projects are evaluated in client organizations, and why some projects appear more successful than others. Her current research is focused on the relation between buyer and seller of complex and knowledge-intensive services. More specifically, she has researched and written about how the purchasing of consulting services is organized, how management consulting services and their quality is perceived by clients, and what the consequences of this are for the consultant-client relationship in both public and private organizations.

Sigrid Quack is a Professor of Sociology at the University Duisburg-Essen and a Senior Research Fellow at the Käte Hamburger Kolleg/Centre for Global Cooperation Research. Her current research focuses on authority and expertise in transnational governance, tensions between intellectual property regulation and organized creativity, as well as the role of cross-border social movements and NGOs in challenging prevailing knowledge paradigms.

Claudia A. Rademaker is Assistant Professor at Fashion Marketing and Entrepreneurship (FAME) at Stockholm Business School, Stockholm University. She is affiliated with the Stockholm School of Economics and Visiting Researcher at Amsterdam School of Communication Research (ASCoR), University of Amsterdam. She holds a PhD in business administration from the Stockholm School of Economics. Her doctoral thesis was entitled "Green Media: Exploring Green Media Selection and Its Impact on Communication Effectiveness". Her current research interests include fashion brands and global business, fashion and sustainability and fashion creativity.

Annika Schilling is Assistant Professor at the Department of Organization and Entrepreneurship, Linaeus University. She holds a PhD from the Stockholm School of Economics. Her research interests include post-merger integration, service innovation and the work of PR consultants. Current research interests include organizing practices and human resource management in knowledge-intensive organizations and the embodiment of knowledge-intensive service work.

Kristina Tamm Hallström is Associate Professor at the Department of Management and Organization at the Stockholm School of Economics, where she also earned her PhD. Moreover, she holds a position as Research Director at the Stockholm Centre for Organizational Research (SCORE). Her research interests include legitimacy and authority in transnational governance with studies of standard-setting organizations and increasingly also of the work of certification and accreditation organizations and the continuous efforts undertaken by such auditing organizations in demonstrating their "independence". She runs several research projects in which the construction of independence is studied within empirical areas such as sustainability certification of products and retailers, LGBTQ certification, and comparisons between accreditation organizations in Europe and the US.

Mats Tyrstrup is an Associate Professor and Researcher at the Centre for Advanced Studies of Leadership (CASL) at the Stockholm School of Economics where he also earned his PhD. His research has focused on the study of managers and managerial work. The past ten years, his focus has been on leadership for renewal in knowledge-intensive service organizations. This research was initiated in collaboration with the Ericsson Corporation and resulted in the "everyday leadership" model ("Well Then What Now?—An Everyday Leadership Approach to Managerial Leadership"; Leadership, 2010). He has also been engaged in the renewal of the health-care sector through the Leading Health Care foundation.

Richard Wahlund is holder of the Bonnier Family Professor in Business Administration, especially media, at the Stockholm School of Economics (SSE). He is also Head of the Department of Marketing and Strategy at SSE and Head of the Center for Media and Economic Psychology at the SSE Institute for Research. He runs a number of research projects, most of them concerning media, marketing and/or economic behaviors and to a large extent related to theories in economic psychology. He has especially studied media-related issues, financial behavior, tax behavior, consumer behavior, economic expectations, cognitive biases in decision-making, branding, market communications, gender issues and corporate ethics and sustainability.

Andreas Werr is Professor at the Stockholm School of Economics (SSE) and Head of its Department of Management and Organization. He is also Head of the Center for HRM and Knowledge work at the SSE institute for Research. He holds a PhD from SSE and his research has focused on different aspects of knowledge work in general and of management consultants in specific. More specifically, he has researched and published on topics including knowledge management, purchasing professional services, HRM in knowledge-intensive organizations, knowledge integration in knowledge-intensive teams and knowledge flows across organizational boundaries. Current research engagements focus on the quantification of competence and qualifications in the context of HRM.

1 The Contemporary Expert Society

Staffan Furusten and Andreas Werr

Telling Good from Bad Experts—A Key Challenge in the Expert Society

We are currently living in an expert society where we are constantly confronted with experts for everything. As individuals, we meet them in media where they provide cocksure analyses of the condition of the world, the world economy, security risks, who to blame when a corporation is not as profitable as expected during the last quarter, how to cook or how to lose weight. We also meet them through various forms of health apps in our smartphones, in fitness blogs, and at the gym where we are not expected to be able to make our own exercises, but need a personal trainer to guide us. To an increasing extent, we also see experts offering their expertise to corporations, governments, public organizations, associations, unions and political parties. They offer expert missions, and processes of assessments, auditing, ranking, certification, authorization, accreditation and standardization. We have experts giving advice, and assist organizations in matters of communication, recruitment, investment, brokerage, analysis, financial investment, intelligence, information, marketing, purchasing, education, sustainable development, staffing, PR, media relations and more. Whatever you do, wherever you turn, as an individual or member or manager of an organization there are experts—individuals with a legitimate claim of superior knowledge in a specific area—ready to guide and support you and as a responsible individual, citizen, organizational member or manager you are expected to relate to this increasing amount of expertise available.

In this book, we address the question what this proliferation of experts and expertise means for contemporary organizations and the people that lead them and work in them. We explore this phenomenon from the point of view of how organizational members navigate in this increasingly complex landscape of experts and expertise. How do they tell good expertise from bad and better experts from worse? How are different fields of contemporary experts organized in order to create a, from the view of the organizational members, desirable order in this landscape? Who are the organizers and what do they do? What kind of order(s) on these expert fields do the organizing attempts by different organizers create?

In this book we view the sorting of expertise as an act of organizing (Brunsson, Ahrne & Tamm Hallström, 2007) in that it provides structure to a field of expertise and thereby hierarchizes expertise not only into expertise vs non-expertise but also into better vs worse expertise. These acts of organizing may take different forms. Some forms of organizing are generally applicable, clear-cut and transparent, like when expert systems are based on the logic of professionalism. Other forms of organizing, however, are based on more tacit and local structures, like when organizations hire consultants for providing services such as organizational development, where experience-based trust and reputation are central organizing mechanisms.

In the cases when attempts of organizing are clear and transparent, represented by classic "professionalism" (e.g., medicine, law and auditing) it is relatively easy to pick an expert if you need one. There are regulations, institutionalized codes of conducts and demands of membership in associations for professionals where there are strict and transparent requirements for becoming a member of the expert community and keeping a membership. If you pick an expert accredited to represent one of these occupations, you can expect to get one that is highly qualified to perform in the expert role, at least formally! Of course, not all are equally good in solving all sorts of problems for all organizations in all situations, but you can be sure that they are representatives of areas of expertise that are strictly organized in terms of institutionalized standards for what sort of expert knowledge they need to master in order to play the role of the expert in practice.

Many experts in the contemporary expert society are, however, not organized in these ways and some describe them as "new" or "entrepreneurial" professions (Reed, 1996; Svensson, 2006; Nordegraaf, 2007) where attributes of professionalism will emerge gradually over time. Still, it has also been argued that some fields of expertise are not entrepreneurial in this meaning, where other modes of organizing, such as commercialism (the legitimation as an expert derives from the ability to sell one's expertise on the market) are more pronounced in practice (Furusten & Werr, 2005, 2009; Furusten, 2009, 2013). In this book, we focus on these types of experts. They are increasing in number and in the knowledge areas they represent, and they are hired in more situations, which also means that they have become potentially more influential in forming social contexts and defining what is relevant information to base decisions on. This is taking place globally and in all sorts of organizational settings, such as business firms, governments, schools, public authorities, municipalities, sports clubs, unions, cooperatives and political parties. These types of experts are given more power in contemporary society, but compared to the more strictly organized professions, there is no formal system for authorization, no formal scrutiny of their practices and no transparency in what their expertise consists of and what they have to do in order to earn their status as experts. In these situations, other modes of organizing expertise are at play—modes that have received less attention in previous research.

These modes of organizing will be explored by studying the organizing of a number of rising forms of expertise. The book contains studies of management consultants, certification bodies, investment bankers, marketing consultants, architects, auditors, lawyers, CSR-consultants and experts in management of modern expert organizations, including the public sector. We will study market conditions for these types of experts, expert organizations where these types of experts work and characteristics of different fields of expertise. By doing so, we aim to develop theory for the organization of rising forms of expertise in contemporary society.

Why a Study of the Organization of Expertise in the Contemporary Expert Society Is Needed

We see three main reasons for why the organizing of expertise in the contemporary expert society needs scrutiny.

First, we see signs of an ongoing turn, where the established knowledge production systems, and the systems for educating, training and controlling professionals are under challenge. University produced science and scientists, as well as governmentally authorized professionalism are today questioned ways to organize what is experienced as relevant expertise and supply of relevant experts. The contemporary expert society offers a number of alternative and supposedly more immediate practically relevant ways for this. This, we believe, increases uncertainty among decision-makers in organizations about trusting their own knowing, who to listen to when societal challenges and solutions are problematized, when to turn to an expert and most important of all, what expert to turn to for assistance or guidance.

Second, there is an increasing lack of transparency in how the expertise these experts represent is built up and about the paths they have beaten in order to reach the expert position. There are no requirements of a special education or formal authorization, and it is becoming increasingly difficult to get visibility and control over what kind of expertise the new representatives of expertise convey. This creates challenges to decision-makers in organizations when trying to understand what all these experts "out there" represent, and how trustworthy their expertise really is.

Third, in more and more situations there are reasons to pose questions such as "who controls the contemporary expert?" and "how can we trust these people?" Experts in the classical sense (such as physicians and lawyers) often have close ties to science as well as strong professions to ensure and protect these ties. They are subject to the norms and control within these systems on a daily basis. Those that do not follow the scientific ethic and professional codes will lose both credibility as a representative for science and formal professional legitimation. Within the traditional professions, expertise and the way it is exercised is continuously monitored and reviewed. Among contemporary experts, these processes are largely implicit, if they exist at all, leaving the question of who has the right to perform in the role of the expert to the market i.e. those that manage to sell their services are the ones that can claim expertise. This, we believe, creates uncertainty among decision-makers in organizations, an uncertainty that triggers organizing processes aimed at resolving this.

These three reasons to engage in a scrutiny of the organizing of expertise in the contemporary expert society are founded on an obscurity in its organization. Compared to experts and expertise that we associate with occupations organized according to a classical professional logic (Freidson, 2001/2007) several conditions and processes for the demarcation between experts and non-experts are missing. The organization of the development of expertise as well as how the work of experts is conducted, and the monitoring and insurance that reasonable considerations are made, follows different paths in the contemporary expert society. This, in itself, calls for research and reflection on its organization. To conclude that many of the contemporary experts do not live up to the norms of the classical professions and thus denounce them as non-experts has been one approach in these investigations (e.g., Kieser, 2002). The current book, however takes a different approach in its aim to understand how order in the contemporary expert society is shaped. While the literature on professions has taken its viewpoint from the perspective of the experts and their struggles to organize and strive for legitimation, we approach the organization of the expert society from the other end, from the view of those confronted by this expertise. Thus the experts may struggle to create a kind of order among experts and their expertise to distinguish what they see as the good ones from the bad, and government may support these attempts by creating structures for authorization or offer education programs (or both), but this intended order emphasized by the experts themselves and governments may not necessarily be the kind of order the users experience or prefer. Moreover, different groups of experts may also compete on representing the best and most trustworthy expert system. Users of expert services live in such crossroads on a daily basis, and our viewpoint in this book is to look upon the contemporary expert society from their position, asking the question "how is it possible to navigate when there are so many experts pointing out different directions"?

Organizing Experts when No One Is in Charge

In the modern society it is deemed rational to have confidence in experts representing abstract systems of expertise, i.e. systems where we trust that others know more about various things then we do ourselves (Giddens, 1990). Giddens suggests that when we, for example, purchase a holiday with flights included, we trust that actors such as travel agents, airplane engineers, airplane constructors, pilots, airhostesses, airport staff and states know what they are doing. The layman has very limited knowledge and competencies in the fields in which these experts work, and it would require a lot of time and effort if each and every one should develop competence within each and every field of practice, to enable them to ensure and monitor the competencies of the various experts. To develop relationships based on individual trust with all the people carrying out the various jobs enabling us to have our vacation would also be problematic. Rather, we trust that the respective expert systems for each occupation has developed the mechanisms necessary for it to regulate itself, or that states and associations for various professions, when required, control that the organization of each expert system is solid and the experts representing them are trustworthy. Previous research on the organization of experts promotes professionalism as the most appropriate and desired ordering logic. Still, critical studies on professionalism argue that the power of professions to monopolize knowledge provision in a knowledge field has decreased. As a consequence, it is argued that there is a risk for de-professionalization (e.g., Burrell, 1996). Moreover, other studies emphasize that expert services are increasingly provided by professional service firms, and that these are a specific kind of organizations for which a new organization theory has to be developed because traditional organization theories are based on observations of organizations in industry or the public sector (Greenwood, Suddaby & McDougald, 2006). Lately, we have also seen studies that bring attention to the practice of experts today, where they argue for a need to see contemporary professional work as organized according to hybrid logics of professionalism where, e.g., expertise in management and a professional occupation such as medicine tend to be combined in practice (e.g., Nordegraaf, 2007, 2015). We will in the following discuss in what way these four approaches to professionalism contribute to the understanding of how experts in contemporary society are organized.

Professionalism

In the literature on professions, expert knowledge is seen as something specifically developed and monitored by the professionals themselves (Freidson, 2001/2007). Classical examples are the organization of occupations such as medical doctors, solicitors and auditors (Larson, 1977; Abbott; 1988; Macdonald, 1995; Ackroyd, 1996; Reed, 1996; Freidson, 2001/2007; Brante, Johansson, Olofsson & Svensson, 2015). The state also provides resources for education and research necessary for these professions to maintain authority over the expert knowledge and the required level of competence among a sufficient number of potential recruits. The state, in cooperation with the professions, guarantees that those who are certified as experts are trustworthy and that those acting under certain professional titles, such as physicians and lawyers, are living up to the demands that are put on these occupations regarding both ethics and competence.

The idea behind organizing an occupation in this way is to install professionalism in its pure form. This means that a profession monopolizes and controls the knowledge content and the level of knowledge required for providing particular services, at the same time as an ethically correct conduct in relation to their role as neutral altruists is guaranteed. Only those living up to specified prerequisites defined by the profession for inclusion, manifested through authorization or certification procedures, are allowed to act in the role of a professional (MacDonald, 1995). In the event of a breach of the code of conduct, the national professional body, in which all professionals have to be a member, will impose sanctions such as a registered admonition or exclusion (Larson, 1977; Collins, 1979; Abbott, 1988; Burrage & Torstendahl, 1990). The argument is that this is a prerequisite for not only obtaining but also assuming the power a profession ought to have, without the involvement of commercial or political interests (Reed, 1996). Only then, the conditions exist for various professions to act as a balanced and objective element of power in societal development with the power to stand up against market pressure.

In practice it has, however, appeared that the professional ideals are not always as robust as we presume. Freidson (2001/2007), for instance, argues that this pure version of professionalism is a pipe dream, a world that does not exist, an ideal type like the free market and the rational organization. By seeing professionalism as an ideal form of organizing, a certain ideal logic for the division of labor in a knowledge area is implied. Where the free market and the rational organization represent two logics, the logic of professionalism is the third and mean that "power of economic support and social organization sustains the occupational control of work" (Freidson, 2001/2007, p. 2). Thus, depending on what logic that rules in a particular social setting, it is either the customer (markets), manager (organizations) or the professional that has the power of division of labor. Professionalism thereby represents the attempts made by the experts and governments in order to mobilize power to take control of the definition of experts and the expertise required to become one. Still, in practice, Freidson argues, these categorizations are not really sufficient. Organizations that operate on markets employ professionals. This means that in practice these logics are often blended which is a threat to the rule of professionalism even in classical professions such as medicine and law (Leicht et al., 2009; Svensson, 2006).

De-Professionalization

The balance between the requirements of professionalism and the conduct of commercial business activity is one of the most debated dilemmas in the literature on professions (Macdonald, 1995). Grey (1998) suggests in a study of accountants that their authorization as holders of professional expert knowledge is one thing, while acting professionally is something entirely different. He concludes that for the accountants employed by one of the largest global accounting firms, the signification of being professional is tied up around various forms of confidence building activities with the aim to be able to sell services, rather than questions related to technical competencies and accreditation. Grey states (p. 584):

> That does not, of course, mean that qualification and knowledge were unimportant. On the contrary, failure to qualify would mean an end to one's career in BSF. However, professional and "appropriate" forms of behavior are used so as to be "taken seriously" by colleagues and clients.

According to Grey, the expertise accountants are required to possess in practice is not solely constructed around technical skills and formal aspects when relationships to clients, who are the ones paying the bills of the accounting firms, are considered. Clients demand more from the expert than excellence and technicalities. However, this does not mean that this specific expert system lacks criteria for who is to be considered professional. No one can fully act as an expert on accounting without the formal authorization from the national association for professionals,[1] yet it takes more to be acknowledged as an expert. Grey claims that accountants, in addition to formal authority, must gain legitimacy as experts from their colleagues and clients. In other words, they must instill respect as professionals in the organizations where they are employed as well as on the market. To succeed with this, they also need to possess social skills, that is, competence to handle relationships and conduct business.

Within research on professions, this development is discussed in terms of de-professionalization, meaning that professionals are losing power to define the role they play and monopolize knowledge development in their field of knowledge (Macdonald, 1995). Here, risks are highlighted that de-professionalization means that other groups than the experts themselves influence areas traditionally monoplized by classical professions (Burrell, 1996). The knowledge-based expert authority that the classical professions had, and which they ought to have according to the logic of the role of balanced professions for the distribution of power in society, risks being eroded and thus opens up for more commercial and political interest to assume power over how expertise is defined. The risk seen by those arguing for the danger of de-professionalization is that the control of knowledge production, codes of conduct and authorization of experts trickles away from the professionals to markets or managers in organizations following different agendas than that of "altruistic service" (Brint, 1994; MacDonald, 1995). There are reasons to take this potential risk seriously because the quality of the services provided by those legitimized as playing the role of the expert in particular decision-making contexts may become more uncertain in times of de-professionalization. On the other hand, as argued by Grey (1998) and Freidson (2001/2007), to balance the three logics of professionalism, markets and organization is nothing new, it is rather a constant dimension for individuals and organizations offering expert services irrespective of their field of expertise. Thus it is not a dimension that is new for this kind of work, although it is important to consider if there are power shifts going on between the three logics. It may also be important to define the power balance in a knowledge area at a specific point in time.

From Occupational Professionalism to Organizational Professionalism

This concurrent development toward on the one hand an increasing importance of experts in all domains of society and on the other hand the fact that a large number of these experts are working under market conditions with a risk for de-professionalization, has fueled a broad concern in society with the quality and efficiency of expert services (Leicht, Walter, Sainsaulieu & Davies, 2009). Research on occupations and professions has for some time observed a move from a focus on guarding the interests of the profession toward cultivating organizations (Svensson, 2006; Evetts, 2011). Evetts (2011) summarizes some of the key changes from "occupational professionalism" to "organizational professionalism" as a shift from notions of "partnership, collegiality, discretion and trust" toward "managerialism, bureaucracy, standardization, assessment and performance review" (p. 407). The latter regime is often also labeled "new" as opposed to traditional professionalism (Svensson, 2006; Leicht et al., 2009; Evetts, 2011) and makes control over the nature of experts and expertise the responsibility of, for example, the organization and its management and control systems.

These circumstances have been in focus in studies of professional service firms where criticism is directed to theories of professions for no longer being appropriate when dealing with changes in the modern society (Greenwood, Suddaby & McDougald, 2006). The main focus in this literature is to develop theory of what they claim to be the contemporary knowledge society (Baradacco, 1991) populated by knowledge workers (e.g., Starbuck, 1992; Alvesson, 1993) working in professional service organizations (Greenwood, Hinings & Brown, 1990). According to Furusten (2013, p. 268) building on Greenwood, Suddaby & McDougald., (2006):

> Their main concern is that the conditions for knowledge-intensive organisations are different from those of the manufacturing industry. Since organisation theory is mainly based on studies of organisations other than knowledge-intensive ones, they argue that there is a need for a new theory for these types of organisations.

Much of their theorizing is based on studies of the modern accountancy profession and they argue that among these firms there are two archetypes: the professional partnership and the managed professional business (e.g., Greenwood et al., 1990; Maister, 1993; Morris & Pinnington, 1999). While the former builds on traditional professionalism, the latter builds on the logic of establishing a commercial business. Still, as we pointed out earlier, while referring to Grey's (1998) study of accountancies, although the ideal is that professionalism should be unaffected by the dynamics of markets, commercialism is a dimension of professional practice that cannot be neglected if we want to understand how the role of the professional providing services to organizations is formed today.

This strengthens Freidson's (2001/2007) argument, that there is a difference between professional ideals and professional practice. Furusten (2013, p. 270) referring to Hanlon (1999), argues that, "over the last decade, professionalism has become more entrepreneurial, "managementized", and commercial, meaning that the packaging and commercialization of the services provided has become more important". This means that professionalism and perceived expertise need not necessarily go hand in hand (Fournier, 1999). Norms can be institutionalized in an occupational group, i.e. for experience-based expertise, even when there is no formal structuring of expert knowledge. Building on these arguments, there do not have to be definite boundaries in practice between markets (where expertise is exchanged), organizations (where expertise is performed) and professions (where expertise is cultivated, constructed and controlled).

Consequently, there is a difference between professionalism as an ideal, and professionalism as a practice. In constructing practice, commercialism and market mechanisms are likely to be considerable components. This suggests that conditions such as competition and trust are important mechanisms to include as organizing forces (Furusten, 2013). This means that, if the service providers want to stay in business, they have to offer what organizations are willing to pay for (Furusten, 1999, 2003). The expertise they offer can, therefore, to some extent, be understood as shaped in business negotiations with their clients—not controlled by the professional community. This suggests that the organizing of expertise must be understood as some form of hybridity between the organizing logics of the organization, the market and the professional community.

Hybrid Professionalism

The tendency for experts to blend different organizing modes is explored in a recent strand of literature where the work of professionals in practice is framed as hybrid professionalism. The concern in this, emerging literature, is not so much with the risks of de-professionalization or organizational professionalism, but with the fact that we see the rise of a new type of professionals, the hybrid professionals, who tend to blend two occupational skills into one professional practice. This fits well with Grey's (1998) and Freidson's (2001/200/) observations of the tendency for professionals to blend the professional logic with other logics for organizing experts. This literature draws attention to a less idealistic and more empirically anchored form of professionalism, where the tendency is noted that classical professionals such as medical doctors, increasingly blend their expertise in medicine with expertise in management (Nordegraaf, 2007, 2015). Hybrid professionalism is by Blomgren & Waks (2015, p. 83) defined as "professionals within an area of expertise who develop a relation capability vis-á-vis expertise in other areas". Thus, the concept "hybrid professionalism" is more connected to the practice of professionals, where blending logics of organizing such as commercialism and managerialism with professionalism has been observed to be normal (e.g., Grey, 1998; Freidson, 2001/2007).

Although not explicitly discussing the challenges of keeping the professional logic clean in practice, authors such as Brint (1994), Macdonald (1995) and Freidson (2001/2007), have indicated that there are challenges for experts in balancing the tree logics of organizing expertise—professionalism, commercialism and managerialism. The understanding of professionals as hybrids in practice is useful in explaining how expertise in contemporary society is organized. Contemporary experts need to be both professionals in a pure sense but also functioning market actors and employees or managers in organizations operating on markets. Still, although being a core dimension in the practice of experts, Freidson claims that it is rare in the literature on professions to search for explanations of how contemporary experts are organized where all three dimensions (professionalism, commercialism and managerialism) are seen as interrelated.

Freidson's quest are supported by Brint (1994), Furusten & Werr (2005), Ernst & Kieser (2006), Leicht & Lyman (2006) and Brante et al. (2015), who all argue that old definitions of professionalism do not represent contemporary processes of how expert work is organized. Thus, fewer members of the contemporary expert society fulfill the criteria of the traditional professions: well-specified knowledge bases, defined educational routes, and strictly controlled entrance criteria. Therefore, central authors in the literature on professions call for broader approaches to the professional layer of society, and for studies on "new types" of professionals and professionalism (Halliday, 1987; Brint, 1994; Macdonald, 1995; Freidson, 2001/2007; Brante, 2014; Brock, Leblebici & Muzio, 2014; Brante, Johansson, Olofsson & Svensson, 2015).

To sum up, experts in the contemporary expert society, the construction of their expertise and the legitimation procedures of representatives of the expert core are not fair to define in terms of classical professionalism only. Neither does the literature on de-professionalization or organizational professionalism explain how contemporary expertise is organized. Still, few studies, analyze the organizing of expertise from other lenses than professionalism, and few analyze professions from a broader societal context, or offer comparisons between categories of experts and types of professionals (Brante et al., 2015). Following from the aforementioned calls for studies of new types of professionals and professionalism, we argue that there is an even greater need to theorize on organizing of expertise in the contemporary expert society, where the meaning of the "expert" concept is growing more diversified; we can, for instance, notice more specialization and more diversification at the same time. A consequence is that we are living in a time when an increasing number of more well-defined expert categories are being established, but where the logic for organizing them varies, and where the element of hybridity between organizing logics may be significant in practice. The literature on hybrid professionalism opens up for a more empirically based theorizing on the organization of experts, but so far this literature has mainly focused on how a single category of professionals, medical doctors, have to balance their occupational expertise with expertise in management. Thus, the literature on hybrid professionalism gives important contribution to the understanding of how expertise in contemporary society is organized, but as we see it, we also need to apply a more fundamental approach on organizing.

Organizing Contemporary Experts in Spirals of Interrelated Actions

As the main concern of this book is the organizing of expertise, a brief positioning of our view on organizing is warranted. Following Brunsson et al. (2007) we view organizing as acts aimed at reducing ambiguity. Organizing is to strive for ". . . a specific order among individuals or organizations, to attribute certain identities and to prescribe certain patterns of behavior" in order to" (Brunsson et al., 2007, p. 619)

> facilitate interaction and communication by making people or organizations behave in predictable ways and by introducing certain identities and common status orders. Another purpose is to instil the order the organizer prefers.

In the context of the current book the individuals in focus of organizing are experts—i.e. those with claimed superior knowledge in a knowledge domain.

As we have discussed earlier, the professional system is one established way of instilling a specific order among individuals, attributing certain identities and prescribing patterns of behavior in order to create predictability and facilitate interaction among, for example, experts and their users. However, we have also argued that professionalism is by no means the only way. As argued by e.g., Grey (1998) and Freidson (2001/2007), professionalism is intertwined with other organizing logics such as those of the market and the organization. This means that even the most rigorous system of professionalism does not automatically create order in practice. Just because someone is formally authorized as an expert, this does not mean that this person also carries relevant knowledge and competence for organizations in need of expert services and thus is able to sell his/her services on a market. Organizing experts and their expertise is thus a complex process involving organizing attempts founded in different organizing logics. Brunsson et al. continues:

> Some forms of global organizing have existed at least since the early 19th century, but after World War II there has been a large increase in the number of attempts at organizing organizations globally. There is often a demand for organizing: when acting on a global arena, organizations benefit from the organization of other organizations that they want to compete or interact with, and they often take active part in such organizing. Several organizers often interact and support each other. In other cases there is a competition among various organizers, which allows organizers to choose how they are to be organized. Far from all organizing attempts are successful.
>
> (Brunsson et al., 2007, p. 620)

While the logic of professionalism thus suggests that there should only be one principal category of organizers, Brunsson et al. suggest that it is likely that a number of organizers are active in parallel on a field, and that they all have ambitions to create their version of order. They may interact and support each other actively or indirectly, but they may also compete with each other. This implies that organizing attempts have no guarantee to succeed in creating order on an aggregate level. If there are many organizers on a field instilling different versions of order, disorder on an aggregate level is a likely outcome. Consequently, we view the organizing of expertise as interconnected activities, more specifically organizing attempts, performed by different actors with potentially different interests. These organizing attempts will create a sense of order for some actors while they may be a source of disorder for other actors. Order, as an outcome of organizing attempts is thus viewed as a primarily local accomplishment that can be more or less shared.

In some cases, organizing attempts may create a temporary, shared sense of order in which we can identify traces of institutionalized organizational elements such as rules, membership, hierarchy and control (Brunsson et al., 2007; Brunsson & Ahrne, 2011). Different organizing attempts may vary in to what extent they manage to establish these different organizational elements. Brunsson & Ahrne (2011) argue that some attempts to organize only end up in an order that can be defined as partially organized, with bits and pieces of some organizational elements being in place while others are not. On a field of expertise, it is thus not unlikely that there are associations for professionals or professional service firms. However, their contribution to order may vary between fields. In some fields of expertise you have to be a member of these associations in order to be allowed to act in the expert role, such as in law, medicine and accounting, but in others, membership is optional (as for example in management consulting). When bits and pieces of organizational elements are in place, it means that some parts of the activities on the field are at least partially organized. This also means that other activities on the field are not organized at the field level, but there might very well be other mechanisms for the creation of local order among both expert service providers and expert service users. Order and disorder may thus co-exist across different actors and levels of analysis. A strong profession may make it rather clear what the basic qualifications of an expert are. However, the individual buyer of a professional may still be struggling with which expert to hire in order to gain most value for money. At the same time, the lack of a strong profession does not necessarily imply that the users of such experts are completely disoriented. They may very well have a trusted network of experts from which they confidently select suitable providers.

The point we want to make here is that order as well as disorder, are potential outcomes of ongoing attempts to *organize*. As Czarniawska (2013, p. 12) points out, organizing attempts are continuously ongoing with order being an ongoing local strive rather than a stable global outcome:

> Organizing is thus an ongoing encounter with ambiguity, ambivalence and equivocality, part of a larger attempt to make sense of life and the world . . . Although organizing is an effort to deal with ambiguity, it never completely succeeds. Furthermore, the ordering it involves does not consist merely of imposing the rules of rationality on a disorderly world: it is a far more complex and inherently ambiguous processes of sensemaking (Weick, 1995).
>
> (Czarniawska, 2013, p. 12)

This makes sensemaking a key aspect of organizing. Sensemaking as organizing takes place in the context of numerous parallel organizing attempts, some of which may have become more generally accepted and thus instilled as institutionalized orders:

> At each place and time one can speak of an institutional order—a set of institutions (not necessarily coherent) that are recognized as prevailing at a specific time and place. Such institutions determine organizing in the sense that certain connections between actions are legitimate while others are not—or not yet.
>
> (p. 13)

Institutionalized orders thus play a role in shaping expectations of appropriateness in behavior (cf. March & Olsen, 1976, 1989), expectations that **create** mental structures from where individuals interpret the level of order in a social setting (Furusten, 2013). The institutionalized order is performative in the sense that it creates expectations among organizers—for examples those that formally give experts their assignments. Following this argumentation, organizing can be illustrated as a spiral of organizing attempts by different organizers (Figure 1.1).

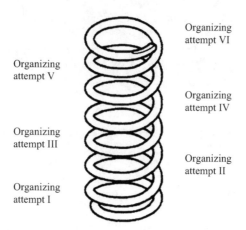

Organizing attempt VI

Organizing attempt V

Organizing attempt IV

Organizing attempt III

Organizing attempt II

Organizing attempt I

Figure 1.1 A spiral model of organizing.

Important to note is that organizing attempts are made by different organizers who may act based on either professional, market or organizational logics. Over time, some may be reified as actors representing attributes of institutional order, meaning that their potential impact on the organization of the field is likely to be higher. Djelic and Quack (2007) talk about path generative actors. They argue that some points in time are more formative than others and call these moments path generating junctures. Actors with strong positions may in these situations be able to influence the organization of the field substantially. Such strong positions may be based on financial power (e.g., ability to give assignments to experts), regulative power (e.g., the state), cultural power (e.g., an established association for experts) or discursive and rhetorical power. Also, the historical background of the field and its institutionalized order may give some actors more influence on forming the direction of the organizing spiral than others. Thus, depending on the situational power structures on a field of expertise, different organizers or attempts to organize may have more or less potential to create order on the field, even if the achieved order may be temporal or local.

Arenas for the Organization of Expertise

Ambiguity regarding experts and expertise thus fuel spirals of organizing attempts, involving different organizers acting on different organizing arenas. Based on what we have seen from the literature on professionalism we will focus on three such arenas—the market, the organization and the field which here represents the attempts to establish a general order for all experts offering particular identifiable and comparable services. These three arenas represent different contexts where self-claimed experts and those with a need to reduce ambiguity around these experts meet. The experts and their "judges" have different labels on the different arenas. On the market, we have suppliers and buyers; on the field, we have different kinds of experts competing and colluding for legitimacy, and in the organization, we have experts and their managers who in the context of performance management, talent management or staffing need to make judgments on the experts' expertise.

Different institutional orders govern these three arenas, and we expect both similarities and differences across them in how expertise is organized. The thorough exploration of these orders, and how they interact with the organization of expertise, is the focus of the upcoming chapters. Here we will just begin highlighting some of their key characteristics.

The Market

The market is possibly the most obvious arena for the organization of expertise. Buyers and suppliers uncertain about what expertise to buy or sell are engaged in a joint effort to establish some kind of order to the different claims of expertise on the market. The closed deal demonstrates that this has been successfully achieved, at least temporarily—that different organizing activities have reduced uncertainty sufficiently for a buyer to dare to exchange a specific expertise for a specific fee. The main question explored in the coming chapters on the market arena is thus:

1   What organizing attempts can be observed between buyers and suppliers in their struggles to establish sufficient certainty to close a deal?

The Field

The field represents the sum of actions taken by actors directly involved in the organization of a domain of expertise. On the field arena, expertise is both made relevant as well as structured into different levels of expertise. Making expertise relevant involves the reorganization of existing fields of expertise in order to create a legitimate space for a new field of expertise. Once established, the field of expertise needs to gain an internal structure. Key actors in these field-organizing processes are often collectives of experts competing and/or colluding in their efforts to reduce uncertainty regarding the specific knowledge domain. Two key questions thus pertain to the field arena:

2   What organizing attempts can be observed among actors on fields of expertise in order to establish legitimate spaces for new fields of expertise?
3   What organizing attempts can be observed among actors on fields of expertise in their efforts to organize established fields of expertise?

The Organization

The organization, finally, is a key actor in the expert society both as a creator and as a guardian of expertise and within the literature on professions it is often claimed that the organization has gained influence at the cost of the influence of other field level actors such as professional associations. In order to fulfill this role, the organization of expertise in terms of developing and judging expertise is central. One important issue is thus identified as follows:

4   What organizing attempts can be observed in organizations' efforts to reduce ambiguity regarding employees' expertise?

Investigating Spirals of Organizing Expertise between Three Interrelated Arenas

Although we will focus on each of these three arenas separately in the chapters to come, they are to a large extent interrelated. The way in which buyers and suppliers organize expertise in trying to make market deals will, for example, be strongly influenced by the way in which the expertise is organized on the field of expertise level. The same goes for the organizing taking place on the organizational arena. Also, the organization of expertise on the organizational and market arenas will affect each other. The way in which expertise is assessed on the market (e.g., a strong focus on interpersonal trust) directly interacts with the way in which expertise is developed and assessed in organizations (e.g., focus on soft skills, relationship building in performance and talent management). Individually, as well as collectively, the different organizing attempts are instrumental in shaping the nature of expertise and experts. Organizing attempts on these three arenas are further viewed as affected by and having impact on change and maintenance of institutional order and thus what is regarded as expertise in a particular area, and how experts and the expertise they represent should be organized in order to be regarded as representative for a relatively recognizable expert culture. This overall framework for investigating the organization of the contemporary expert society is summarized in Figure 1.2.

Based on the earlier discussion and the framework summarized in Table 1.1, we are in each chapter to come approaching the organizing of expertise in the contemporary expert society as consisting of four analytical dimensions, each with specific characteristics. There are (1) likely to be different organizers on all organizing arenas, who make (2) different attempts of organizing based on their views, positions and ambitions. These attempts lead to the emphasis of particular (3) characteristics of the organized expert, that in turn create certain (4) characteristics of the expertise that is emphasized. These dimensions of organizing and the three levels of analysis create an overall investigative framework (Table 1.1) that will be filled by the

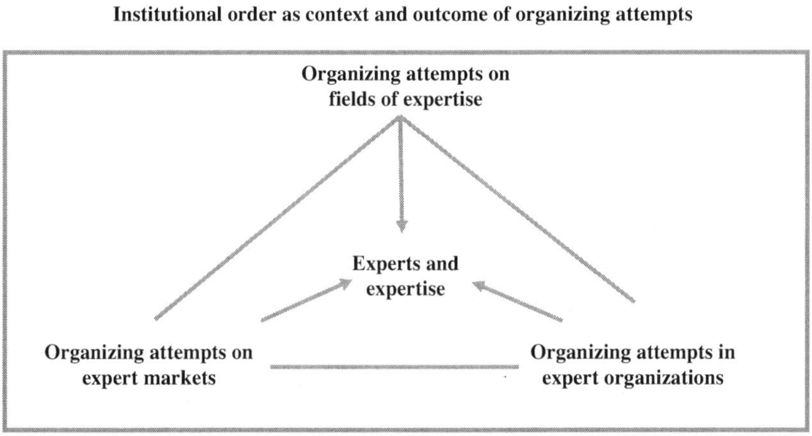

Institutional order as context and outcome of organizing attempts

Figure 1.2 Three interrelated arenas on which expertise is organized.

Table 1.1 Dimensions of organizing at organizing arenas

Dimensions of organizing ———— *Organizing arenas*	*Organizers*	*Organizing attempts*	*Characteristics of organized expert*	*Characteristics of organized expertise*
Field				
Market				
Organization				

different chapters of the book. In a concluding chapter, we will come back to these discussions and analyze how spirals of organizing actions on and between different arenas shape some form of order among experts and for users of their expertise.

Structure of the Book

The overall approach of this book is explorative, and the aim is to develop theory for how expertise in contemporary society is organized. The different chapters therefore have the character of different illustrations of the overall phenomenon. Hereby, we aim to cover presumed variation in type of organizers and organizing attempts on different arenas. The chapters are structured according to the three organizing arenas. We will start with an investigation of the field level, where we in Chapters 2 and 3 study two extreme attempts to organize. In Chapter 2, Susanna Alexius analyzes organizing attempts in the field of management consulting, where attempts to organize according to professional logics are made at a global level but with little success. Instead, local trust building is a more commonly used organizing principle. In Chapter 3, Kristina Tamm Hallström studies the organization of experts in certification and accreditation. In this case, the organizers manage to install a global system for singling out the experts based on the logic of professionalism. In Chapter 4, Jesper Blomberg studies an emerging field of experts, stock analysts where achieved reputation in networks plays an important role in organizing experts on the field level. Another emerging field of experts and expertise is studied in Chapter 5 by Susanna Alexius, Staffan Furusten and Andreas Werr, regarding the field of expertise in sustainability. Here attempts made by the market actors toward productification and standardization of services become important for organizing efforts. In Chapter 6, the emerging field of experts in marketing is studied by Claudia Rademaker, Carl-Patrick Nilsson and Richard Wahlund. They discuss the emergence of different specialized expert roles in expert fields. A forth analysis on emerging expert fields is followed in Chapter 7 by Sigrid Quack who discusses the rise of critical professional communities who from changing background conditions challenge and disrupt established knowledge orders in transnational governance fields. She does that based on studies of experts on copyright and corporate financial reporting while discussing the tendency of broad participation between actors from different policy fields, triggering events and coalition building.

Next, follow two chapters focusing on the arena of the market exchange. First, Lovisa Näslund and Frida Pemer in Chapter 8 analyze organizing attempts made in business relations between buyers and providers of management consulting services. Second, In Chapter 9, Staffan Furusten analyses attempts made by providers of management consulting services to develop skills in improvisation in order to make themselves hirable.

In the next section of the book, a number of attempts to organize expertise on the organizational arena are studied. Pernilla Bolander studies procedures of recruiting experts in Chapter 10, and Annika Schilling compares attempts to create expert identities within management consultancies, PR consultancies and law firms in Chapter 11. In Chapter 12, Andreas Werr and Annika Schilling compare two types of organizing logics in management consultancies. Next Savita Kumra and Andreas Werr in Chapter 13 study the managerial attempts to organize expertise manifest in the performance management system of a management consultancy and discuss how the consultants deal with these attempts. This is followed by an analysis of attempts to change the role of internal experts in public organizations by Mats Tyrstrup and Ingalill Holmberg in Chapter 14. Staffan Furusten and Andreas Werr, finally, in Chapter 15 offer a concluding analysis of how expertise in contemporary society is organized.

Note

1 In Sweden referred to as FAR (Professional institute for accountants C/R webb).

References

Abbott, A. (1988). *The System of Professions.* Chicago, IL: University of Chicago Press.

Ackroyd, S. (1996). Organization contra organizations: Professions and organizational change in the UK. *Organization Studies, 17*(4), 599–621.

Alvesson, M. (1993). Organizations as rhetoric: Knowledge-intensive firms and the struggle with ambiguity. *Journal of Management Studies, 30*(5), 997–1015.

Baradacco, J. L. (1991). *The Knowledge Link.* Boston, MA: Harvard Business School Press.

Blomgren, M. & Waks, C. (2015). Coping with contradictions: Hybrid professionals managing institutional complexity. *Journal of Professions and Organization, 2*(1), 78–102.

Brante, T. (2014). *Den professionella logiken: hur vetenskap och praktik förenas i det moderna kunskapssamhället.* Stockholm: Liber.

Brante, T., Johansson, E., Olofsson, G. & Svensson, L. G. (2015). *Professionerna i kunskapssamhället: en jämförande studie av svenska professioner.* Stockholm: Liber.

Brint, S. (1994). *In an Age of Experts.* Princeton, NJ: Princeton University Press.

Brock, D., Leblebici, H. & Muzio, D. (2014). Understanding professionals and their workplaces: The mission of the Journal of Professions and Organization. *Journal of Professions and Organization, 1*(1), 1–15.

Brunsson, N. & Ahrne, G. (2011). Organization outside organizations: The significance of partial organization. *Organization, 18*(1), 83–104.

Brunsson, N., Ahrne, G. & Tamm Hallström, K. (2007). Organizing organizations. *Organization, 14*(5), 619–624.

Burrage, M. & Torstendahl, R. (1990). *Professions in Theory and History: Rethinking the Study of the Professions.* London: Sage.

Burrell, G. (1996). Hard times for the salariat. In Scarbrough, H. (ed.), *The Management of Expertise.* London: Macmillan, 48–64.

Collins, R. (1979). *The Credential Society: An Historical Sociology of Education and Stratification.* New York: Academic Press.

Czarniawska, B. (2013). Organizations as obstacles to organizing. In Robishaud, D. & Cooren, F. (eds.), *Organization and Organizing: Materiality, Agency and Discourse.* New York: Routledge, 3–22.

Djelic, M. L. & Quack, S. (2007). Overcoming path dependancy: Path generation in open systems. *Theory and Society, 36*, 161–188.

Ernst, B. & Kieser, A. (2002) In search of explanations for the consulting explosion. In: Sahlin Andersson, K. & Enwall, L. (eds.), *The Expansion of Management Knowledge: Carriers, Flows, and Sources.* Stanford: Stanford University Press, 47–73.

Evetts, J. (2011). A new professionalism? Challenges and opportunities. *Current Sociology, 59*(4), 406–422.

Fournier, V. (1999). The appeal to professionalism as a disciplinary mechanism. *Sociological Review, 47*(2), 280–307.

Freidson, E. (2001/2007). *Professionalism, the Third Logic: On the Practice of Knowledge.* Chicago: University of Chicago Press.

Furusten, S. (1999). *Popular Management Books: How They are Made and What They Mean for Organizations.* London: Routledge.

Furusten, S. (2003). *God Managementkonsultation?* Lund: Studentlitteratur.

Furusten, S. (2009). Management consultants as improvising agents of stability. *Scandinavian Journal of Management, 25*(3), 264–274.

Furusten, S. (2013). *Institutional Theory and Organizational Change.* Cheltenham: Edward Elgar.

Furusten, S. & Werr, A. (eds.). (2005). *Dealing with Confidence—The Construction of Need and Trust in Management Advisory Services.* Copenhagen: Copenhagen Business Press.

Furusten, S. & Werr, A. (2009). The need for management advisory services: A consequence of institutionalization, organization and trust. In Bouno, A. F. & Oulfelt, F. (eds.), *Client-Consultant Collaboration—Coping with Complexity and Change.* Charlotte, NC: Information Age Publishing, 179–197.

Giddens, A. (1990). *The Consequences of Modernity.* Stanford: Stanford University Press.

Greenwood, R., Hinings, C. R. & Brown, J. (1990). P2-form strategic management: Corporate practices in professional partnerships. *Academy of Management Journal, 33*(4), 725–755.

Greenwood, R., Suddaby, R. & McDougald, M. (2006). Introduction. In Greenwood, R. & Suddaby, R. (eds.), *Research in the Sociology of Organizations: Professional Service Firms, Volume 24.* Bingley: Emerald, 1–16.

Grey, C. (1998). On being a professional in a 'Big Six' firm. *Accounting, Organization and Society, 23*(5/6), 569–587.

Halliday, T. (1987). *Beyond Monopoly: Lawyers, State Crises, and Professional Empowerment.* Chicago: University of Chicago Press.

Hanlon, G. (1999). *Lawyers, the State and the Market: Professionalism Revisited.* Basingstoke: Macmillan.

Kieser, A. (2002). Managers as marionettes? Using fashion theories to explain the success of consultancies. In Engwall, L. & Kipping, M. (eds.), *Management Consulting: Emergence and Dynamics of a Knowledge Industry.* Oxford: Oxford University Press, 167–183.

Larson, M. S. (1977). *The Rise of Professionalism.* Berkeley: University of California Press.

Leicht, K. T. & Lyman, E. C. W. (2006). Markets, institutions, and the crisis of professional practice. In Greenwood, R. & Suddaby, R. (eds.), *Professional Service Firms (Research in the Sociology of Organizations, Volume 24).* Bingley: Emerald, 17–44.

Leicht, K. T., Walter, T., Sainsaulieu, I. & Davies, S. (2009). New public management and new professionalism across nations and contexts. *Current Sociology, 57*(4), 581–605.

Macdonald, K. (1995). *The Sociology of the Professions.* London: Sage.

Maister, D. H. (1993). *Managing the Professional Service Firm.* New York, NY: Free Press.

March, J. & Olsen, J. P. (1976). *Ambiguity and Choice in Organizations.* Oslo: Universitetsforlaget.

March, J. & Olsen, J. P. (1989). *Rediscovering Institutions: The Organizational Basis of Politics*, New York: Free Press.

Morris, T. & Pinnington, A. H. (1999). Continuity and change in professional organizations: The evidence from law firms. In Brock, D., Powell, P. & Hinings, C. R. (eds.), *Restructuring the Professional Organization: Accounting, Health Care and Law*. London: Routledge, 200–214.

Nordegraaf, M. (2007). From pure to 'hybrid' professionalism: Present-day professionalism in ambigiuous public domains. *Administration & Society*, 39(8), 761–785.

Nordegraaf, M. (2015). Hybrid professionalism and beyond: New forms of public professionalism in changing organizational and societal contexts, *Journal of Professions and Organizations*, 2(2), 187–206.

Reed, M. (1996). Expert power and control in late modernity. *Organization Studies*, 4, 573–597.

Starbuck, W. (1992). Learning by knowledge-intensive firms. *Journal of Management Studies, 29*(6), 713–740.

Svensson, L. G. (2006). New professionalism, trust and competence: Some conceptual remarks and empirical data. *Current Sociology, 54*(4), 579–593.

Weick, K. E. (1995) *Sensemaking in Organizations*. Thousand Oaks: Sage.

2 Experts without Rules— Scrutinizing the Unregulated Free Zone of the Management Consultants

Susanna Alexius

As discussed in the introductory chapter, traditional experts' characteristics need not always be a prerequisite for achieving expert status. In fact, it may even be the opposite. In this chapter, I look closely at management consultants, some of the most well-paid experts of our times, and ponder how and why they have managed to retain their comparatively unregulated "free zone" in the otherwise so regulated expert community. How can we understand that the backbone of other modern experts' special position and authority—the common professional rules—still *languishes* in the management consultancy field? What consequences do these special conditions bring about for their expert practice, clients and society in general?

In the first part of the chapter, I discuss these issues in light of research on attempts to regulate the management consultants' expertise and of resistance to such attempts. I start by discussing what makes someone an expert in the management-consulting field, noting that in comparison to the professional foundation of traditional experts, there is a striking diversity and openness that apply to both management consultants and their knowledge. How come then, that the codified has not supplanted the personal in this field of expertise? Why has diversity not given way to uniformity and openness not been diminished by stricter border controls? In the second part of the chapter, I present arguments for and against three common understandings of the management consultants' rare exception from codification: 1) rules are not needed because other options to secure expertise are sufficient, 2) it is an impossible task to regulate consultation and 3) rules will come with time.

A Smorgasbord of Knowledge

Experts belonging to classic professions such as the medical profession, derive their status of expertise from a fairly clear core of recognized, codified knowledge. The prefix "management" may be interpreted to suggest that management, as in knowledge on business administration, should be a core knowledge base for management consultants. However, when looking closer at actual consultants and their offers, it is fair to say that they represent a large open smorgasbord for managers to choose from—a metaphor that captures that in principle there are as many business definitions as there are consultants.

Most consultancy services are intangible and very difficult to put into words, measure and evaluate (Alexius & Furusten, 2005; Alexius, 2007; Sturdy, 2011). Definitions of what consultants do and what they sell are typically open and ambiguous, as the definition by the British consultancy association MCA (Management Consultancies Association), cited in O'Mahoney (2010, p. 14) shows

> the creation of value for organisations, through the application of knowledge, techniques and assets, to improve business performance. This is achieved through the rendering of objective advice and/or the implementation of business solutions.
>
> (O'Mahoney, 2010, p. 14)

As is clear from this definition, management consultants are not restricted to a common knowledge base. On the contrary, diversity proves to be the hallmark of consultancy. As a telling illustration in the aforementioned definition, the MCA deliberately refrains from trying to define what kind of knowledge, technologies and resources the consultant should base its offer on. Consultant Researcher Joe O'Mahoney develops this idea as follows (O'Mahoney, 2010, p. 180):

> Consultancy tools and techniques, therefore, are not scientific instruments and are closer to the instruments of art: they can be used in many different ways, their use is highly subjective, they are interpreted differently by varying groups, and they can be used to produce an infinite number of outcomes. Moreover, as with artists, the hundreds of thousands of tools, techniques and frameworks that consultants use are less important than the consultant that uses them.

In essence, successful operation is based on a set of vague and non-solid capabilities such as openness to diversity and improvisation (Furusten, 2003; Alexius, 2007; Whittle, 2008). Improvisation is always based on basic knowledge adapted to the demands and conditions in the specific context where the consultant makes assumptions, builds on, interprets and invents "variations on a certain theme", much like a jazz soloist would (Furusten, 2003; Furusten, 2009).

Many consultants are generalists rather than specialists. They have a broad set of basic knowledge that can be made relevant in different situations and they have developed a sense of knowing just when and where different skills are relevant to the client. It can often be the case that different skills are combined in new ways or small additions are made here and there and it is generally a pronounced advantage if the offer is perceived as unique in some respect (Alexius, 2007). This opens up opportunities for people with very different educational and experience backgrounds to work as consultants (Furusten, Werr & Alexius, 2012). Many management consultants have studied economics, management or technology related topics. Others have their theoretical background in subjects such as theology, sociology, political science, medicine, psychology or pedagogy (Furusten, 2003; O'Mahoney, 2010). Some practice without a formal degree, but with long experience from leadership positions. Two consultants I interviewed for my dissertation project expressed it as follows (translated quote from Alexius, 2007, pp. 78, 81):

> We have different approaches, different foci, different motivations, too. Thus, consultant, anyone can become a consultant or call themselves a consultant.
>   Consultation is not just knowledge. It is skills paired with personality and that combination is found in so many variations that it is almost impossible to describe it.

As seen in the earlier quotes, a clear common, codified knowledge base is not central to the management consultants' expertise. Quite the contrary—it is all about consultants' ability to improvise and create attractive deals based on the smorgasbord of knowledge available to them. In addition, the first of the two quotes tells us another fundamental truth about this unusually unregulated expertise; it lacks clear, formal boundaries between experts and non-experts. The consultant interviewed reminds us that as anyone can become and call himself or herself a consultant, it is up to the rest of us to tell the better from the worse.

Openness to Newcomers

A second key characteristic of traditional experts is the existence of clear boundaries to non-experts who are sometimes called quacks. To get a ticket to one of the traditional areas of expertise, the applicant must demonstrate that he or she has theoretical knowledge and practical skills core to the profession.

As discussed in Chapter 1, specialized professional associations usually monopolize the organization of a pure profession (e.g., associations of authorized public accountants, bar associations and medical associations). The professions' frontiers are hence defended and protected, not only by the associations' own rules (e.g., ethical codes of conduct and professional standards) but also, and ultimately, by government regulation and sanctions. If, for instance, someone attempts to practice medicine without a valid doctor's ID, this is a crime with punishment.

Unlike individuals who practice traditional expert occupations, there is no requirement for a consultant to be a member of a professional association. In fact, anyone may attempt a consultancy career because, unlike the titles chartered accountant, lawyer or doctor, the titles consultant and management consultant do not have any statutory protection (Kyrö, 1995; O'Mahoney, 2010). Partly following from this difference, the consultancy associations are comparatively weak expert organizations with few members and relatively little influence (Groß & Kieser, 2006; Alexius, 2007; O'Mahoney, 2010). For, in the absence of legislation that could make it mandatory to join the professional consultancy association, the hope is to attract members on a voluntary basis. So far, however, this has proven quite difficult.

In the mid-1990s, less than half a percent of the management consultants worldwide were members of any professional association (Kubr, 1996). Two decades later, the representation remains weak. The International Council of Management Consultancy Institute (ICMCI), the international professional association, is representing around 30,000 consultants worldwide. It may sound a lot but this figure represents only about 2 percent of all potential members (O'Mahoney, 2010, p. 26). The Federation of Management Consultancy Associations (FEACO) represents some 15 European countries' national consultant associations. Most of these national organizations (like the English professional association for management consultants MCA, the German equivalent BDU and the Swedish SAMC) have very few members. In 2002, for example, only 0.4 percent of Germany's 14,440 consultants were members of the BDU. In 2007, the Swedish Association SAMC had 20 member companies only (Alexius, 2007). Today, after rising to over 40 in the last recession, the number of member organizations in SAMC has decreased a bit to 34 where the majority of the member firms are small companies, including many one-person consultants.[1] We must also bear in mind that during this past decade, the number of consultants in Sweden has increased substantially. An estimate from 2010 states that at least 10,000 individuals work as management consultants in Sweden (Wihlborg, 2010) and after consulting a number of influential industry seniors, I conclude that it is reasonable to assume that this figure has probably risen to at least 15,000 during the past five years.

In addition to the professional associations, there are attempts to codify the consultancy expertise in professional standards. There is an international personal certification for consultants called CMC (Certified Management Consultant) which is linked to and evaluated according to the methods adopted in the international standard ISO 17024, and an international accreditation called ACP (Accredited Consultancy Practices) developed specifically for consultancy firms (for details see www.exmi.se/samc). The latest addition to this collection of professional rules is a European Standard, published in 2011, on public procurement of management consultancy. The standard, called SS-EN 16114:2011, was developed by the Swedish Standards Institute, SIS, as part of the International Standard Organization network, ISO (for more information see http://www.

sis.se/en/sociology-services-company-organization-and-management-administration-transport/company-organization-and-management/general/ss-en-161142011).

The requirements for obtaining a personal CMC certification are the following; firstly, that the candidate must have at least five years of professional experience including three years as an independent management consultant with about 1,200 hours of work per year, and an academic degree or equivalent. The candidate must also undergo a certification program for verification of his or her competence to ensure that the candidate meets the requirements for how one should act in relation to the clients. Presentation of credentials from assignments, and a personal interview are also included in the requirements. As an illustration, the Swedish Association SAMC presents the CMC certification's "benefits to you" in five points aimed at attracting consultants to certification (www.exmi.se/samc):

*   Assures professional status that differentiates you in the market.
*   Facilitates customer quality controls and reduce costs.
*   Increases your confidence and ensures that your experience and your skill level is right in order to give customers increased value.
*   Provides you with an internationally recognized certification in over 40 countries.
*   Offers access to the international CMC network that facilitates business in different countries.

However, the question remains. Are there any consultants who voluntarily certify and accredit their work? From the time when the CMC certification was introduced in Sweden in the early 2000s, until 2007, only a handful consultants—fewer than 20—of the about 4,000 Swedish management consultants had got a certification (Alexius, 2007). Three years later, the number of certified consultants had risen significantly to about 300 in Sweden and the Swedish management consultant association SAMC set an ambitious goal to certify about 5000 Swedish consultants by 2015. However, the increase to 300 before 2010 took place in an uncertain time with a strong economic downturn—a context that traditionally encourages more people than usual to seek safety, for example through a personal certification like this. In mid-2016, the number of Swedish CMC-certified consultants has dropped down below 100 due both to low interest to get a first certification and to individuals leaving the profession and hence not getting the follow-up certification due every three years to keep the certification. For these reasons, the number of professionally active CMC-certified consultants worldwide has remained at a very stable figure of approximately 10,000 since 2010 (http://www.samc.se/certifiering/certified-management-consultant-23656510).

One argument often put forward to explain why the professional consultant associations remain weak, refers to the leading consultancy organizations' size and influence (Muzio, Kirkpatrick & Kipping, 2011). According to a report from Kennedy Information in 2004, the ten largest consultancies account for around 40 percent of industry revenues (O'Mahoney, 2010, p. 25). The argument is classic for associations that often struggle to balance and reconcile between the interests of its small and large members, where the larger are able to organize many of the association's services on their own, such as industry-PR, industry research and lobbying. O'Mahoney (2010, p. 24) notes:

> If one examines many of the national associations of management consultancies across the globe, there will usually be a notable exception to their member lists. The large strategy consultancies like McKinsey, Bain & Co. and Boston Consultancy Group are often conspicuous by their absence.

While the professional associations representing traditional experts have an obvious identity as mandatory rule setters, the consultancy associations face the challenge to sell their membership and rules on a voluntary basis (see Greiner & Ennsfellner, 2009; Alexius & Pemer, 2013).[2] The only Swedish state regulation with a direct impact on the consultants—the Public Procurement Act (LOU)—has also been met with considerable opposition from both consultants and their clients (Lindberg & Furusten, 2005; Furusten, 2015). To sum up, several attempts have been made to establish a traditional professional basis for management consultants. There are efforts to create an interest for membership in professional associations such as SAMC as well as in the CMC certification, the SIS-standard and the ACP accreditation. However, progress is slow, to say the least. How can we then make sense of the struggles encountered by those attempting to formalize and codify the consultants and their consultancy expertise?

Expert without Rules—But Why?

Why do management consultants continue to be experts without common professional regulation? Previous research on the topic may be divided into two main wings. The first and currently dominating represents what I here call a functionalist understanding of consultants' exemption from formal regulation. Its' three arguments are that 1) rules are not required because there are good alternatives, 2) it is impossible in practice to formulate effective rules for management consultancy, and 3) rules will be established with time, as the profession and market "mature". A common underpinning of the three functionalist arguments is the view of the regulatory exception as something natural, fitting or at least relatively unproblematic. This view is often voiced as an empty counter-argument along the lines of, "But *why* would consultants require formal regulation?".

The second, still poorly represented and more critical perspective, views the consultants' unique position not as natural but rather as the outcome of

Table 2.1 How can we make sense of the unregulated professional status of the management consultant as an expert without rules?

Understanding	Functionalist arguments	Critical arguments
Rules are not required!	*The informal alternatives to formal regulation, such as shared norms and mutual adjustment between consultants and their clients, are sufficient.*	*Says who? Note that the consultants' own perspective dominates the discourse. The very lack of rules makes it difficult to gain insight into the consequences of their operations. It is difficult to detect scandals and make consultants responsible.*
It is impossible to regulate consultants!	*Although rules would be desirable, it is too difficult to set and administer rules for consultants and consultancy.*	*It is a myth! Certainly, it is possible to regulate consultants. Perhaps the easiest way would be by way of mandatory legislation and frequent monitoring. Note that the tenacious myth of the impossibility of regulating consultation is recreated actively by consultants and some clients who reproduce a notion of conflict between the rules and consultation.*
Rules will come!	*The profession is young. Rules will be established and accepted in time, as the profession matures.*	*When? Management consultancy has been around for nearly a century. Other much younger industries, such as staffing and coaching already have much more established and accepted regulation.*

a tenacious myth fueled by claims to power and a successful rule resistance. Table 2.1 summarizes the main features of these functional and critical arguments.

Rules Are Not Required—Says Who?

The most common understanding of the management consultants' regulatory exception claims that formal professional regulation is not required because there are alternative, informal mechanisms sufficiently able to arrange market exchanges. The main alternatives include the normative community and mutual adaptation between consultants and their clients. If we scrutinize these in turn, we find that there clearly is a normative community within which a management consultant becomes socialized according to institutionalized expectations of how a professional management consultant should behave. As a couple of consultants I interviewed described it (translated quote from Alexius, 2007, p. 59):

> There are informal rules that I've learned in projects. I've learned them through colleagues at work so to speak.

> The consultancy firm develops a certain culture. There's some sort of common framework—a common, informal backbone.

When it is difficult to assess the quality of a service, we expect conceptions of the person selling it to become more important as a guideline of service quality (Alvesson, 2004). Therefore, it is no surprise to find that it is perceived as essential for consultants and their clients to put much effort into developing personal relationships, and to act convincingly in the absence of a clear knowledge base or common professional rules that otherwise would have granted them credibility. The consultant and client constantly evaluate each other through so-called mutual adaptation (cf. Lindblom, 2003, for a general discussion of this mechanism of social order). As a rule of thumb, the consultant needs to qualify and pass this informal evaluation in a smaller project before possibly moving on to greater cooperation in larger client projects. A consultant I interviewed put it in the following way (translated quote from Alexius, 2007, p. 60):

> You can tell immediately if the customer's confidence begins to wane. The most important thing about the consultancy industry, compared to the line organization, is that you always have to measure up and deliver in each assignment. If you fail to make the customer happy, you may not get paid. Thus you get rapid feedback, a correction if something goes wrong. If you make crazy mistakes all the time, you'll lose your assignments and any additional assignments.

The consultant expertise is earned in every situation when the consultant manages to convince the client that the proposed and delivered services are worth the invested money. Personal relationships, trust and reciprocity created between the market actors, according to this view, are central to the understanding of how consultants can be perceived as professional experts, even though they lack the traditional expert's characteristics (cf. Chapters 1 and 9). In short, it is the client perception that determines the expert status of the consultant, not the presentation of a certificate or membership in a professional association. As a consultant I interviewed put it (translated quote from Alexius, 2007, pp. 82–83),

> If you sell a business system that is known, it may be that the customer comes from a company where they had just that business system, so she knows the product and wants it. For a management consultant it is almost 100 per cent trust built on a personal relationship. It is not so that you call up a company and ask them to send over a consultant. That is extremely rare. It is more like "I want Paul because I know Paul from working with him before. I can accept Paul plus some people he thinks will be good for this project. And then I trust Paul, that he has some good people with him".

The shared norms and mutual adaptation between the parties also affect the perception of boundaries between the consultant and the client—where the boundaries are typically perceived as both unclear and fluid—both at the organizational and individual level. In many cases, the similarities outweigh the differences and the collaboration may be governed in a mode of mutual respect on the basis of shared values rather than formal rules (Sturdy, Clark, Fincham & Handley, 2009; Sturdy, 2011).

This sounds amazing, but what say the critics of the notion that rules are not required for management consultancy? Are the informal alternatives really sufficient? A critical understanding notes, first of all, that the consultants themselves have long retained the grip over the discourse of the dominant images of the industry. It is primarily the consultants' voices about the state of the industry that we hear, and they affect our perceptions of what happens and does not happen there (cf. Sturdy, Werr & Buono, 2009, which specifically highlight lack of clients' perspective on the industry). For example, there is a widespread perception that consultants' rules are not required because there is no weak individual to protect (as in the case of the doctor and the patient), nor any affected third party (such as the many stakeholders of the organization, in the auditor's case). However, management consultants' work does, of course, bring about great consequences and at times risks and costs for millions of individuals and third parties around the globe (O'Mahoney, 2010). The difference compared to doctors and accountants is that in the consultants' case, any negative outcome will most likely have a slight negative impact on the consultants, as their client typically takes the blame in accordance with the institutionalized belief in rationalist decision-making.

The consultants' power over the discourse of their practice may be seen in how suggested professional regulation more often is associated with problems than with solutions to problems of coordination. Typically, consultants treat all types of formal rules with the same skepticism, rather than differentiating between better and worse rules as is more common among rule skeptics in other areas of social life (Alexius, 2007). The consultants' power over the discourse also makes it more difficult for critics to be heard and to initiate a balanced discussion about the pros and cons of professional regulation.

Researchers specializing in procurement have long stressed costly uncertainty problems associated with procurement of consultancy services. An uncertainty that is linked to the complex, intangible and heterogeneous nature of the service (Clark, 1995; Axelsson & Wynstra, 2002; Axelsson, 2005; Furusten, 2015). Other researchers have questioned whether consultants are able to follow a personal ethical internal compass, given the lack of professional regulation (Kitay & Wright, 2004; Hagenmeyer, 2007). Of course, there are also consultants, especially those new to the industry, who are experiencing the current regime as problematic. It usually takes a long time and requires significant efforts for a new consultant to earn confidence from clients. This is the type of coordination cost that the introduction of rules can typically reduce.

There are a number of ex-consultants who have made it their mission to describe the downside of consultancy (see, for example, Craig, 2005). But it is as if these critical accounts—e.g., of consultants who "plunder" the public sector—not really are taken seriously but rather may be dismissed as tabloid literature and after effect reasoning (Craig, 2005 and Craig & Brooks, 2006). The notion of rules as superfluous is protected by the mighty. A good example is BDU. In the 1990s, the German consultancy association launched campaigns to try to bring about legislation on formal tests and compulsory membership (the same status as the traditional professions' associations enjoy). In 1997, however, the Minister of Commerce rejected the proposal. Three reasons were advanced for the decision: Such a law would limit the selection of the clients, it would limit German consultants to sell their services abroad, and third; the law was considered unnecessary because the consultants' reputation was considered to work well enough as a quality regulator in the market (Groß & Kieser, 2006). This is yet an example of the influential notion that consultants and their clients—unlike other experts and their stakeholders—are able to solve any eventuality and controversy without professional regulation.

Another illustrative example is taken from the ISO/SIS-standard on "effective delivery of management consultancy services", developed in 2011. After four years of work, the technical committee developing the standard offers a truly broad and open rule that may be interpreted in numerous ways. Interesting is also the outspoken claim that the standard should not be used as a benchmark for certification (quotes from the standard summary, see http://www.sis.se/en/sociology-services-company-organization-and-management-administration-transport/company-organization-and-management/general/ss-en-161142011):

> This European Standard is applicable to all MCSPs: public and private companies, government entities, not-for-profit organizations and internal consultancy units, regardless of their ownership, structure, size or specialism. This European Standard applies to any type of assignment for any type of client. It does not place any obligations on the client.
>
> Any offer to certify, or claims to be certified, to this European Standard would be a misrepresentation of the intent and purpose and a misuse of this European Standard. As this European Standard does not contain requirements, any such certification would not be a demonstration of conformity with this European Standard.

The traditional regulatory research has assumed that rules are set when and where they are "needed", typically in response to a high-profile scandal or crisis such as a "market failure" (Nordström, 2004). But reasonably, one can also imagine the opposite. The presence of rules is in fact a prerequisite for many scandals to be detected. Policy remedies not only scandals but also fulfills a function to detect any anomalies. For what do management consultants usually receive public criticism? Mainly, the (high) fees. One can then ask whether this critique may be related to the fact that fees are detectable in the client organization's accounting, which is formally regulated by laws and standards. It is very likely that there are problems and scandals in the consultancy field, which today remain hidden efficiently due to the lack of transparency derived from the consultants' exception from formal professional regulation.

A second core argument in the functionalist understanding of the management consultants' free zone in the otherwise regulated expert community, is to judge any formal codification attempts beforehand as hopeless failures. In essence: although it would be desirable to try, it is not worth the effort because it would be impossible to create an effective professional regulation for management consultants. Some of the consultants I interviewed reasoned as follows (translated quote from Alexius, 2007, pp. 64–65):

> "Consultant", that can mean virtually anything. So it gets very difficult to make rules for it.
> The only thing we can agree on is claptrap. In fact, we can't even agree on basic ethics. There have been several attempts over the years to regulate consultants but they've never been successful.

Is it then really the case that it is impossible to set rules for management consultancy? Or, should we perhaps understand the difficulties of regulating consultants as an expression of the power of an influential elite over the discourse about their business? Can it be that consultants in general are motivated by freedom and actively shun both bureaucracies and other types of formal regulation? Management consultants are quick to tell their clients what to do, but when the rules apply to themselves, they show reluctance.

In Alexius (2007) I analyzed the consultants' rule-skeptical discourse in terms of an elusive "rule resistance", which contributes to making it difficult to create rules that are able to visualize potential problems and scandals. As discussed earlier, consultants have a lot to gain from keeping clear of formal regulation. By consistently describing themselves as unique and independent of individual organizations, consultants gain a greater personal freedom in their work. In addition, consultants have better opportunities to charge higher fees as the reference to unique and personal features of the services make it more difficult for clients to compare offers systematically. It can also be difficult for the consultancy association to identify who can be expected to become members and what constitutes "good" consultation. While regulation is facilitated by *explicitness*, *generality* and *stability*, consultation is typically described as *vague*, *unique* and *changeable*. Simply put, this constantly reproduced gap makes consultants and consultation appear elusive for rule setters (Alexius, 2007).

It is fair to assume that it would be in the clients' interest to regulate consultants and standardize consultation to be better able to compare services, reduce prices, pointing out the shortcomings in quality, etc. Some such more or less failed attempts have been conducted. However, it is crucial to ponder whether not also the clients themselves have a lot to gain from safeguarding the regulatory free zone of management consultancy (especially the clients who work closely with consultants on strategic matters). It is a fact that both parties—consultant and client—enjoy the benefits of the unregulated free zone where they are able to act more freely within their personal networks and temporary project whose events can "fall between the cracks" in relation to the consultant and the client organization's direct control capabilities, and hence escape regulation all together. I suspect that many clients are prepared to face the disadvantage involved with greater uncertainty and inefficiency that can follow when you deal with a nearly unregulated industry, in order to avoid transparency in their own most delicate matters. Pointing in this direction, privacy procedures and arbitration practice in conflicts already help to keep the innermost cooperation between customer and client shaded to the outside world, even if the clients' purchasing departments have advanced their positions a bit during the latest recession (Werr & Pemer, 2007; O'Mahoney, 2010). Based on this power-centered understanding, there is reason to be critical to the "myth" that management consultants "do not require" or "cannot" be formally regulated and we must focus more attention on how and why such myths are maintained.

RULES WILL COME, IN TIME—BUT WHEN?

The third common functionalist argument about the unregulated free zone of management consultants regards the exception as a temporary, transient condition. Viewing management consultancy as a young and "immature" industry in an "entrepreneurial" phase, one can choose to assume that traditional experts' characteristics—a clear knowledge, clear rules and limits to non-experts—will come in time, as the industry and its actors grow and mature (see, Giddens, 1990; Kubr, 1996; Reed, 1996; Abbot, 1998). This evolutionary hypothesis presupposes that older organizations tend to become more bureaucratic. Not only because of their often larger size but also by way of so-called path dependence—the idea that the creation and maintenance of formal rules and structures is facilitated if there are already established rules and structures to build on. So how about this argument? Is it reasonable to regard consultancy as a young profession? Can we expect that over time it will "mature" and evolve toward a higher degree of established and accepted formal rules?

First and foremost, it is important to note that the elite of all times has hired "management" experts for advice and implementation. Biblical kings had their prophets, the Greek sovereign states hired the Oracle at Delphi and the mafia has had its consigliere (O'Mahoney, 2010, p. 16). Even if we restrict ourselves to the common idea that management consultancy like we think of it today began to develop in earnest around 1920, we find that this is an industry of a respectable age, a century after all (cf. Kipping, 1999; McKenna, 2006 on historical industry development). The consultant role is therefore not new in the historical sense, but the field is still regarded as young as it has remained so comparatively informally arranged. Some consultant associations are over 60 years old—but they have remained weak. Is this because the profession is still "young"? If we compare the development of much younger but closely related industries, such as the staffing and coaching industries, these have clearly and strategically evolved in the direction of the traditional professions' formal characteristics. The difference seems to be a willingness and an interest in the potential benefits of regulation, while most management consultants are unwilling because they cherish their freedom and flexibility and see more downsides than upsides with the formal professionalization attempts in the field.

As we have seen in this chapter, management consultancy is characterized by diametrically opposite conditions to those of traditional experts; a vague knowledge base with a smorgasbord of skills to choose from—rather than a uniform common knowledge base, and more open and informal boundaries between experts and non-experts active in the field—rather than formal control of the border between experts and non-experts (see Table 2.2). And yet—despite the highly unsuccessful attempts at establishing traditional professional expert characteristics accounted for in this chapter (like those of professional associations, standards and certification)—there is order in this field, an informal trust-based "new professional" order that is different, but not evidently better nor worse.

It remains to be seen, however, how long the management consultants retain the discursive and rhetorical power over the discourse that their free zone from rules is a "natural" and unproblematic one. Perhaps public procurers' growing demand for a formal consultant legitimization will eventually give the challenged rule setters wind in the sails. Time will tell. In closing, I would

Table 2.2 What makes an expert an expert? Traditional and new professional characteristics

Traditional professional experts characteristics for example a lawyer, accountant and doctor	*Uniform common knowledge base*	*Formal control of the border between experts and non-experts*
Non-traditional experts (new) professional characteristics for example a management consultant	*Unclear knowledge base—a smorgasbord of knowledge*	*Open, informally arranged boundaries between experts and non-experts*

like to leave the readers with some questions for further reflection: What would happen to management consultation as an expertise if it were regulated and codified in accordance with the standards of traditional professions? Is a uniform knowledge base always preferable to a diversity smorgasbord? What, if anything, do we lose if strict guards close off the open and flexible boundaries of the field and the playful improvisation that has good chances to thrive in a less restricted environment becomes limited in favor of a standardized approach? Dare we continue to rely on the "new professionally" ordered experts, or has the time come for the consultants to step into line?

Notes

1 In addition, SAMC has accepted four individual consultants, all senior male consultants, as honorary members (http://www.samc.se/medlemmar-24084030, 31 March 2016).
2 In a comparative study of a number of different associations for consultants in Sweden (Alexius & Pemer, 2012), we found that the associations were typically ambivalent to their rule setting. The associations that succeeded in acquiring the most members and resources appeared rather as CEO clubs or service partners than as formal rule setters for their members' professional practice.

References

Abbot, A. (1998). *The Systems of Professions: An Essay on the Division of Expert Labor*. Chicago: University of Chicago Press.

Alexius, S. (2007). *Regelmotståndarna—om konsten att undkomma regler*. Dissertation in Business Administration. Stockholm: EFI Publishing, The Stockholm School of Economics.

Alexius, S. & Furusten, S. (2005). Dealing with values. In Furusten, S. & Werr, A. (eds.), *Dealing with Confidence- the Construction of Needs and Trust in Management Advisory Services*. Copenhagen: Copenhagen Business School Press, 201–216.

Alexius, S. & Pemer, F. (2013). Struggling to challenge an informal field order—professional associations as standard-setters. In Buono, A., Stoppelenburg, A. & de Caluwé, L. (eds.), *Exploring the Professional Identify of Management Consultants*. Greenwich: Information Age Publishing Inc., 119–138.

Alvesson, M. (2004). *Knowledge Work and Knowledge-Intensive Firms*. Oxford: Oxford University Press.

Axelsson, B. (2005). Purchasing as supply management. In Furusten, S. & Werr, A. (eds.), *Dealing with Confidence—The Confidence of Need and Trust in Management Advisory Services*. Copenhagen: Copenhagen Business School Press, 39–58.

Axelsson, B. & Wynstra, F. (2002). *Bying Business Services*. Chichester: Wiley.

Clark, T. (1995). *Managing Consultants: Consultancy as the Management of Impressions*. Buckingham: Open University Press.

Craig, D. (2005). *Rip Off! The Scandalous Inside Story of the Management Consultancy Money Machine*. London: The Original Book Company.

Craig, D. & Brooks, R. (2006). *Plundering the Public Sector*. London: Constable.

Furusten, S. (2003). *God Managementkonsultation—Reglerad Expertis Eller Improviserat Artisteri?* Lund: Studentlitteratur.

Furusten, S. (2009). Management consultants as improvising agents of stability. *Scandinavian Journal of Management, 25*(3), 264–274.

Furusten, S. (2015). *Dåliga kunder gör bra affärer—Ett dilemma i offentlig upphandling*. Stockholm: Liber.

Furusten, S., Werr, A. & Alexius, S. (2012). *Idealist Innovations and Emperor's New Clothes—CSR and the Consultancy Sector: What Services are Offered and by Whom?* Paper Presented at EGOS 2012, Sub-theme 50 Management Consultancy: Exploring the Boundaries and Alternatives, Helsinki 5–7 juli.

Giddens, A. (1990). *The Consequences of Modernity*. Stanford: Stanford University Press.

Greiner, L. & Ennsfellner, I. (2009). Management consultants as professionals, or are they? *Organizational Dynamics, 39*(1), 72–83.

Groß, C. & Kieser, A. (2006). *Are Consultants Moving towards Professionalization?* In Greenwood, R. & Suddaby, R. (eds.), *Professional Service Firms (Research in the Sociology of Organizations, Volume 24)*. Bingley: Emerald, 69–100.

Hagenmeyer, U. (2007). Integrity in management consultancy: A contradiction in terms? *Business Ethics: A European Review, 16*(2), 107–113.

Kipping, M. (1999), American management consultancies in Western Europe. 1920 to 1990: products, reputation, and relationships. *Business History Review, 73*(Summer), 190–220.

Kitay, J. & Wright, C. (2004). Take the money and run? Organizational boundaries and consultants' roles. *Service Industries Journal, 24*(3), 1–19.

Kubr, M. (1996). *Management Consultancy—A Guide to the Profession* (3rd revised edition). Genève: ILO.

Kyrö, P. (1995). *The Management Consultancy Industry—Described by Using the Concept of Profession*. Helsinki: Helsinki University, Department of Education.

Lindberg, K. & Furusten, S. (2005). Breaking Laws—Making Deals: Procurement of management consultants in the public sector. In Furusten, S. & Werr, A. (eds.), *Dealing with Confidence—The Construction of Need and Trust in Management Advisory Services*. Copenhagen: Copenhagen Business School Press, 169–183.

Lindblom, C. E. (2003). *Marknad och samhälle*. Stockholm: SNS.

McKenna, C. (2006). *The World's Newest Profession*. Cambridge: Cambridge University Press.

Muzio, D., Kirkpatrick, I. & Kipping, M. (2011). Professions, organizations and the state: Applying the sociology of the professions to the case of management consultancy. *Current Sociology, 59*(6), 805–824.

Nordström, A. (2004). Reglerare reglerade och regelskapande processer. In Ahrne, G. & Brunsson, N. (eds.), *Regelexplosionen*. Stockholm: EFI, 9–44.

O'Mahoney, J. (2010). *Management Consultancy*. Oxford: Oxford University Press.

Reed, M. I. (1996). Expert power and control in late modernity: An empirical review and theoretical synthesis. *Organization Studies, 17*(4), 573–597.

Sturdy, A. (2011). Consultancy's consequences? A critical assessment of management consultancy's impact on management. *British Journal of Management, 22*, 517–530.

Sturdy, A., Clark, T., Fincham, R. & Handley, K. (2009). Between innovation and legitimation—Boundaries and knowledge flow in management consultancy. *Organization, 16*(5), 627–653.

Sturdy, A., Werr, A. & Buono, A. (2009). The client in management consultancy research: Mapping the territory. *Scandinavian Journal of Management, 25*, 247–252.

Werr, A. & Pemer, F. (2007). Purchasing management consultancy services—From management autonomy to purchasing involvement. *Journal of Purchasing and Supply Management, 13*, 98–112.

Whittle, A. (2008). From flexibility to work-life balance: Exploring the changing discourses of management consultants. *Organization, 15*(4), 513–534.

Wihlborg, A. (2010). En yrkesroll med snabbt växande krav. *Konsult, 2*, 2010.

3 Watchdog or Business Partner?
The Dual Role of Certification Auditors

Kristina Tamm Hallström

Experts with Multiple Audiences

This chapter is about the construction of expertise within *certification* auditing, that is, the expertise required to perform certification auditing based on standards such as ISO 9001 on quality assurance, ISO 14001 on environmental management, the Forest Stewardship Council (FSC) standards on sustainable forestry, and the like. Compared to the previous chapter on management consultants in which the author constructed their expertise in an informal way, there is an elaborate set of formalized rules that structure this field. In the chapter, I will discuss the character of these formalization efforts and structures that have evolved around this type of expertise, how they are justified, who is involved in organizing them, and some of the consequences of this way of organizing certification auditing expertise.

The work of certification auditors has a dual character. On the one hand, it serves a "public watchdog" function on behalf of the public interest representing consumers, investors and society at large, to check whether companies are performing well in relation to a certain standard. In this role, distance and objectively performed auditing are part of the work although the result of such auditing may upset the organization audited. On the other hand, certification auditors sell their auditing services on the market and to attract customers—the companies paying for the service of being certified—they need to be perceived as a trustful business partner who signals benevolence rather than mistrust and who does not cause dissatisfaction. The following quote illustrates this second dimension of "the business of auditing".

> [I]f you are Coca Cola and you are inviting someone to come and do your audits, then you've got a conflict of interest because of the huge amount of money and the very powerful client name that the certification body will lose if it upsets that client. And one way you can upset the client is by giving them lots of major non-conformities.
> (Interview with certification auditor working for the membership organization IRCA in London, February 2013)

The topic addressed in this chapter is about the very tension between independent auditing and the economic dependency of certification auditors. The question posed is as follows: *How do certification auditors manage the task of convincing about both their legitimacy as independent auditors and their trustworthiness as business partners?*

Before discussing this question, we will give a short description of the work of certification auditors, followed by an account of the political developments that constitute a background and driving force behind the expanding markets for certification auditing.

The Practical Work of Certification Auditors

Certification auditors are external experts that are hired by a company that wishes to be certified against a certain standard. The certification auditor conducts audits against a standard and in case of compliance with the requirement stated in the standard used for the certification, the certification auditor may issue a certificate that the audited company may use towards stakeholders to communicate a "proof" or approval that the business activities are performing well in terms of the requirements in question. A well-known example of a certificate is the ISO 9001 that may be found on the websites and contracts of, for example, automotive manufacturers, health-care centers and dental practices. Certification is not a new phenomenon, but it is diffusing and applied in an increasing number of empirical settings such as manufacturing companies, service providers, governmental as well as non-governmental organizations, childcare providers, and grocery stores. There are also standards that address an increasing number of organizational aspects: work safety, sustainability, equality, fairness, human rights, etcetera.

The standard behind the ISO 9001 certificate, to take just one example, is the ISO 9001 standard on quality management systems issued by the International Organization for Standardization (ISO). This particular standard, but also many others, is a management system standard. Put simply, a management system is a documented framework of policies, processes and procedures that should guide an organization in its daily work of fulfilling decided tasks required to achieve the goals it has set. The ISO 9000 series of management system standards, initially issued in 1987, was the first standard of this type that became a global success, and there are today numerous management system standards that followed suit, although with diverse values in focus (e.g., environmental management, social responsibility, sustainable forestry).

The main task of a certification auditor checking compliance with such a standard is to check that a documented management system is in place, that it is coherent and articulate, and to make a judgment about whether this system is integrated in the daily practice of the certified company. More specifically, depending on the size of the business activity being audited, a certification auditor, or a team of such auditors, go through all documentation of the drafted management system together with a selection of managers, to check whether the documented processes and routines are rational, coherent and well-articulated in accordance with the requirements of the standard in question. The audit process may take place in a meeting room with the auditor going through the paragraphs of the standard, step by step, and posing questions to the representatives of the certified organization about the practical work with the management system developed by the client organization.

Political Dimensions of Auditing Expertise

Certification auditors, being an expert group that during the past decades has increased considerably in numbers, play a crucial role in contemporary markets by their contribution to the assurance of crucial financial and non-financial values in market transactions, quality and safety, for example. More specifically, there is an increase in certification auditors working for private inspection companies, typically labeled 'certification bodies' that may be large multinationals active in several countries certifying against a broad array of standards and possessing certification expertise for several types of businesses. There are also smaller certification companies whose business activities are limited to the national, or even local level, and to certification against a smaller number of standards with smaller businesses among their clients.

The expansion of privately employed certification auditors is linked to the trend for governments to liberalize, deregulate, privatize and delegate numerous responsibilities to the private sector. In turn, this has led to a shift from inspection organized as a state-run function, to a greater emphasis on organizational solutions of self-inspection based on standards complemented by certification services provided by specialized certification auditing companies (Power, 1997; Bernstein & Cashore, 2007; Mennicken, 2010; Bartley, 2011; Tamm Hallström & Gustafsson, 2014).

Parallel to this political trend, is the increased interest, in times of intense global transactions, in regulatory solutions with a transnational reach (Brunsson & Jacobsson, 2000; Tamm Hallström, 2004; Djelic & Sahlin-Andersson, 2006; Tamm Hallström & Boström, 2010), as well as an increased interest in non-financial values, such as sustainability, human rights, fair trade, occupational health and safety. Often such values are articulated and pushed for by social movement organizations, for example through the development and promotion of eco-labels with a certification mechanism (Dubuisson-Quellier, 2013). Well-known examples are the Fairtrade label found on coffee and tea, organic labels on fruit and vegetables in grocery stores, or sustainability labels on toilet paper and stationery.

As a consequence, when values such as human rights, safety and labor rights increasingly are regulated through certification standards, it becomes all the more obvious that the work of certification auditors is of high societal value. It is not only the certified companies that may improve their reputation and be seen as trustworthy by various stakeholders in the market through demonstrating that they are certified (Lindeberg, 2007). Certification may also be seen as a tool to exercise politics (Tamm Hallström, 2006; Bartley, 2007), not least regarding business relations and transactions across national borders. Thus, there is an inherent political dimension in certification auditing, as is also the case in financial auditing (Humphrey & Moizer, 1990; Gendron, Cooper & Townley, 2001).

In this political role, acting in the public interest, certification auditors contribute to the assurance of values that are publicly articulated as crucial to consider. If an auditor audits and approves a company's work on occupational health and safety, and later on it is revealed that several employees are hurt due to bad working conditions, there are consequences at many levels: at the level of the individual workers, of the individual auditor, and at the societal level in terms of health care, for example. Thus, as the work of auditors has clear implications at the societal level it is crucial that there is a perception about auditors making correct judgments and acting with professionalism. If it is not believed that they possess sufficient expertise and are capable of doing independent audits, their authority as experts may be endangered.

The practice of organizing inspection and auditing as a commercial commodity fits well with the contemporary belief in market solutions, which thus strengthens the support for this type of regulation (Rose & Miller, 1992; Power, 1997; Higgins & Tamm Hallström, 2007). However, the very fact that market actors perform auditing and inspection activities also poses challenges to the auditing companies providing such services. In order to convince about their purpose to serve the public interest by assuring that companies comply with certain standards, there should, according to contemporary auditing ideals, exist no dependencies between the auditing firm and the company being audited (Humphrey & Moizer, 1990; Sikka & Willmott, 1995; Power, 2003). However, as certification auditors have a business relationship with the audited companies, they are economically dependent on them, in turn contradicting the necessary independence and this problem is often exacerbated when the audited company sells additional advisory services to the audited party (cf. Power, 2003; Hatanaka & Busch, 2008; Boiral & Gendron, 2011). As argued earlier, an interesting question then becomes how this type of expertise is constructed both as legitimate in the eyes of society at large, and as trustworthy and valuable to the customers paying for the auditing services. In the remainder of the chapter, we will discuss this question. First, however, we provide a brief account of the methodology used for the studies used to illustrate the reasoning.

Methodology

The discussion draws on qualitative research made during the years 2009–2014[1] of the organization and conduct of certification practices, including interviews with a large number of certification and accreditation auditors in Sweden, the Netherlands and the UK and representatives of state agencies responsible for approving the mandate to perform accreditation in these three countries, with international membership organizations for standard setters, certification bodies and accreditation bodies within the field of sustainability and organic farming, with business associations of both certification bodies and certification auditors, and with companies being audited for standards such as ISO 9001, ISO 14001, PEFC (the Programme for the Endorsement of Forest Certification) and FSC (Forest Stewardship Council). Participant observations have also been conducted of certification processes, including observations of the work of conducting office audits with audit team discussions, auditors' presentations of their audit reports to the management team of audited companies, and of auditors doing field visits in certified forest areas as part of the certification process. Questions posed have regarded the interviewees' experiences about challenges involved in organizing for trustworthiness and performing auditing work, about who has been involved in establishing this organization and the justifications behind such organizational decisions.

Finally, analysis of written documentation, found through websites, investigations made by involved stakeholders, as well as certification and accreditation standards were also made.

In Search of Legitimacy—Organizing for Independence

In the field of critical accounting studies, it is widely acknowledged that there is a complexity, or tension, at the heart of the auditing business—that auditing is a business at the same time as it is a function that serves the public interest. The main way of handling this tension, and of constructing an image of "independent auditing", is through the professionalization of financial auditors (Humphrey & Moizer, 1990; Sikka & Willmott, 1995; Humphrey, Loft & Woods, 2009; Sikka, 2009). The idea is that auditors, through their professionalism, should be able to perform "objective" and "neutral" audits.

With reference to this literature, one could expect that certification auditing would share similarities with financial auditing in the ways of establishing legitimacy and competitive advantages through professional authority (cf. Abbott, 1988; Tamm Hallström, 2004; Humphrey et al., 2009; Botzem, 2012).

This is not the case, however. Certification auditors do not have their background in financial accounting and audit, and there is no formal requirement regarding their education or background in the same way as for financial auditors. Many certification auditors conducting management system certification based on standards such as ISO 9001 and ISO 14001 have an engineering background, but there are also many auditors with another academic and professional background, within environmental legal studies or general management, for example. Certification auditors could rather be seen as a professional group composed of a variety of competences. Still, we may observe other organizational solutions in this emerging field. One main organizational measure has been identified: accreditation of certification organizations.[2]

Accreditation of the Certification Body

Accreditation is an auditing activity, but with the purpose of assuring the quality of certification. Thus, accreditation is an organizational solution developed to install legitimacy in certification as an "independent" auditing activity. Accreditation may be compulsory, for instance for certain product areas or purchasing situations decided by the EU. However, in many auditing contexts accreditation has remained a voluntary regulatory activity. Still, during the past decade accreditation has become an institutionalized practice for certification companies, as described by an interviewed certification auditor.

> Most clients want a certification body with accreditation. If you want someone to audit your company, then you want a proper "receipt". Otherwise you might as well do it yourself or ask your neighbor to do it.
> (Interview with certification auditor, September 2010)

In the accreditation standard ISO/IEC 17021:2011 used to accredit certification organizations working with management system certification based on ISO standards, for example, there are detailed rules about how the accredited certification organization should be organized in order to be truly independent, such as having routines for how to identify and sanction nonconformities; the recommendation to avoid consultation services, or at least to organize consultation and training departments separately and staff these departments by other employees than the ones working with audits; the establishment of a committee of external experts for safeguarding impartiality; and rules about time limits of contracts between an individual auditor and a customer firm (3–5 years). All these rules are about safeguarding the value of independence. Some of these requirements are similar to the ones applied in the field of financial auditing, such as the separation between auditing and consultancy services, and the recommended time limit for an individual auditor to work with one and the same client.

Moreover, the value of competence is specifically highlighted in the accreditation standard, that is, the use of proper competence and certification expertise and documented auditing experience from the type of businesses being certified. Within certification with reference to ISO standards, it often means, as noted earlier, that certification auditors are trained as engineers, but other backgrounds are also common such as scholars of management or legal studies. Going through the paragraph on "resource requirements" in the 2011 accreditation standard for management system certification firms, it is notable that it has been substantially extended from the previous version of 2006, implying that the requirements on the certification auditors' competence have been raised. Moreover, it is required that the certification firm documents its processes both for determining the necessary competence of its personnel, and for initial competence evaluation as well as ongoing monitoring of competence and performance of all personnel involved in the management and performance of audits and certification (ISO/IEC 17021:2011). In practice these requirements, that are directed toward the management of certification organization, are translated into internal policies about the competence and experiences of employed auditors, which also is a requirement stated in the accreditation standard ISO Guide 65. Many certification companies have set up internal training activities and courses for employed auditors and have policies about the length of experience from a certain field of practice or business in order to be able to work independently as an auditor in that field or type of business. Still, as noted earlier, there are no strict requirements regarding specific training or academic background, which thus means that the requirements differ from the ones used in the field of financial auditing where affiliation with a professional auditing organization with more standardized criteria for auditing competence is required as an assurance mechanism for their independence.

When it comes to the actual accreditation audit, there are many similarities with the practices of certification audits. One auditor working with both FSC and ISO 9001 certification audits describes how accreditation audits are performed.

> As a certification body we have accreditation audits once a year, both office audits and field visits. There are different accreditation bodies [and auditing processes] depending on what standard it concerns but in principle these accreditations are all based on ISO standards [such as ISO 17021 and ISO Guide 65]. There is Swedac [the Swedish state-run accreditation body], but then there are others for FSC, for example. Then it's ASI [Accreditation Services International]. ASI and Swedac work in the same way with office audits and field audits.
>
> (Interview with certification auditor, December 2011)

According to the EU regulation 765/2008, decided by the EU commission to be applied within the internal market, accreditation should be run by a state agency. Moreover, all national accreditation bodies of the member countries should be members of the meta-organization European Accreditation (EA). EA audits its members through a peer review procedure based on the ISO

17011 standard. In addition to the EA membership, accreditation bodies are members of the International Accreditation Forum (IAF), which thus means that there are three layers of control to establish legitimacy for the practice of certification auditors (Gustafsson & Tamm Hallström, 2013).

Accreditation and meta-accreditation are found also in fields and countries where the rules about EU accreditation structures do not apply, such as in the sustainability field where certification often is based on other standards than ISO ones, such as the FSC forestry standards, the Marine Stewardship Council (MSC) standards, the Aquaculture Stewardship Council (ASC) standards, and the Social Accountability International (SAI) standards on sustainable working conditions. These standard setters are not part of the EU regulation for accreditation, but have instead decided to establish their own accreditation structures, which means that an international non-governmental organization performs accreditation worldwide. In the case of FSC, MSC and ASC standards, it is the Accreditation Services International (ASI) that accredits all certification firms around the world wishing to obtain the right to conduct this type of certification. In the SAI case it is the Social Accountability Accreditation Services (SAAS) having this role. Both ASI and SAAS were established in 2007 and the accreditation procedure is mandatory. In the promotion of their accreditation services, arguments about guaranteeing competence and impartiality reoccur. Many of these organizations, both standard setters and accreditation bodies, are also members of the international organization ISEAL Alliance that performs audits of its members as a measure to establish legitimacy for their standard setting and auditing activities respectively. Thus, there are many organizations, to say the least, that perform various auditing procedures to assure the value of independence within certification auditing.

So far, the focus on the accounts made in this chapter has been placed on the expansion of certification auditing and the escalating control structures that are developed to legitimize these practices and the competence of auditors involved in them. What is lacking, still, is an understanding of how certification auditors, promoting their independence and purpose of serving the public interest, manage to establish and maintain a trustworthy, and, hopefully, long-term, business relationship with the companies they sell their services to. To provide some insights in this dimension of the construction of auditing expertise, the following section accounts for the relationship between the auditor and the paying customers, that is, the audited companies.

Maintaining a Trustworthy Business Relationship with the Client

One interviewed certification auditor describes how a good way of maintaining a trustworthy relationship with the client organization, is to play down the appearance of being a "public watchdog" and rather to integrate the checking activities into a constructive dialogue.

> The best audit, according to me, is when I manage to talk to the staff of the client organization and they perceive that they've had a lot of nice conversations without feeling that I've actually checked them straight through the requirements of the standard.
>
> (Interview with certification auditor, May 2010)

There were also several examples in the material of how the auditor showed benevolence toward the client through letting the client participate in the organizing of the audit work. One example regards the selection of specific business activities to audit during a certification visit, or the selection of managers to interview at this occasion regarding the daily work with the management system.

More specifically, at a certification visit the auditor may ask the client to display the documented routine for handling complaints, or the routine for follow-ups and evaluation of actions taken, and then ask to meet the managers responsible for such routines for further descriptions and illustrations of recent examples of how the organization works with these processes in practice. According to auditing practice, it should be the auditor who chooses what routines to look at specifically. However, the company to be audited often prepares before the auditor's visit by choosing the managers who are "appropriate" for use in such interviews and determining specific and good examples to use for illustrations. One interviewed quality manager at a certified company gave the following account of how the company usually prepared for a certification audit.

> The quality manager and the environmental manager make these plans [regarding what ought to be audited during the certification processes] and we coordinate the plans before they are finally set together with the external auditors. We always discuss what we want the auditors to focus on.
>
> (Interview with quality manager at a Swedish telecom company, May 2010)

During an interview, the environmental manager of the same company confirmed that the certification, on the one hand, could be seen as a control made by the external auditors, but that the company paying for this service, on the other hand, often has a very clear idea about what ought to be checked. During a participant observation of a FSC certification process in a Swedish forest company, a similar situation was observed during a discussion about what specific forest areas were to be visited as part of the field audit of the company. The representatives of the forest company that were in charge of the certification process had before the auditor's visit prepared a route for the afternoon with planned visits to four different forest areas and explained that the chosen areas represented an interesting variation of different forestry activities: clearing, thinning, burning and felling. The auditor accepted the proposed plan but commented that, according to the certification rules, it really should be the auditor, not the client, deciding about the spots for the field audits.

Another type of situation observed regarded the choice of auditor to conduct the audits. The environmental manager at a studied telecom company described how they sometimes were not satisfied with an auditor because that person did not possess the "right" qualities in terms of perceived knowledge, or posed questions and communicated with the client in an unsatisfactory way, which usually lead to a replacement of the auditor. Other auditors were highly appreciated and kept for a long time. However, as stated in the relevant accreditation standards, for the risk of losing the necessary independence an individual auditor may not work for the same client for too long (typically a maximum of 3–5 years in a row). Still, in practice, certified companies may find ways of keeping the auditors they prefer, as explained by an interviewed certification auditor who had worked for the same client for 20 years. As it was a fairly large company that had hired this auditor, the auditor had worked with an auditing team, which enabled the auditor to stay for all these years as the other auditors of the team were changed on a regular basis.

Yet another type of situation illustrating how a certification auditor works to maintain a good business relationship with the client was found during a certification process, and more specifically during participant observations of a pre-meeting between the team of auditors and a few representatives of a client company. During this meeting, the auditors were to present the preliminary results of the four days long audit process that was just finished. A few days after this pre-meeting, the team of auditors would meet the top management of the company to present the final audit report.

During the pre-meeting Auditor 1 and Auditor 4 raised the point that they both had made notes about a minor deviation (a non-conformity) from the standard. It concerned the company's purchasing function: in the documented management system, there were no criteria articulated regarding the choice of suppliers and the evaluation of the purchase after delivery. Furthermore, the auditors could not find any trace (verifications) of what criteria had been used by the company in these situations, nor any trace of how the company had evaluated the purchases made during the past period. The auditors argued that this non-conformity was about the lack of document control, which according to the standard is a requirement; criteria and routines for the evaluation should be clearly identified and placed on the company's intranet, together with visible traces of decisions taken in such purchasing processes. Auditor 1 explained that one example identified of this type of non-conformity regarded how the company managed dissatisfied customers in situations when the company had outsourced a service to a sub-contractor. In the management system, it was stated that complaints from dissatisfied customers should be attended to within eight hours, but the auditors could not find any trace of measurements made by the company regarding how well their subcontractors kept the eight-hour time limit.

When the quality and environmental management group, representing the audited company at this pre-meeting, heard about this non-conformity, they protested loudly. It was not reasonable, according to them, to define this as a non-conformity, because they claimed that the company indeed had such routines that were used, but they were not visible on the intranet. After some discussion about the practice of document control between the auditors and the company representatives, the auditors decided to turn this "minor non-conformity" into an "improvement suggestion", which is a more positive category in an audit report, and concluded the discussion by making a note that at the next certification audit the auditors would specifically follow-up on these routines for document control.

What these findings confirm is that the certification auditor, having a business relationship with the client organization that is certified, in practice makes an effort to keep a good relationship by showing benevolence, for example by letting the client organization have an influence in various decisions regarding the certification process and the choice of auditors. Thus, when examining the practical work of auditors in relation to individual clients, it becomes evident that the role as a business partner (and not only the role as a "public watchdog") is highly present.

In the first part of the chapter, I discussed how the expertise of certification auditors is constructed through elaborated organizational structures and procedures applied by the certification organization employing the auditors, which to a large extent serve to signal the legitimizing and highly cherished value of independence. In this section, I have discussed how certification auditors also need to convince about their role as a trustworthy and valuable business partner in relation to individual client organizations. In this dimension of their work, the economic dependency between auditor and auditee is highly present and influences the relationship. It may seem difficult, or even paradoxical, to cope with these diverging dimensions embedded in the construction of certification auditing expertise. However, as I will discuss in the final section, it is far from impossible. There is one more dimension regarding the construction of certification auditing expertise that is worth highlighting here, namely the management system character of the standards used for both certification and accreditation. Thus, it regards the character of the standards used to structure the meeting between auditor and auditee in both certification (e.g., ISO 9001, ISO 14001, FSC) and accreditation (e.g., ISO 17020, ISO 17021).

Constructing Expertise through Reliance on the Formal Organization

In the introduction to this chapter, reference was made to accounting research on auditing practices made from a critical perspective (e.g., Humphrey & Moizer, 1990; Power, 2003, 2011). In this literature, the quest, and social construction, of legitimacy within the business of auditing is thoroughly discussed and a crucial value in this context is auditors' independence. The focus of attention in regards to assurance mechanisms has mainly been placed on how the profession of auditors strives to strengthen the status of the profession and the individual members and in this way assure the value of independence.

What has become clear from the studies presented in this chapter from the field of certification auditing is that the solutions used to handle such legitimacy problems differ. Although the competence, professionalism and independence of auditors are still focused within certification auditing, the means of assuring such values is different as there is no requirement of individual membership or affiliation with a professional association of auditors. Rather, competence and independence are assured through accreditation of the certification organization, meaning that the organization employing certification auditors is expected to develop routines for the employment of people with relevant competence and for the maintenance of their competence, as well as structures for safeguarding independence of the auditing work. Such routines and structures become part of the management system of the certification organization, and it is that system with formalized structures, objectives and organizational routines that is checked during a yearly accreditation audit.

Within the field of certification auditing, there is thus a strong belief in, and responsibility for, the formal organization to solve, or at least handle, the legitimacy problems that are related to the fact that certification auditing is a service provided through the market. The idea is to require that the certification organization develops a relevant management system, ensures that it is kept updated, and then it is assumed that the practical work conducted by employees of the certification organization will follow the instructions of the management system.

The expertise that is prioritized and nurtured through contemporary certification practices, with the focus on structures and procedures, tends to be of a general character, and the auditors become generalists in checking routines with reference to a broad range of standards. The generalist character is reinforced by the fact that certification organizations typically employ auditors that may work with several standards, which is advantageous for many of the clients wishing to engage an auditor for joint-certifications (i.e. certifications against several standards through one and the same auditing process). In the same way as certification needs to be done for each standard, a certification organization that wishes to become accredited needs accreditation for each certification standard. As many accreditation organizations also work with a broad range of standards, both certification and accreditation auditors become generalists—being specialists in the act of checking—although they should have specific competence about all standards they work with.

Whether it is realistic to assume that there is a direct link between the formal management system of an organization and its daily practice is of course questionable (cf. Meyer & Rowan, 1977; Walgenbach, 2001). Still, the popularity of management system standards combined with third-party certification is by no means decreasing. One possible explanation to this development lies in the widespread belief and hope that organizations could be more rational and actually follow decisions they take regarding rationalization efforts (Meyer & Jepperson, 2000; Brunsson, 2006; Bromley & Meyer, 2015), in the form of a documented management system, for example. With such an understanding of the strong hope in formalized structures for a rational business activity, it becomes less of a problem that a certification auditor spends most of the time checking the documented management system of their clients. As long as there is a certain level of decoupling between the formalized structures and routines developed by decision-makers in organizations becoming audited, and the everyday practice of these organizations, the "watchdog" role of auditors is not as problematic as it may seem at first glance. However, if it is mainly the polished surface of an organization that is audited, the legitimacy of this type of auditing might become a target of questioning.

Notes

1 I am grateful for the generous financial support from the Swedish Research Council Formas for research conducted in 2009–2011 on the practice of management system certification, from Riksbankens Jubileumsfond on the organization of markets in 2008–2015, and from the Swedish Retail and Wholesale Development Council for research conducted in 2012–2014 on the organization and trustworthiness of eco-labels.
2 A parallel, complementing attempt to overcome legitimacy problems articulated within the business of certification auditing comes from associations of professional certification auditors performing ISO management system certification. The International Register for Certificated Auditors (IRCA), founded in London in 1984, is one such organization that certifies auditors based on proven work experience including a certain number of audits performed during a certain number of years in practice in different subject areas, as well as sector awareness from different industries. There are also competing registers, such as the American-Australian auditor certification body RABQSA and the Japanese equivalent JRCA. As these attempts are still emerging and are far less institutionalized as a legitimizing device compared to accreditation, they are left out of the discussion in this chapter.

References

Abbott, A. (1988). *The Systems of Professions—An Essay on the Division of Expert Labour*. Chicago: The University of Chicago Press.

Bartley, T. (2007). Institutional emergence in an era of globalization: The rise of transnational private regulation of labor and environmental conditions. *American Journal of Sociology, 113*(2), 297–351.

Bartley, T. (2011). Certification as a mode of social regulation. In Levi-Faur, D. (ed.), *Handbook on the Politics of Regulation*. Cheltenham, UK and Northampton, MA, USA: Edward Elgar, 441–452.

Bernstein, S. & Cashore, B. (2007). Can non-state global governance be legitimate? An analytical framework. *Regulation & Governance, 1,* 1–25.

Boiral, O. & Gendron, Y. (2011). Sustainable development and certification practices: Lessons learned and prospects. *Business Strategy and the Environment, 20*(5), 331–347.

Botzem, S. (2012). *The Politics of Accounting Regulation: Organizing Transnational Standard Setting in Financial Reporting.* Cheltenham, UK and Northampton, MA, USA: Edward Elgar.

Bromley, P. & Meyer, J. W. (2015). *Hyper-Organization: Global Organizational Expansion.* Oxford: Oxford University Press.

Brunsson, N. (2006). *Mechanisms of Hope: Maintaining the Dream of the Rational Organization.* Copenhagen: Copenhagen Business School Press.

Brunsson, N. & Jacobsson, B. (eds.). (2000). *A World of Standards.* Oxford: Oxford University Press.

Djelic, M. L. & Sahlin-Andersson, K. (eds.). (2006). *Transnational Governance: Institutional Dynamics of Regulation.* Cambridge: Cambridge University Press.

Dubuisson-Quellier, S. (2013). A market mediation strategy: How social movements seek to change firms' practices by promoting new principles of product valuation. *Organization Studies, 34*(5–6), 683–703.

Gendron, Y., Cooper, D. J. & Townley, B. (2001). In the name of accountability—State auditing, independence and new public management. *Accounting, Auditing and Accountability Journal, 14*(3), 278–310.

Gustafsson, I. & Tamm Hallström, K. (2013). The Certification Paradox: Monitoring as a Solution and a Problem. In Reuter, M., Wijkström, F. & Kristensson Uggla, B. (eds.), *Trust and Organizations: Confidence across Borders.* New York: Palgrave, 91–109.

Hatanaka, M. & Busch, L. (2008). Third-party certification in the global agrifood system: An objective or socially mediated governance mechanism? *Sociologica Ruralis, 48*(1), 73–91.

Higgins, W. & Tamm Hallström, K. (2007). Standardization, globalization and rationalities of government. *Organization, 14*(5), 685–704.

Humphrey, C., Loft, A. & Woods, M. (2009). The global audit profession and the international financial architecture: Understanding regulatory relationships at a time of financial crisis. *Accounting, Organizations and Society, 34*(6), 810–825.

Humphrey, C. & Moizer, P. (1990). From techniques to ideologies: An alternative perspective on the audit function. *Critical Perspectives on Accounting, 1*(3), 217–238.

Lindeberg, T. (2007). *Evaluative Technologies: Quality and the Multiplicity of Performance.* Copenhagen Business School. PhD Series 7. 2007.

Mennicken, A. (2010). From inspection to auditing: Audit and markets as linked ecologies. *Accounting, Organizations and Society, 35*(3), 334–359.

Meyer, J. W. & Jepperson, R. L. (2000). The 'actors' of modern society: The cultural construction of social agency. *Sociological Theory, 18*(1), 100–120.

Meyer, J. W. & Rowan, B. (1977). Institutional organizations: Formal structure as myth and ceremony. *American Journal of Sociology, 83*(2), 340–363.

Power, M. (1997). *The Audit Society: Rituals of Verification.* Oxford, UK: Oxford University Press.

Power, M. (2003). Auditing and the production of legitimacy. *Accounting, Organizations and Society, 28*(4), 379–394.

Power, M. (2011). Assurance worlds: Consumers, experts and independence. *Accounting, Organizations and Society, 36*(4–5), 324–326.

Rose, N. & Miller, P. (1992). Political power beyond the state: Problematics of government. *British Journal of Sociology, 43*(2), 172–205.

Sikka, P. (2009). Financial crisis and the silence of the auditors. *Accounting, Organizations and Society, 34*(6), 868–873.

Sikka, P. & Willmott, H. (1995). The power of "independence": Defending and extending the jurisdication of accounting in the United Kingdom. *Accounting, Organization and Society, 20,* 547–581.

Tamm Hallström, K. (2004). *Organizing International Standardization: ISO and the IASC in Quest of Authority.* Cheltenham: Edward Elgar.

Tamm Hallström, K. (2006). ISO Enters the Field of Social Responsibility (SR)— Construction and Tension of Global Governance. In Schuppert, F. (ed.), *Vol. 4, Contributions to Governance—Global Governance and the Role of Non-State Actors.* Berlin, Germany: Nomos Publishers, 117–156.

Tamm Hallström, K. & Boström, M. (2010). *Transnational Multi-Stakeholder Standardization: Organizing Fragile Non-State Authority.* Cheltenham, UK and Northampton, MA, USA: Edward Elgar.

Tamm Hallström, K. & Gustafsson, I. (2014). Value-neutralizing in verification markets: Organizing for independence through accreditation. In Alexius, S. & Tamm Hallström, K. (eds.), *Configuring Value Conflicts in Markets.* Cheltenham, UK and Northampton, MA, USA: Edward Elgar, 82–99.

Walgenbach, P. (2001). The production of distrust by means of producing trust. *Organization Studies, 22*(4), 693–714.

4 Stock Analysts—Experts of the Financial Sector

Jesper Blomberg

This chapter addresses professionalization in and by the financial sector, or more specifically stock analysts, which have recently become, and today remain, the most professionalized profession in this industry. The analyst has, in the last two or three decades, obtained an increasingly influential and central position as being an expert in the financial sector.

In what is often referred to as investment banking, we find a variety of professional groups: brokers (or *sales*), traders, company bankers (or *corporate bankers*) and analysts (or *research*). The stock analysts are, out of these professional groups, the group that can be said to have advanced the most in their role as an expert group and a developed profession. They have a common training in terms of financial economics, a subject that is also considered superior in scientific content; they are certified; their profession is regulated by law, and they are very much looked upon as experts, both within and beyond the financial sector. The purpose of this chapter is to try to understand, and even explain, why the analysts have obtained this expert status. What role do they play in investment banking and in the financial sector? What "causes" analysts, in a double sense: How can we understand both its establishment and its impact? Investment banking is an extremely profitable business, albeit one also characterized by powerful, and regular, recessions, which are commonly described as financial crises. Can we maybe understand both the profitability and the recurrent crises by means of shedding a new light on the analyst and his/her role as an expert?

A possible approach to shed such a new light is to create a detailed historical description of the birth of the analyst. How did the analyst arise and gradually acquire its present expert role? Such a history would, if it were told seriously, be quite comprehensive, but that is not the way in which it will be told here. Instead, we will here look at the analysts' practice today and a little further back in time, i.e. delimit the analysis to the analysts' recent history. Through an analysis of the analysts' contemporary history, the chapter aims to shed new light on the analyst as being the financial sector's primary experts.

Brief Historical Background

The history of the financial sector is well studied and substantially described in other contexts. However, an extremely short summary of it benefits the subsequent recent history:

The financial and economic history is intimately connected with the development of society as a whole. The distinct lines of development toward a modern financial industry, and investment banking and analysts as an expert group, can be seen with the emergence of the medieval Italian city states and their banking communities (Kindelberg & Aliber, 2005; Morrison & Wilhelm, 2007; Blomberg, Kjellberg & Winroth, 2012). The history of the analyst encompasses the establishment of the Italian trading cities, with their influential and innovative banks. This is in conjunction with, many hundred years later, increasingly stronger European nation states and their financing of bolder commercial projects and warfare against other nations, along with the new industrial companies, in the early 19th century, and their increasingly popular forms of organization and financing, as well as the discovery and exploitation of the new world. This, among other aspects, meant that the United States, 100 to 150 years ago, took over as the economic world power. In the midst of this history of princes, kings, industrialists, central bank governors, war, economic growth, financial crises, regulations and deregulations, we today find, like in the medieval Genoa and Venice in the 18th century Central Europe, and in the early 20th century Wall Street, various kinds of bankers, traders and brokers whose profession is to deal in stocks and other securities. There are also counselors: experts providing investors, entrepreneurs and agencies advice on how the financial system can be designed, managed and exploited.

Right from the start, these advisors based their advice upon local knowledge of how the local markets worked, and how various business owners and entrepreneurs operated. Through this local knowledge, advisors could reduce the risk of investment, as well as help the business owners find financiers. Analysis and brokerage were not clearly divided services. Local knowledge, as a knowledge base, has gradually been supplemented throughout history: primarily by knowledge that sprung from the achievements of the economic sciences, the legal and institutional environment (what we often discuss in terms of standardization, regulation and deregulation), and later in the handling of new digital media and computers.

Accordingly the French King Louis XIV hired Scottish economic theoretical expertise (with practical experience from the Amsterdam Stock Exchange) when he wanted to modernize the French financial system in 1717 (complete failure). Similarly, the US president Roosevelt was heavily influenced by the prominent British Economist Keynes when he launched his

"New Deal" during the 1930s great depression (its impact is very disputed). The economic and financial theory has therefore increasingly expanded to become one of the foundations of the stock analysts.

In addition, new technology has shaped the analysts' expertise, ranging from the telegraph, the Atlantic cable, and later, the phone's emergence, allowing faster and more comprehensive information flows. Computerization of the administration of the ever-growing stock exchanges, and later trading, and later again, the capacity of PCs to keep track of vast amounts of information and trading, as well as allowing for ever more advanced calculations and instruments, have also had a significant impact on the analysts' expert role. Today, the range of information of which the analyst is expected to have knowledge is almost infinite, as well as the management of advanced financial valuation models and programs being seen as the analyst's natural domain.

In the following, we will go into much more detail concerning what analysts actually do today and what kinds of expert roles they hold. However, from a long-term perspective, we can already now say that the analysts' history continues to be written and that the financial world order, at its best, is to be radically reformed. Analysis, based on science with the help of computers and regulated by law—in spite of investment banking activities—continues to be alternately extremely profitable and in crisis, and the financial markets continue to be characterized by high volatility.

Investment Banking

Investment banking operations, or, in short, investment banking, is a business activity that is undertaken by all from the global big banks to more specialized independent investment banks and brokerages. During the last two or three decades, the secondary stock market has transformed from consisting of local stock exchanges, with a small number of members who have bought and sold stock certificates and government debt securities face-to-face, to becoming a system of global virtual marketplaces where anyone with Internet access can participate. Today, stocks are just a small component among increasingly numerous, more abstract and technically complex products, instruments or investment objects. Human traders have taken on advanced mathematical models and increasingly technologically advanced information technologies to assist them. At the same time, much of the trade is fully automated. Computers, that are programmed to react to market movements, trade rapidly and widely, without human intervention. Transaction costs for buying or selling, for example a share, have, despite the explosion of available information and data declined radically, thanks to technology and large-scale production, while trading volumes have increased (Figure 4.1).

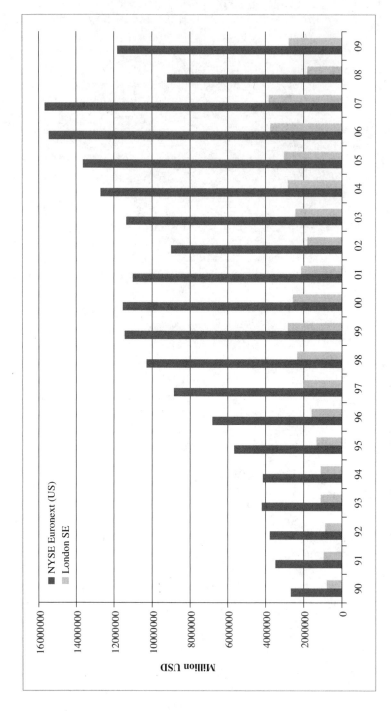

Figure 4.1 The total share value of the New York and London Stock Exchange respectively (in addition to increasing in value, you can also clearly see the last two major financial crises in the form of two sharp drops).

Investment Banking of Today

Investment banking consists, broadly speaking, of two main activities (Figure 4.2). It is partly the so-called corporate bankers who offer their services to companies for issuing new shares, buying back shares or introducing previously non-listed company shares on different stock exchanges. This is called the primary market, i.e. when parts of the company are split up, merged or introduced and sold on stock exchanges for the first time. The second main activity is securities trading in the so-called secondary market. In the case of stocks, it is in the secondary market that stocks change hands or become redefined, without the involvement of the company that the stock represents. The organizational part of the investment banking business that manages the secondary market is often referred to as *securities* or *equities*, also in the all-Swedish banks. Securities are, in turn, organized in the professional groups brokers/sales, (sell-side) analysts/researchers and merchants/traders. Twenty-five years ago, it was not uncommon for the same person to act as both broker and trader, and the analyst was only seen as an internal, and not very important, support person for brokers, i.e. the broker was usually fine with his/her own analyses. Today however, these activities are therefore largely divided processes and technified machineries.

This increased specialization is to be seen in the light of the financial sector's strong historical growth: the increase in volume, the high volatility and the enormous quantities of information simply require a different organization than the slower, smaller and more local stock markets needed a couple

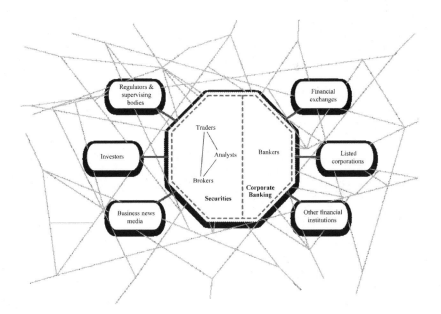

Figure 4.2 An elementary picture of the investment banking operations' different parts.

of decades ago. Without taking a position on the cause and effect, chicken or egg, both the financial sector and its key practice—investment banking—have developed greatly.

Analysts—The New Financial Stars

Twenty-five years ago, the focus was upon investment banking, both in the financial sector, in the media and among the public, and primarily directed toward brokers and traders. Brokers and traders were even the lead characters in Hollywood movies, like Wall Street (Stone, 1987), and the subject of ethnographic studies (Abolafia, 1996; Bruegger, 1999). The number of studies of brokers and traders (e.g., Smith, 1981; Abolafia, 1996; Knorr Cetina & Brueggers, 2000, 2002a, 2002b; Blomberg, 2004; Fenton-O'Creevy, Nicholson, Soane & Willman, 2004) exceeded by far the number of studies on analysts and bankers. However, this is also undergoing a change today, and the focus has shifted since the mid-1990s. The analyst has won a great deal of attention, both in the financial sector, media and in research. The number of studies of analysts grows (e.g., Zuckerman, 2000; Hägglund, 2001; Rao, Greve & Davis, 2001; Mouritsen, 2003; Fogarty & Rogers, 2005; Beunza & Garud, 2007; Blomberg et al., 2012; Blomberg, 2016), as does the analysts' self-image:

> Well, we have taken the fast elevator up in the hierarchy, straight up to the work of CEOs and investors.
>
> (*Chief Analyst, investment bank*)

The analysts' increased status can be explained in many ways and from different theoretical perspectives (we will return to this later in the chapter). Independently of these explanations, however, it can be noted that the first big star analysts were created during the dot-com bubble of the late 1990s. This boom (and subsequently bursting bubble) is considered to partially have been pushed by a number of analysts, who became both very famous and rich, and later on, infamous and convicted (Fleuriet, 2008, pp. 151–158; Blomberg et al., 2012, p. 67). Even if there is today a certain amount of caution among the leading banks for profiling their securities transactions with the help of a number of star analysts, their current position is completely different from previously: a good analysis unit is considered something that every serious investment banking operation must include. Analysts are ranked by all kinds of ranking institutions, individually as a team, and on the basis of the industrial sector and employer.[1] [2] However, what is it that analysts do, and what can possibly form the basis of this increased attention?

Collect Data, Analyze Companies and Present Assessments

In conjunction with the analysts' higher status, the content of their work has changed radically. A couple of decades ago, the analyst often spent his time alone in his room. He, or very rarely she, collected public information about companies, mainly accounting data, when requested to do so by a broker or trader. A single analyst could be a support function, not always in such high demand, for a group of ten to 15 more high-profile brokers.

> I remember how we used to work. Suddenly, a broker came by with an annual report which we had not seen or knew about. Look at that, we thought a little surprised.
>
> *(Analyst)*

Analysts still collect information and analyze companies and industries. However, today their work is far more structured, it includes many more information sources, involves a large and heterogeneous group of people, and it is much more technologically advanced. Instead of working as before, analyzing companies when ordered by brokers, the analyst's work of today is made up by a proactive, structured, specialized and standardized process.

The vast majority of stockbrokers specialize in a number of companies and in one industrial sector, such as metal and mining, health, banking and financial, among others.[3] In the global big banks, the analyst often works in a team of analysts that are specialized in a specific sector. Each team consists of a chief sector analyst, some senior sector analysts, and a few less experienced assistant analysts. As a general rule, the senior analysts have more contact with clients, while the less experienced (but most often trained in the latest methods of calculations) perform most of the technical analysis. In smaller enterprises, an analyst is usually the only one in his sector, and in the smallest enterprises, the analyst is responsible for several sectors. Regardless of the size of the investment banking operations, one can see a clear trend toward greater standardization, both within and between firms, in respect of how the technical analysis work is actually performed:

> The standard way to work with business valuation is to gather industry and company information, anything that can be used to build an analysis product. Then the information is used to forecast future results and balance sheet. Typically, the numbers are discounted in a DCF [Discounted Cash Flow]. Values come out, and you argue about the value and the estimates that led to the result.
>
> *(Analyst)*

Although stock analysis has become increasingly standardized with respect to the use of, among other things, DCF models, the model development is still something that may vary between analysts, teams and banks. Analysts make use of several models, which are customized based on the companies and the sectors that are being analyzed:

> First we have models to estimate the company's turnover and profitability. Then we put the data into a standard model that all analysts use. This second model gives us profit and loss, balance sheet and cash flow.

So, the only model that is unique to the analyst is the one that is used to estimate revenues and profitability for the actual company. Then the estimates are standardized into models, that we can store in our databases and use as data for different purposes.

(*Analyst*)

Seasons, Views and News Flashes

Today, the analyst's work is largely structured by the so-called four seasons. The four seasons culminate in the weeks when the companies in an industry sector publish their quarterly and annual reports. For a limited time, the analysts have to write so-called previews, reviews and other comments, and, moreover, those must also be well anchored in the comprehensive analysis of companies, sectors and global trends.

Today, everything is centered on the four seasons. If you work in a sector where reports are coming in close to each other, then it is enough to work yourself to death for a couple of weeks, it is worse for those who cover sectors where the reports are coming in over a longer period of time.

(*Chief Analyst*)

All analysts are expected to stay up to date on their respective companies and within their sectors, both before and after working hours. Normally, the analyst takes part in the economic news flow before, or on his or her way to, work. If there is something that has a bearing on the analyst's company or sector, he or she immediately types it in on their tablet or phone, a so-called flash, and sends it to his company's intranet. This comment contains a brief message addressing the previously prevailing recommendation (buy, sell, hold) for a particular stock to be reconsidered. A little later, the flash is followed up with a slightly longer reasoning, a so-called on-the-spot analysis, and if the news is considered important for the stock's future value, further analysis will follow within a couple of hours.

The Analyst's Main Product—The Case

Although the analyst's work is mainly structured around the four seasons, the main product is neither the important previews, nor the daily analyses. The main product is, according to the analysts themselves, their *case*. When the analyst is not working with quarterly reports or news flashes, he/she devotes the time to creating interesting cases, i.e. descriptions of companies or constellations of companies that may be of interest for investors looking to buy shares, and hopefully through the bank or brokerage firm for whom the analyst works.

The case is our main product. Everything is about producing better, more convincing cases.

(*Analyst*)

The work with cases is not as time-limited as work on quarterly reports. In the work with cases, there is more room to collect data and analyze it in a more personal way:

> You need a creativity of your own; you can't search for information via directives. The thing is to find your own ways, your own sources. Because you need primary information. But it is up to each person to decide what kind of primary information.
>
> *(Analyst)*

The work on cases also differs from the work with the quarterly reports in that it is easier to get information from the companies you analyze. A couple of weeks before a company publishes its quarterly report, it is more or less impossible to get any new information from executives and IR people at the listed companies. The closer to the publication, the more sensitive the limit for what is considered insider information, and the flow of information from the companies is therefore consciously stopped (known as the black-out period). When the quarterly report becomes public, the doors gradually open again to this important source of information.

Analysts spend much time analyzing public data, but they do not hesitate to use more personal, and perhaps unorthodox, methods to get a better feel for the sector and the companies they follow:

> I have a habit of going up to NK (Stockholm's most prestigious department store) and going through the different clothing brands. I look at their pricing and the quality of the goods. It gives me a sense of what each company is doing.
>
> *(Analyst)*

Organized Social Interaction

Although the analysts' cases do not generate transactions by themselves, they form a basis for further discussions between investors and representatives of the investment bank. It is therefore of great importance that the analysts manage to construct a case that makes an impression. Subsequent interaction with real and potential customers includes typical brokers and traders, and leads, at best, to stock trading via the bank's trading function and hence to revenues for the bank. Today, analysts are also very much involved in this interaction and sales process of the bank's trading operations. Even the bank's corporate banking sector (see Figure 4.2), benefits from potential clients having a good relationship with the bank's analysts.

Interaction within the Bank

First of all, analysts interact with each other. They talk about everything from news, ideas, the quality of the data, to trends and more. Analysts are usually placed relatively close to the brokers with whom they interact on a regular basis. Most often, the brokers ask the analysts for expert opinions with regards to the values of a company, and sometimes, the analysts ask the brokers about their perceptions of where the market is heading, about a specific company or a specific client. In addition, each business day's initial morning meeting always consists of a more structured knowledge exchange. This is mainly between analysts and brokers, but traders can also be included:

> Whether the brokers and the traders are attentive to what I have to say depends largely on which corporation I'm talking about. If it is HM, everybody listens, and I get a lot of questions. If it is 24Hpoker, maybe one is listening. It also depends on who is talking, like if Chris is talking, there will usually be discussion, most brokers are interested in his sector, and he is also a top ranked analyst.
>
> *(Analyst)*

The analysts' interaction with the company bankers or "corparna" (common title in the Swedish banks and an abbreviation of corporate bankers), is a somewhat touchier subject. Corparnas work in the primary market (to help business leaders and principal owners with company funding) and must be kept separate from analysts, brokers and traders' activities on the secondary market (to help investors to buy and sell stocks and other securities). This is to avoid a conflict of interest (company owner wants a high valuation of his company, investors want to find low-valued companies) and illegal use of information. This regulated border between activities, information and interests is the most established, so-called Chinese wall, in investment banking operations.

However, from the analysts' position, the relationship with corparna is relatively uncomplicated. A banker who needs help with a specific business analysis usually initiates the interaction. No matter what kind of analysis, and what potentially share price sensitive information it includes, all analysts consider that they can handle it correctly—i.e. they will not let the information be affected by their analysis:

> One has to have integrity. If you start to compromise your own valuations and give in to some pressure to raise a target price on a stock, you will not last long as an analyst.
>
> *(Analyst)*

At the same time, they have no problems in pointing out colleagues in other banks that have not demonstrated such integrity but, on the contrary, adjusted their recommendations to the bank's current business financing projects:

> Well, there are cases, for instance one quite obvious one a few years back, when Deutsche Bank, or rather the analyst at Deutsche Bank here in Stockholm, overnight and without any real new information, raised their buy price on Saab quite a bit. This happened just before their

bankers started to distribute a new issue of Saab shares. That one was a little bit too much.

(*Analyst*)

The Analysts' Interactions with Operators Outside the Bank

The analysts' work includes direct communication with investors/clients, both via phone, e-mail and face-to-face. Nowadays, the analysts spend up to half their work time interacting with investors and business representatives (see also Fleuriet, 2008, p. 136). They make visits to the professional investors' offices and talk about their last cases, all in order to get the investors to buy (and sell) shares through the analysts' bank. Some clients, especially large fund managers, are primarily interested in the analysts' future scenarios, rather than how they argue that these scenarios will affect the price of a particular stock. This is partly a consequence of these clients increasingly having developed their own analysis methods. The big institutional investors have become progressively more sophisticated and hired their own analysts (see also Hägglund, 2001; Beunza & Garud, 2007; Fleuriet, 2008). These "buy-side" analysts also collect information; they use the same analytics tools as the banks "sell-side" analysts, in addition to talking to analysts at several banks in order to be able to compare several analysts' scenarios and valuations.

Other clients, mainly more risk-averse investors, such as hedge fund managers, are often more interested in the individual analysts' perceptions of specific stocks and their possible future values:

Some customers just want to talk estimate and industrial data, others want to go all the way and discuss the arguments for a specific valuation.

(*Analyst*)

Today the analyst's work is, thus, largely based on communication via texts, different media and face-to-face interaction with colleagues and clients. Investors who visit the bank have often been invited to industry-specific seminars or company specific breakfast or lunch meetings. They also have individual meetings with analysts or meet with them in the context of "road shows"—i.e. events where a company goes around to important financial centers and invites investors to tell them more about their activities and the bright future. These road shows are arranged together with the investment bank branch with whom they have a good relationship and that they think has the best contact with the investors with whom they want to come into contact.

However, analysts do not only have contact with colleagues at their bank and with clients and investors, they also regularly meet executives and key personnel in the companies they analyze:

I have regular contacts with 'my' corporations and at times I set up visits at their facilities for interested investors. [. . .] It provides them with a 'flavor' of reality, shows them that it's not just a spreadsheet in Excel, you know, but allows them to see what it really is. Verbally, the investors are very interested in these events. But it takes a lot of time, of course, so in the end we typically have only a small group with us.

(*Analyst*)

As a general rule, I meet all the corporations I follow in connection to their quarterly reports. Plus, I call them whenever there's a development.

(*Analyst*)

The conversations between analysts, investors and executives mean that information, ideas and experiences are flowing in all directions. The conversations and meetings are not only about the exchange of experience but also about creating experience, i.e. creating perceptions of companies, shares and values in this interaction. It also creates more than beliefs, as it is on the basis of these that investors buy and sell shares. In other words, this means that the market, in itself, is partly created by analysts' interactions, with the help of mainly analyst colleagues, brokers, traders, corporate bankers, investors and clients, as well as executives and key personnel in listed companies.

Therefore, the analysts' relationship with other operators has changed radically over the past two or three decades. From having been in an internal support function (see Figure 4.3), the analysts have become one of the

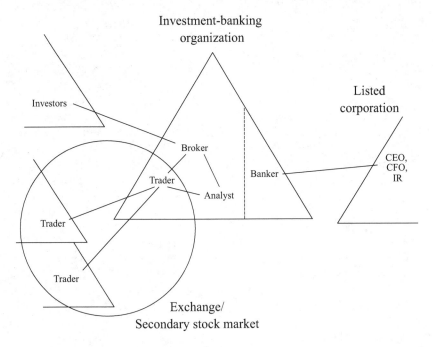

Figure 4.3 The analysts' position in the late 1980s: internal role without contact with external operators and low status in relation to brokers, traders and bankers.

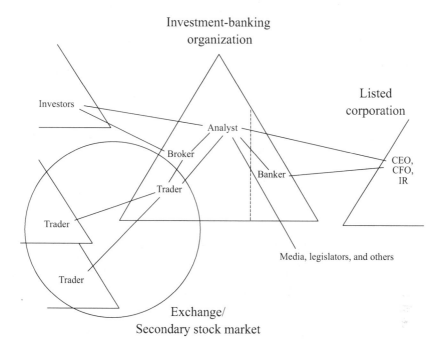

Investment-banking
organization

Listed
corporation

Investors

Analyst

Broker

Banker

Trader

CEO,
CFO,
IR

Trader

Trader

Media, legislators, and others

Exchange/
Secondary stock market

Figure 4.4 The analysts' position today: have high internal status with a practice guided by "their own" logic (not on behalf of brokers, traders or clients) and with regular and structured interaction with several of the key external actors in investment banking.

investment banks' most prestigious professions. They now have a high status within their investment banking operations, as well as having regular contact with both investors and senior executives in listed companies. In addition, they often perform the role of expert commentators in the news media, as well as acting as advisors to both legislators and government agencies (Figure 4.4).

An Increasingly Complex Network

The list of key operators that interact with the analysts could be made even longer. Not least because a considerable amount of technology is involved in analysts' work. Ranging from today's fairly sophisticated financial theories and valuation models, the continually globally connected IT-network and computers' calculation capacity both enable and restrict the analysts' work. In addition, there is the news media, both in terms of financial journalists (with similar education and backgrounds as the analysts themselves) and their various outlets, which is also fast and international. In conjunction with events that attract the attention of the media, it is usually the analysts who will be interviewed about the causes and consequences. In addition, legislators, and related supervisory and inspecting authorities, have frequent contact with analysts. Even within the banks, there are now more operators with great influence on, and dependence upon analysts. Today's growing internal monitoring systems, in the form of risk control and "compliance" functions, have, and will continue to have, major implications for all operators in the field of investment banking. What the consequences are, or will be, is however an unresolved question. The network of actors that operate in the analysts' absolute proximity is, to say the least, extensive and complex when compared to the same professional group only two, three decades ago.

Why Analysts?

That analysts have evolved to become perhaps the foremost experts in investment banking and in the financial sector is a fact; however, why this has happened has only been postulated. To answer the question solely on an empirical basis is somewhat difficult. There are many possible explanations, which are all based on different theoretical and ideological grounds.

Investors' Growing Needs of Analysis

Starting from a financial theory and microeconomic perspective, investment banking is presented as a more or less neutral and effective lubricant that helps investors to find undervalued investment opportunities, and entrepreneurs to obtain funding for their promising projects. The analysts' role is to communicate knowledge of investments and thereby help investors to allocate their resources and, in that way, create an efficient market. The larger and more coherent the market is, the more analysis is required to inform the growing number of investors about the growing number of investment objects. The analysts' increased expert status is explained by an increased need for analysis. The analysts' practice, as described in this chapter, speaks sharply against this explanation. Analysts cannot be said to passively communicate any kind of objective information on different investment objects. Rather, they are very active in trying to contradict, not only the current valuation of the stock market but also other analysts. Analysts try, with their recommendations and valuations, to brand themselves and their investment bank so that they appear interesting and seem to have different ideas and perspectives from other banks and analysts. The analysts' recommendations are just as much an active social process, in which they try to position themselves and their bank in opposition to other analysts and banks, as some sort of neutral information gathering and informative organ. By contradicting the market and the consensus of opinion, analysts rather try to generate volatility, i.e. their valuations and recommendations are designed to get investors to change their positions by buying and selling shares (see also Zuckerman, 1999, 2004; Blomberg, 2016). They cannot make up everything, but their recommendations are just as much shaped by other analysts as they are based on information on investment objects and financial theory:

> If I do an analysis of a large, well analyzed share and come up with a 200% up side. Then I will put, let's say 30 or 40%. People will say that I am crazy. Even if you want to be a little provocative, you cannot disagree too much or too often with consensus.
>
> (*Analyst, manufacturing industry*)

Efforts to Reduce Transaction Costs and Risk Levels

In economic historical research (Basking & Miranti, 1997; Morrison & Wilhelm, 2007) the financial sector's creation and development is explained, in broad terms, as being about reducing risks and transaction costs for investors and entrepreneurs. The practice described in this chapter, however, almost points at an opposite role for analysts. They devote an enormous amount of work to information gathering, theoretically sophisticated and very comprehensive analyses, and writing lengthy reports and cases. However, most of these analyses and reports are never actually read. If they are shown, they must maintain a very high standard, but investors and other related parties rarely bother to read through the extensive reports, regardless of whether they are previews or cases. They look at summaries, listen to briefs and talk with each other, but almost never scrutinize the voluminous analyses in detail. The dire reports function more like material to start from, or as an excuse for the analysts to converse and interact with investors and corporate executives. What is produced in these conversations and interactions are images of companies, investment objects, risks and values, and perhaps in the end, stock trading, but it is an extremely expensive method of conducting trade. Stock trading can be entirely automated and has previously been carried out by brokers and traders without the costly involvement of analysts. It is easy to see what costs the analysts cause, but not as easy to see what revenue they generate. In a slightly exaggerated way, the costs that the analysts cause could be viewed as an administrative additional cost and thus lead to increased, rather than reduced, transaction costs. Because the analysts' recommendations and cases are designed to generate trade rather than to communicate some sort of neutral image of companies and markets, it would also be possible to argue that they create trade, and thus risk that would not be present without their work. Consequently, the analysts are rather co-producers of risk, than producers of analysis to help investors and businesses to lower their risks (Blomberg, 2016).

Following Trends without Reflecting

Based on organizational theory, a few clear and partly different explanations can be found in the aforementioned concerns. One is rooted in a socio-logical neo-institutional perspective on organizing (Meyer & Rowan, 1977; DiMaggio & Powell, 1983) and in analysis of, among others, measuring- and risk management trends (Power, 1997, 2004). This perspective is simply meant to explain business and industrial activities on the basis that there are always vast norms, cultures and assumed values that guide our actions and us without us really being aware of them. From this perspective, the change in the analyst's role is an uncritical and non-strategic alignment to the external "institutional pressure" from "the environment". Neither exec-utives nor experts in investment banking operations, or other actors, have any influence over the fact that the banks, both internally and externally, invest more and more resources to measure, analyze and forecast all sorts of activities. Nobody really knows why the analysts do what they do, and nor do they question it. Assumed standards govern us all and analysts adapt and translate these norms, without reflecting over them, in relation to their own practice. This explanation, however, ignores the fact that both analysts and others in investment banking and in the financial sector quite clearly express what they are doing and why they do it. Analysts know that they have to justify their presence in the face of traders and brokers. Unless the analysts deliver great ideas that traders and brokers can use in their work, they will be called into question. The same is true in relation to investors and other operators; unless the analysts can come up with something new, or if they are unable to explain what happened in an unexpected stock market development, then they will be pulled up upon it. This leads into the second version of this more organization theory explanatory model.

Look Good and Make More Money

This more economical business perspective gives actors more reflective capacity and a higher explanatory value, and it is, to a greater extent, based on "interactionist" or "micro sociological" theory (Schutz, 1962; Knorr-Cetina, 1994). Based on this explanatory model, analysts can rather be seen as a strategic resource for profitable investment banking operations. The analysts' activities play a critical role for themselves, for investment banking and for the financial sector in general. For themselves, as individual ana-lysts and as an expert group, they must constantly prove their worth, even internally in the investment bank. However, this has become easier because the stock markets opened up at the start of Internet trading. Today, any-one who can afford and has access to the Internet, can, via online traders, buy and sell shares in a few keystrokes. The investment banks and broker-age houses' monopoly of carrying out stock trading is history. This means that the investment banking operations must be able to offer something more than the trade itself. Through this, the analysts' expertise becomes the offered added value.

From the commercial reasoning of the investment bank operation, the analyst today fills a role that significantly overlaps that of the broker's. That analysts are referred to as "sell-side" and the brokerage "sales" speaks for itself. Commercially, the main role of brokers and analysts is to generate stock trading. The difference, however, is that the analysts' sales work has more of a scientific character than a focus on the individual investor. Analysts' sales work, in the shape of general corporate values and recommendations, comes across more as an objective science in comparison to the brokers' customer specific and subjectively customized advice. Analysts appear less as salespeople and more like objective knowledge-based representatives. The practice of analysts thereby covers the investment banking operations commercial and strategic sales processes with a mantle of objective science and analysis.

Therefore, analysts' practice seeks to generate trade by convincingly arguing that there are imbalances in markets and hidden values in a variety of business/investment objects. Whether there are some kinds of objective values, beyond the technical, social and commercial practice of which analysts are a part is questionable, but that is what analysts argue for. By constantly demonstrating that investors and other analysts incorrectly value different investment objects, the analysts can be said to create volatility, i.e. changes in those markets:

> Today we have reached a level similar, or not far from, the brokers, in terms of assuming a lot more responsibility for the sales work, for our ideas [. . .] that are both in short, middle and long term so much more important to generate trade, because you cannot . . . only be an order central, that doesn't work anymore. Then people go to the net-brokerage houses and do the trade themselves. This has created a metamorphosis of the analyst trade. We are necessary to profile, not only ourselves but also the whole investment banking industry.
>
> (*Chief Analyst*)

A closely related task that analysts as an expert group have is marketing, or legitimization, of the investment banking operations and also the financial sector in a broader context. The analysts' work is also a kind of "window dressing" for the entire financial sector. Through its comprehensive information gathering and by using relatively sophisticated models founded in financial theory, the analysts give the impression that the financial sector, investment banking and trading are standing on a solid scientific foundation. That the financial markets are as volatile as ever and that investment banking, including analysts' own practices, rather increases than reduces this volatility is hidden by analysts' expert opinions with reference to financial theory and extensive knowledge about companies and markets. Analysts predict the market but when they turn out to be wrong, they can always subsequently explain the rapid changes by referring to scientific models and established correlations. As a result, investors, legislators, supervisory government agencies, pension savers and media, despite high volatility, dare to hand over their money to the financial sector's seemingly secure custody. Only a few decades ago, we understood shares to be an inappropriate form for pension savings, yet today we take it for granted.

This declaration means that analysts and other operators in the financial sector are not seen as passive or that they are adapting to some kind of external pressure or trend. Rather, they are active creators of both their expertise and the needs of others of this expertise. They *create* the trend rather than describe, translate or adapt to it.

Notes

1 Influential international rankings can be found in the business journals Euromoney and Institutional Investor. The most influential Swedish ranking is published by the journal Affärsvärlden.
2 The most important international rankings are the ones published in the magazines *Euromoney* and *Institutional Investor*, and in Sweden—*Affärsvärlden*.
3 The majority of all operators in the financial sector make use of similar sectoral divisions. The two leading classification systems are *The Industry Classification Benchmark* (ICB) supported by Dow Jones and the FTSE Group, and *The Global Industry Standard* (GICS) developed by Morgan Stanley and Standard & Poor's. The two classifications are very similar to each other and consist of several levels of industries, industry groups, and super sectors and sectors.

References

Abolafia, M. Y. (1996). *Making Markets—Opportunism and Restraint on Wall Street*. Cambridge, MA: Harvard University Press.
Basking, J. B. & Miranti, P. J. J. (1997). *A History of Corporate Finance*. Cambridge: Cambridge University Press.
Beunza, D. & Garud, R. (2007). Calculators, lemmings, or frame-makers? The intermediary role of securities analysts. In Callon, M., Millo Y. & Muniesa, F. (eds.), *Market Devices*. Chichester: Wiley, 13–39.
Blomberg, J. (2004). Appreciating stockbroking: Constructing conceptions to make sense of performance. *Journal of Management Studies*, 41(1), 155–180.
Blomberg, J. (2016). The multiple worlds of equity analysts: valuation, volume, and volatility. *Journal of Cultural Economy*, 9(3), 277–295.
Blomberg, J., Kjellberg, H. & Winroth, K. (2012). *Marketing Shares, Sharing Markets: Experts in Investment Banking*. New York, NY: Palgrave-Macmillan.
Bruegger, U. (1999). *Wie handeln Devisenhändler? Eine ethnmographische Studie uber Akteure in einem globalen Markt* (How do Traders Trade? An ethnography of the Actors on a Global Market). Bamberg: Difo-Druck OHG.
DiMaggio, P. J. & Powell, W. W. (1983). The iron cage revisited—Institutional isomorphism and collective rationality in organizational fields. *American Sociological Review*, 48, 147–160.

Fenton-O'Creevy, M., Nicholson, N., Soane, E. & Willman, P. (2004). *Traders: Risks, Decisions, and Management in Financial Markets*. Oxford: Oxford University Press.

Fleuriet, M. (2008). *Investment Banking Explained: An Insider's Guide to the Industry*. New York: McGraw-Hill.

Fogarty, T. J. & Rogers, R. K. (2005). Financial analysts' reports: An extended institutional theory evaluation. *Accounting, Organizations and Society*, 30(4), 331–356.

Hägglund, P. (2001). *Företaget som investeringsobjekt: Hur placerare och analytiker arbetar med att ta fram ett investeringsobjekt*. Stockholm: EFI.

Kindelberg, C. P. & Aliber, R. Z. (2005). *Manias, Panics, and Crashes: A history of Financial Crises* (5th edition). Hoboken, NJ: Wiley.

Knorr Cetina, K. (1994). Primitive classification and postmodernity—Towards a sociological notion of fiction. *Theory, Culture & Society*, 11, 1–22.

Knorr Cetina, K. & Bruegger, U. (2000). The market as an object of attachment: Exploring postsocial relations in financial markets. *Canadian Journal of Sociology*, 25(2), 141–168.

Knorr Cetina, K. & Bruegger, U. (2002a). Global microstructures: The virtual societies of financial markets. *The American Journal of Sociology*, 107(4), 905–950.

Knorr Cetina, K. & Bruegger, U. (2002b). Traders' engagement with markets: A postsocial relationship. *Theory, Culture and Society*, 19(5–6), 161–185.

Meyer, J. W. & Rowan, B. (1977). Institutionalized organizations: Formal structures as myth and cermony. *American Journal of Sociology*, 82(2), 340–363.

Morrison, A. D. & Wilhelm, W. J. (2007). *Investment Banking: Institutions, Politics, and Law*. Oxford: Oxford University Press.

Mouritsen, J. (2003). Intellectual capital and the capital market: The circulability of intellectual capital. *Accounting, Auditing & Accountability Journal*, 16(1), 18–30.

Power, M. (1997). *The Audit Society: Rituals of Verification*. Oxford: Oxford University Press.

Power, M. (2004). The risk management of everything. *The Journal of Risk Finance*, 5(3), 58–65.

Rao, H., Greve, H. R. & Davis, G. F. (2001). Fool's gold: Social proof in the initiation and abandonment of coverage by wall street analysts. *Administrative Science Quarterly*, 46(3), 502–526.

Schutz, A. ([1940–1959] 1962). *Collected Papers I: The Problem of Social Reality*. The Hague: Martinus Nijhoff.

Smith, C. W. (1981). *The Mind of the Market – A Study of Stock Market Philosophies, Their Uses, and Their Implications*. Totowa, NJ: Rowan and Littlefield.

Stone, O. (1987). *Wall Street*. Los Angeles, CA: 20th Centrury Fox.

Zuckerman, E. W. (1999). The categorical imperative: Securities analysts and the illegitimacy discount. *American Journal of Sociology*, 104, 1398–1438.

Zuckerman, E. W. (2000). Focusing the corporate product: Securities analysts and de-diversification. *Administrative Science Quarterly*, 45(3), 591–619.

Zuckerman, E. W. (2004). Structural incoherence and stock market activity. *American Sociological Review*, 69(3), 405–432.

5 As Flies around Goodies—The Rise of Experts and Services in the Emerging Field of CSR and Sustainability

Susanna Alexius, Staffan Furusten and Andreas Werr

A never-ending barrage of management ideas bombards managers. Total Quality Management (TQM), Lean, E-business, digital transformation and HR transformation are some examples of ideas that managers have been expected to respond to over the past decade. This chapter concerns the question of how experts relate to popular management ideas with a focus on how ideas affect the development and offer of expert services in an emerging field of expertise. A first aim is to scrutinize what happens to already established experts when a particular idea becomes popular and a new field of expertise is emerging. What kinds of expert services emerge in response to an increasingly more popular management idea? A second aim is to scrutinize what kinds of experts that offer services related to an increasingly popular management idea. Do new ideas also create new experts?

In the study reported in this chapter, we focused our attention on the responses to one popular management idea—the management idea of Corporate Social Responsibility (CSR) and its associated idea of corporate sustainability—in the Swedish context (cf. Windell, 2006). Following previous research on similar topics (Windell, 2006; Whittle, 2008; Frostenson, 2010), we identify core organizers and organizing attempts and analyze the kinds of experts and expertise emanating from such efforts. The chapter largely confirms findings in previous research (Windell, 2006; Whittle, 2008; Frostenson, 2010) but makes a new contribution by way of two empirically grounded categorizations of experts and expert services (see Tables 5.1 and 5.2).

The chapter is based on a series of empirical studies of the supply of CSR-services among consultants in the Swedish consultancy market. Consultants relating to the popular ideas of CSR and sustainability were identified using the local *Yellow pages*, *Eniro*—a web based search service of individuals and organizations, *Konsultguiden*—an established guide to the Swedish consultancy market, and various lists provided by actors such as *Standardization in Sweden (SIS)*—that manages the CSR standard ISO 26,000 in Sweden and *CSR Sweden*—a Swedish business network for CSR issues. In the search for relevant organizations, we started from the concept of CSR but also included a number of related keywords such as sustainable development, social responsibility, environmental management and ethics. In a first round of analysis of these sources, we identified 88 consulting organizations that offered some form of CSR-related service. Fifty of these were then selected and asked via e-mail if they would agree to give an interview. Eventually, 22 interviews were performed, transcribed and analyzed along with corporate self-presentations of the selected 50 firms. This first study was conducted between December 2008 and March 2009. A second and third follow-up study of the selected organizations websites were then conducted in January 2010 and May 2012 to follow the development from the emerging to the established field of CSR-consulting. All empirical illustrations selected for this chapter have been translated from Swedish by the authors.

Expert Services Offered

In order to investigate if new management ideas lead to the development of new expert services or rather a re-labeling of already existing services, we studied how Swedish consultancies advertised and promoted their CSR-related services. It was clear that new types of services did appear, but also that more traditional consulting services were increasingly advertised under labels such as "CSR" and "sustainability". That a service is presented in terms of CSR or sustainability does not say much about its content. We rather found that the vague yet popular labels offered ample opportunities for consultants from a range of disciplines and backgrounds to engage in "CSR-consulting". This suggested, in turn, that the emerging field of expertise, at the time of our first study, was not yet standardized. As illustrated empirically next, not even consultancies that explicitly positioned themselves as "CSR-specialists" shared profound similarities.

Although no clear standardized set of services could be identified in the empirical material, an analytical categorization of the following five broad categories of "CSR-services" was constructed based on the findings in the interview- and web studies of 2008–2009: 1) Education, 2) Traditional consulting/advice, 3) Investigation and assessment, 4) Auditing and reporting and 5) Certification. Needless to say, in actual service construction and delivery, boundaries were blurred and consultants often combined traits of several analytical service categories.

Education

The popular management idea of CSR attracts many educators. A large part of the Swedish consultants' service offerings in the emerging CSR-field consisted of education services of various kinds. Almost everyone who claimed to sell CSR-services provided education. It seemed widely recognized that CSR requires new knowledge and changing attitudes and consultants were ready to remedy these assumed knowledge deficiencies.

Table 5.1 Five categories of CSR-related consulting services

Categories of CSR-related consulting services	Empirical illustration
Education	*Education on corporate responsibility for human rights*
Traditional consulting (advice)	*Advice on strategy, risk analysis, procurement, health and safety, equality and diversity*
Investigation and assessment	*Sustainable footprint assessment*
Auditing and reporting	*Preparation of external communication and CSR/sustainability reports*
Certification	*ISO 26 000, GRI*

The range of training services was broad. One common label on these services was the seminar. Observed examples included a breakfast seminar on the theme "What responsibility do companies have when human rights are violated?", offered by *Enact* as of May 21, 2012 (www.enact.se) and the full-day seminar "Responsibility in the Supply Chain" offered by *TEM* as of November 8, 2012 (http: //www.tem.lu.se/). There were also consultancies, such as *the Natural Step Sweden* that through partnerships with university colleges (in their case Blekinge Institute of Technology), offered longer educational programs such as in applied information technology, and innovation and sustainable development of industry and society (www.bth. com/sustainability; www.naturalstep.org/sv/sweden/ partners). This type of education often aimed to increase the general awareness in society of corporate social responsibility or sustainability issues such as climate change, human rights, environmental protection or diversity. But the empirical material also offered ample examples of more niche and customized courses, workshops and webinars such as, for example, on "sustainable health care" or "management of chemical risks" (www.lu.se).

Traditional Consulting/Advice

A second broad category of services that engaged most experts in our sample was "traditional" consulting in the sense that managers hire consultants for advice. As illustrated next, vague and inclusive concepts such as CSR and sustainability, invite a multitude of consultants to offer advice from quite different perspectives. As in the case for education services, at the time of study, as there was no standard for consulting in CSR and sustainability, the advice could be about almost anything. Advice on strategy, risk analysis, procurement, health and safety, equality and diversity issues were offered under CSR and sustainability labels, e.g., by *Goodpoint* and *Sustania* (www.goodpoint.se; www.sustania.se). Advice on accounting in line with the GRI standard (Global Reporting Initiative)—a UN supported international standard for sustainability reporting in organizations—or the standards on G3 reporting and SRI (Social Responsible Investments) were offered early on by *Ernst & Young* (www.ey.com/se). Also, advice on public relations, branding and communications were dressed up in CSR and sustainability costumes, for example, by *Halvarsson & Hallvarson* and *Kreab Gavin Andersson* (www.halvarsson.se; www.kreabgavinanderson.com). CSR labeled advice could also be about how customers implement and monitor an ethical or environmental code of conduct. Such advice was offered by, among others, *Ethos International* (www.ethosinternational.se).

Investigation and Assessment

A third category of observed CSR and sustainability services were investigations and assessments of various kinds. The contemporary society and business stakeholders require more information about corporate environmental, ethical and social conditions and their "footprints". A first step to meet these requirements that was often suggested by consultants was to consider investigations and assessments of how the organization performs in terms of values and goals related to CSR and sustainability. Such services were offered by audit and accounting consultants, such as *PWC, Deloitte* and *KPMG*. Engineering service firms, such as *ÅF consultants*, offered to help customers improve their energy efficiency and to identify environmental, social and ethical risks and consequences of their investments in technologies and production processes. Their offer of investigations and various monitoring services included web tools (e.g., ÅF consultant "Energy Controller", www.energieffektivitet.se/en/). Another example is the so-called SFAS (sustainable footprint assessment) that can involve measurement and reporting about how much energy and other resources an organization uses in its operations worldwide. Using these tools, energy consumption and carbon dioxide emissions can be analyzed on an aggregated or local level, and be specified to cover everything from individual properties to transport.

Auditing and Reporting

A fourth broad category of CSR and sustainability services, which is closely linked to the third (Investigation and assessment), relates to the preparation of accounting and other reports and external communication on corporate environmental, ethical and social conditions and footprints. CSR and sustainability reports are usually based on criteria from so-called soft regulations such as GRI and the Global Compact principles. The reports may be included as part of the organization's annual report or issued separately.

Certification

A fifth, and somewhat more innovative, category of services concerns certification of responsible and sustainable business processes. *PWC* and *Ethos International*, for example, advertise certification services as a way for customers to obtain greater legitimacy. The certification is communicated as an independent "guarantee" that the organization's production processes of goods and services are conducted in a responsible and sustainable manner, with respect for environmental, social and economic criteria. More precisely, the clients receive a certificate stating that the organization subscribes to a specific CSR or sustainability standard, such as the ISO 26000 for CSR and the GRI standard for sustainability. The service can also be about certifying that the organization adheres to other predefined obligations, such as particular codes of conduct or industry standards from organizations such as the *Swedish professional institute for authorized public accountants (FAR, see* www.far.se of FAR SRS). The CEO of *Ethos International*, Anna Lindstedth, wrote on their website in a communication dated January 25 2012 that "We are proud to be one out of only three companies with a license to certify sustainability reports according to the international standards AA1000 (2008)" (www.ethosinternational.se). The company also emphasized on its website that "an independent third-party audit is the key to a credible sustainability report" and that "AA1000AS provides a better assurance of the sustainability reports than traditional accountant audits by not only reviewing that the figures in the report are correct but also guaranteeing that the company reports relevant information based on the company's operations and stakeholders' views" (www.ethosinternational.se).

As seen in the empirical illustrations earlier, we found that CSR and sustainability was similar to other popular management ideas, such as TQM, Lean and BPR, in so far as consultants do not just jump on and carry forward these ideas (Whittle, 2008). They rather actively relate to and modify an idea to suit their own profile and agenda. As expected, we found a large variation in how and to what extent consultants relate to ideas on CSR and sustainability. As we shall see next, some consultancies chose to develop and offer new services while others offered their existing portfolio of services as solutions to CSR and sustainability issues. While some use the labels CSR and sustainability explicitly, others chose to downplay them.

Who Is Offering CSR-Consulting?

Who are the consultants translating the popular CSR-idea and can we identify a pattern as to what type of actor is offering what category of services? When analyzing our Swedish sample of CSR-consultants, two main categories of providers were identified. A first group of CSR-consultancies took on a *specialist* CSR profile. They related explicitly to the CSR-concept and used the CSR-label for their entire service portfolio. As described in Table 5.2, two

Table 5.2 A categorization of CSR-consultants

Categories of CSR-consultants	Definition	Empirical illustration
SPECIALISTS	Consultants that relate explicitly to the CSR-concept and use this label for their entire service portfolio.	
Idealist specialists	Consultants with a clear aim to prioritize social and altruistic values over economic profits.	Services aimed to create awareness, commitment and expertise for sustainable development in society (The Natural Step Sweden)
Business-oriented specialists	Consultants with a "win win"-aim to balance potentially conflicting values and goals, rather than assuming a hierarchy of values.	Assistance in creating business value and enhancing client reputation by developing strategies and systems to proactively manage corporate responsibility (Enact)
DIVERSIFIERS	Consultants that offer CSR-services as a complement to or minor part of their service portfolio.	CSR and sustainability services are described as grounded in other "core skills", e.g., in assurances, tax, transactions and advice. (Ernst & Young)

subcategories were identified among the specialists: the *idealist specialists* and the *business-oriented specialists*. The second group of consultancies, the *diversifiers*, did not specialize in CSR-services, but were CSR-consultants in the sense that they offered services under this label as a complement to and minor part of a broader, often functionally focused, service portfolio (see Table 5.2).

Idealist CSR-Specialists

Both categories of specialists commercialized CSR—they sold CSR-services to clients. The main difference between the two specialist categories was seen in their approaches to the plurality and complexity of drivers, as expressed in organizational values and goals. Characteristic for the idealist specialist consultants, as reflected in their self-presentations on websites and in interviews, was their clear aim to prioritize social and altruistic values over economic profits. As exemplified by the self-presentations that follow, the idealist specialists' activities were primarily driven by a wish to further sustainable development for all and by a commitment to knowledge development and dissemination in the broader CSR-field:

> We show the way to an ecologically sustainable society.
>
> *(Eco Centre, www.ekocentrum.se)*

The purpose of The Natural Step is to create awareness, commitment and expertise for sustainable development.

(The Natural Step, www.thenaturalstep.org./sv/sweden)

Many of the idealist specialists offered education as a means to realize their ideals. They offered courses aimed at raising the awareness and involvement in the community on environmental and CSR-related issues. Courses were typically aimed at a broad audience; emphasis was on contributing to a more sustainable society by creating insights not only among business leaders and managers, but on a broad scale including employees and the general public. The core of the idealist specialist service portfolio was thus awareness building learning events of various kinds.

Eco Centre is the learning platform . . . Environmental Education in the form of itinerant lectures in the exhibition is aimed at both businesses, administrations, students and the public.

(Eco Centre, www.ekocentrum.se)

Since 1989 we have inspired decision makers, entrepreneurs and academics to make the world more sustainable and at the same time we have developed and disseminated a science-based framework which currently has several millions of active users worldwide. Welcome to become a change agent, you too!

(The Natural Step, www.thenaturalstep.org/sv/sweden)

TEM offers open training courses on our own premises, training tailored to customers' needs, lectures and workshops. Our courses are very popular and in demand, both by private companies and public organizations. Whether you need an hour of inspiration for the management team or a three-day training, we can offer our assistance at competitive prices.

(TEM, www.tem.lu.se)

Idealist specialists like *TEM*, *Eco Centre* and *The Natural Step* all drew on their own active research in their courses. *TEM*, for instance, offered courses and related services in their main areas of expertise which are energy and climate change, social responsibility and environmental laws, regulations and permits. Courses were also offered on more specific topics such as chemicals management and sustainable health care (www.tem.lu.se).

Another characteristic of the idealist specialists which differentiated them from the business-oriented specialists (see the following) concerns their organizational traits. CSR and sustainability practices have come to blur the boundaries between various institutional fields and practices and have united a variety of stakeholders in this development (e.g., Jutterström, 2006; Windell, 2006). As explained by one anonymous consultant (Ardenfors, 2011, p. 10):

CSR can be a very sensitive area. It is still controversial whether companies are welcome to join in this area of social responsibility. We have had this debate going for a while now . . . it is still a controversial field for some.

Possibly relating to this anxiety we found that while the business-oriented specialists typically drew on the ideal-typical traits of the market and private firm, the idealist specialists could be described as *organizational hybrids* in the sense that they took on ideal-typical traits from not only the private company but also the political organization and the association (Brunsson, 1994). For example, in terms of *purpose*, idealist specialist organizations *Ekocentrum*, *the Natural Step Sweden* and *TEM* are nonprofit organizations (rather than for profit). Employees of the *Natural Step Sweden* openly described its nonprofit orientation as a strategy which they believed enabled client companies to trust *the Natural Step Sweden* and to listen to its advice. In terms of *target groups* and *relation* to these, the idealist specialists resemble ideal-typical public agencies or associations more than private firms in the sense that they make active efforts to turn to audiences beyond the traditional crowd of client managers. TEM Foundation at Lund University for example, described itself in the following words:

> We are an interdisciplinary link between universities and society. We are offering consulting and education in parallel with research within the area of sustainability.
>
> *(www.tem.lu.se)*.

The idealist specialists were often connected to both civil society and academia and presented themselves as a "meeting place", "exhibitions", "learning platform" or "networking hub"—words that connote as much to citizens and members as to clients, and which suggest a relation ideal of a more long lasting type than is characteristic for the private firm. For some, such networking opportunities could even be considered their main "service", alongside education.

Several of the idealist specialist consultants interviewed had a background in the nonprofit sector and viewed CSR as a concern and professional field linked to human rights organizations and other NGOs active in the environmental movement and the trade union movement. As suggested by one of our interviewees from an idealist specialist consultancy, many CSR-consultants are activists at heart:

> I think many who work on these issues are a bit of activists themselves. They could just as well have been working for Greenpeace or another similar NGO. But it may be that you have a background, perhaps in terms of education, that makes consulting work well.

In line with previous studies (e.g., Windell, 2006 on "world saviors") our material reveals that idealist specialists among the CSR-consultants associated their work with a personal commitment, a compassionate mission. To continue along these lines, some consultants also took active part in round table discussions and committees aiming to develop CSR-standards and other related regulations (cf. Tamm Hallström & Boström, 2010). These findings indicate that idealist specialists directly or indirectly referred to and made use of their organizational hybridity (organizational traits such as a nonprofit purpose), as a differential resource for authority, credibility and attention. Perhaps experimenting with organizational traits in such a way could even be analyzed in terms of service innovation?

Business-Oriented CSR-Specialists

The business-oriented CSR-specialists were defined by their emphasis on, or in many cases prioritization of, business, as seen in the self-presentations that follow:

> Natlikan have a positive business case for improving results in the environment . . . Through analysis of the economic benefits and the right tools our customers can work result-oriented and structured with environmental and sustainability issues.
>
> *(Natlikan, www.natlikan.se)*

> We assist in the efforts to create business value and enhance its reputation by developing strategies and systems to proactively manage corporate responsibility.
>
> *(Enact, www.enact.se)*

Although the business-oriented specialists clearly differed from the idealists in that idealists claimed to prioritize social values before profits, many business-oriented specialists drew on the popular "win-win" discourse of possibilities of *balancing* or aligning potentially conflicting values and goals, rather than assuming a hierarchy of values:

> Our services are based on the assumption that healthy people, healthy environment and a healthy organization increase the confidence in our customers and strengthen their brand and profitability.
>
> *(Good Point, www.goodpoint.se).*

> Our passion is to combine sustainability and profitability.
>
> *(Respect, www.respect.se)*

Business-oriented specialists often described themselves as important cogs in a long time sustainable perspective. But in essence, they typically did not engage in CSR for the good cause and long-term sustainability *only*. They were in it to increase clients' business success—and their own, also in the short run. Like one of our interviewees put it:

> If you attempt to do something else, if you try to save the world without making money—then you can go and work for an NGO instead. There is nothing wrong with that. When you run a company you do it to make money.

Business-oriented specialists (such as *Good Point* and *Sustania*) were defined by their commercial focus where the business idea was to provide services—usually advisory services—that relate directly to CSR or related concepts such as sustainability. Informants from this category of CSR-service providers carefully pointed out that CSR and its related concepts are universal but most of all economically viable for their clients. As a clarifying illustration, while both idealist specialists and business-oriented specialists stressed that clients needed to re-use their resources in order to become more sustainable, an idealist like *The Natural Step Sweden* claimed the consultancy business to be a *means* to make the whole community/world sustainable, while business-oriented specialists and diversifiers (described in the next section) highlighted their business as an end in its own right. In this latter stance, the consultants may for example emphasize how companies will not be able to do business in the future because resources are scarce and costly.

In terms of services offered, a few of the business-oriented specialists, like *GES Investment Services* and *ETIX SRI advisor* chose to focus on specific services (assistance and advice on sustainable and responsible investment decisions) and a specific client category (institutional investors). However, the vast majority of the business-oriented specialists aspired to offer a "one stop shop" for a collection of CSR-services. These providers may thus be distinguished from the idealists by offering a broader range of services, including but not mainly focusing, education. The business-oriented specialists rather promote themselves through a range of services that spans various disciplinary boundaries, but where all services are still related to CSR and its different facets. One empirical illustration is collected from *Goodpoint* that explicitly emphasized the company's diversity of services and roles on its website:

> Goodpoint consultants work in a variety of roles depending on the task at hand. For example, we can work as a strategic advisor and business partner, change manager, evaluator, project manager, trainer, environmental manager, quality manager, health coach, expert or auditor.
> *(Goodpoint, http://www.goodpoint.se/english/index.html)*

When opening the specialists' service portfolios the content is not standardized. When looking closer at the service portfolios of the business-oriented specialists it becomes clear that the field, at the time of study, was still in an experimental state. As seen in Table 5.3, increasing your client's business success (and your own as consultant) can be achieved in various ways, for example by cost savings from energy efficiency or by communications, boosting brand awareness. We found business-oriented specialists' service portfolios extending over the entire service spectrum. Specialist portfolios could include services ranging from environmental impact assessment to legal advice to change management services related to the implementation of CSR. Compared to the idealist specialists who used the CSR-label explicitly and who "lived and breathed" CSR and aimed to become closely associated with the concepts, the business-oriented specialists tended to avoid "putting all their eggs in the CSR-basket".

The wide span of specialized CSR-services that is depicted in Table 5.3 was also reflected in the employees' backgrounds in the business-oriented specialist firms which were typically relatively small and employed up to 30 employees (not including subcontractors and professional networks). Competencies that were highlighted in the business-oriented specialist firms ranged from management and economics, public relations and communications, to toxicology and other biological and ecological expertise, political science, law and more. As a business-oriented CSR specialist, being specialized did not mean offering the same services as other CSR-specialists. Compared to "traditional experts" who earn legitimacy for their expertise

Table 5.3 Examples of service portfolios of business-oriented CSR-specialists

Sustainia (www.sustania.se)	Goodpoint (www.goodpoint. se)	Respect (www. respect.se)	Natlikan Sustainability solutions (www. natlikan.se)
Environment process & quality	Strategy & Organization	Sustainable development	Sustainability reporting
Health & safety in the workplace	Performance Management	Business development	Climate
CSR for vigorous, proactive organizations	Health, Safety and Environment	Communication	Environmental legal advice
Measurements	Procurement	Key issues	Education
Education	Social Responsibility	Review and verification	
E-services	Sustainability communications	Climate neutral events and products	
International services (subcontractors in Asia help out with investigations/inquiries)	Education	Climate estimates	
		Carbon offsetting	
		Climate Strategy	
		Education	

by drawing upon a united knowledge base for the profession (cf. Chapter 2 in this volume) CSR-consultants are expected to improvise on the CSR theme (cf. Chapter 9 in this volume).

CSR-Diversifiers

We defined a second main category of CSR-consultants as CSR-*diversifiers*. As stated previously, the organizations in this category of suppliers do not specialize in CSR-services, but rather offer services under this label as a complement to and minor part of a broader, often functionally focused service portfolio. As an illustration, the Swedish *Ernst & Young* division presented its "Climate change and sustainable development" offer under the heading of "specialist services" on the same level as services concerning "French Business Network". But looking closer at their "specialist" offerings, it is clear that, at the time of study, CSR and sustainability was not a specialty of *E&Y's* in the same way as they specialized in insurance, tax, and transaction lines. Rather, *E&Y* translated and transposed (Whittle, 2008; Frostenson, 2010) their traditional services under the label of CSR and sustainability. Among the *E&Y* "climate change and sustainability development services" we found "strategic advice", "global reporting initiative", "environmental auditing" and "risk analysis" (www.ey.com/SE).

Although expanding at different rates and to different degrees into the business area of CSR, diversifiers could generally be identified as companies which referred to their entire skills base when pitching their "CSR-offers" to clients. This stance is illustrated next by a selection of diversifier firms' self-presentations:

> Deloitte can assist your business with environmental and sustainability reporting. . . Our specialists will assist in the accounting issues and identify environmental, social and ethical risks associated with acquisitions and divestitures.
>
> *(Deloitte, www.deloitte.se)*

> Our climate change and sustainability services team is grounded in our core skills in assurances, tax, transactions and advice. In addition to that we have the specific knowledge to help you understand business and regulatory threats and opportunities, to explore and execute commercial transactions, to monitor performance and assure public disclosures and progress.
>
> *(Ernst & Young, www.ey.com/SE)*

A specialized, well-defined service portfolio for CSR was less common among more traditional management consultants (such as *Accenture* and *BCG*) and technology consultants (with *ÅF* as an exception). Diversifiers were also found among the large auditing and communication consulting firms such as *PWC*, *Ernst & Young*, *Deloitte* and *Halvarsson & Hallvarsson*. Just like Frostenson (2010), we found diversifiers translating or *transposing* CSR in such a way as to match and be able to draw on their existing service portfolios. On a general note, and in line with similar findings reported by Frostenson (2010), we conclude that the consultants who diversified into the sub-field of CSR and sustainability consulting tended to offer about the same types of services as they did previously in other sub-fields. Communications consultants offered CSR communication services, strategy consultants offered CSR strategy services, technical consultants offered technical inquiries and measurements in the CSR area, etc. That is, CSR and sustainability were translated and packaged to fit with the consultancies' existing knowledge and experience.

For some, CSR became just another sales argument for the same old services: risk management with a CSR twist or branding with a CSR twist. Along these lines, one of our specialist informants even likened diversifier CSR-services to "the Emperor's new clothes" as a critique of the fact that the CSR-services did not add substantially more than a new label to what the diversifiers had previously been offering. This response allows diversifiers to be "money makers" (Windell, 2006) who "cash in" (Whittle, 2008) in relation to the CSR and sustainability trend with only slight changes to the contents of their service portfolios.

By re-labeling traditional services, or by offering them as complements to their actual specialties, the diversifiers were able to keep a distance to the CSR and sustainability concepts. This distance could prove healthy in case the popularity of the concepts would wane and the consultants would be forced to adjust their tools and service offers to the changing fashion. Generally, when a connection to a framework is vague, this allows for more freedom for individual consultants (cf. Alexius, 2007).

In cases where a more elaborate and specific CSR-service portfolio was created by a CSR- diversifier, this often followed a key recruitment of a recognized CSR specialist with an established network and credibility in the expert area. This was the case in *ÅF*, one of the largest engineering consulting organizations in Sweden, which in 2009 took the initiative to promote and position their existing services in a CSR and sustainability discourse. Key to this process was the creation of a new coordinator role for "environmental and CSR-services". The recruitment of Alice Bah Kuhnke, a well-known media person with a strong record in the nonprofit sector (and since 2014 the Swedish Minister of culture and democracy), was communicated in the following words in a press release from April 2009:

> ÅF is one of the leading technical consulting firms on climate change but we can get better at coordinating, packaging and communicating our expertise to customers.
>
> *(ÅF, www.afconsult.com)*

Key individuals such as Bah Kuhnke may thus become a hub to which additional CSR-experts can join to develop a specialized section. In the ÅF case, following the recruitment of Bah Kuhnke, the firm stepped up and successfully advertised itself as the "Green advisor".

All in all, we found that the CSR-concept generated a comprehensive range of services, perhaps one of the broadest service output volumes that has been generated inspired by a recent popular management idea? Similar to other popular management ideas, CSR and sustainability demonstrate an exceptional "generative capacity". Few management ideas have created a platform for professionals from as many disciplines—managers, engineers, communicators, lawyers and others—and generated such a broad set of different types of services.

Does the CSR-Idea Create Experts?

Our study of the range of services that emerged in response to the related management idea of CSR and sustainability shows that these ideas indeed gave rise to a wide range of services—such as education, consulting, investigations, auditing/reporting and certification (see Table 5.1). A larger number of different types of experts and expert organizations offer these services (see Table 5.2). The popular management ideas of CSR and sustainability served as a platform for experts from different disciplines and experience— managers, PR-experts, engineers, communicators, lawyers, auditors and others—to expand their portfolio of expert services to new areas. The entrepreneurial opportunities that the CSR and sustainability ideas offered thus not only resulted in many different types of services but also invited actors with very different disciplinary backgrounds, from business to biology, engineers, lawyers and environmental science. For some, the CSR-concept was seen as an opportunity to transform specialist issues to management issues, with greater attention and budget as a result. In some cases, completely new services were created, meaning that new areas of expertise emerged (such as different types of CSR certifications). In other cases, already existing and well established and demanded services (such as implementation support and change management) were related to the CSR-idea, most likely in order to ride on its popularity and extend the possible scope and target audience for the traditional lines of expertise. All in all, our study indicates that management ideas indeed create experts.

Although our study shows that many experts linked their services to the CSR-idea, they did not automatically and uncritically "jump on" the bandwagon (Whittle, 2008). Rather, we found that the experts had a reflective and thoughtful relation to new popular ideas when advantages and disadvantages to associate themselves with the idea were openly considered and at times debated. The 22 consultants interviewed for the study explained how they acknowledged the business potential of relating to CSR (or ability to influence society for idealist specialists), but they also expressed an awareness of the risks of tying their services to a popular management idea that sooner or later might lose in popularity. Our findings further indicate that opportunities for entrepreneurial initiatives were most actively exploited by smaller expert organizations, particularly in the category of the specialists, where the CSR-idea acted as an impulse to create a number of new organizations. Established actors, primarily found in the diversifier category, were generally more wary of tying up too closely and exclusively to the CSR-idea.

All in all, our study also points at great possibilities for the creation of new services, possibilities, which were seized by the many different consultants. Characteristic of the flora of emerged services was a focus on different types of "visibility services", including the assessment, financial reporting, certification and advisory services in communications and public relations around which a whole new cadre of experts emerged (Jutterström, 2013). CSR as an idea is largely dependent on communication, because oftentimes, it is the visibility of CSR initiatives that create goodwill among stakeholders, which then in turn increases the organizations' competitiveness. This reasoning may explain why the novel kinds of CSR-services focused on creating visibility for clients as corporations with morality.

Bringing this chapter to a close, a striking finding from this study is the multiplicity of actors that crop up around a popular management idea— much like flies around goodies. We have illustrated how popular ideas create entrepreneurial opportunities for diverse experts and how their expertise not only differs in the services provided but also in the types of organizations that offer them. We have shown that the management idea of CSR serves as a breeding ground for new expert services produced by "new" categories of experts, as well as a sounding board for already established experts, expanding the boundaries and relevance of their services (for example by making some expertise—such as environmental expertise—relevant to new groups such as general managers). Not least the presence of idealist specialists (see Table 5.2) is interesting because they represent an atypical agenda for management consultants as "goodness-oriented" rather than "efficiency-oriented" (Frostenson, 2010). This is also reflected in their often atypical hybrid organizational form (this category of experts are likely to run their business in the form of a foundation or an association). Idealist specialists thus borrow characteristics from other types of organizations that are directly associated with an altruistic mind. This type of hybridity (Brunsson, 1994) might be seen as a way for the expert organizations to profile themselves and create legitimacy around the idea that they in fact have a pure interest in saving the world.

The example of an emerging field of expertise in focus here—CSR—may seem as an extreme example considering the generative capacities of an idea that is possible to relate to underlying values of both kindness and efficiency. Still, we believe that the basic mechanisms underlying the relationship between new ideas and emerging fields of expertise identified here are also valid for other emerging fields of management related expertise.

References

Alexius, S. (2007). *Regelmotståndarna: Om konsten att undkomma regler* [rule-resisters—on the art of escaping rules]. Stockholm: EFI.

Ardenfors, M. (2011). CSR-konsulter—Idealister Och Opportunister? *Score Report Series*, 2011:1. Stockholm: Stockholm Centre for Organizational Research.

Brunsson, N. (1994). Politicization and 'company-ization'– On institutional affiliation and confusion in the organizational world. *Management Accounting Research*, 5(3–4), 323–335.

Frostenson, M. (2010). How consultants contribute to CSR innovation: Combining competences and modifying standards. In Louche, C., Idowu, S. O. & Leal Filho, W. (eds.), *Innovative CSR—From Risk Management to Value Creation*. Sheffield: Greenleaf Publishing, 352–373.

Jutterström, M. (2006). Corporate Social Responsibility—The Supply Side of CSR Standards. *Stockholm: Score Report Series*, 2006:2. Stockholm: Stockholm Centre for Organizational Research.

Jutterström, M. (2013). Organizations that set CSR standards. In Jutterström, M. & Norberg, P. (eds.), *CSR as Management Idea – Ethics in Action*. Cheltenham: Edward Elgar, 52–74.

Tamm Hallström, K. & Boström, M. (2010). *Transnational Multi-Stakeholder Standardization: Organizing Fragile Non-State Authority*. Cheltenham, UK and Northampton, MA, USA: Edward Elgar.

Whittle, A. (2008). From flexibility to work-life balance: Exploring the changing discourses of management consultants. *Organization*, 15(4), 513–534.

Windell, K. (2006). *Corporate Social Responsibility Under Construction: Ideas, Translations and Institutional Change*. Uppsala: Uppsala University.

6 On Experts in Marketing

Who's in the Driver's Seat and What's Love Got to Do with It?

Claudia A. Rademaker, Patrik Nilsson and Richard Wahlund

Introduction

It is common practice among companies to engage various types of external marketing consultants from advertising, media, PR, DM, web, event, brand, marketing research and other marketing expertise agencies, even when they already have a marketing department led by a marketing manager. In 2001, there were about 43,000 such agencies in Sweden (Statistics Sweden, 2001). Wahlund, Rademaker, Nilsson & Svahn (2013) showed that the amount spent (real value) on some such services in Sweden almost tripled from the early 1990s to over ten billion SEK in 2010 (still not including all types of marketing expertise hired). In recent years, many new types of experts have appeared on the market following the IT development (Nilsson, Rademaker, Svahn & Wahlund, 2013). Research has shown that marketing managers often work with different external consultants simultaneously and that these managers often wish they could reduce the number of cooperating consultants or agencies. In addition, marketing managers also wish that agencies would cooperate better with each other and listen more to their clients, the marketing managers (Rademaker, 2013).

The purpose of this chapter is to explore the rather extensive consulting industry in marketing by addressing the following questions: a) Why do companies hire various external consultants for their marketing tasks? b) What types of consultants are hired and what competences do they possess? c) What do these consultants actually deliver and how do they supplement the existing competences in companies? d) How is the coordination of internal and external marketing tasks organized? There will be a focus on marketing communication and the media selection process, but we start by discussing some general motives for hiring external marketing consultants.

Marketing—A Complex Task Becoming Even More Complex in a Changing World

Marketing plays a key role in business because it is responsible for attracting and retaining customers, thus being responsible for a firm's income and profit (Drucker, 1999). The concept of marketing is essentially to achieve corporate goals by meeting and exceeding customer needs and expectations better than the competition. Nonprofit organizations also need and use marketing, both for their offerings and to attract needed resources (members, money, gifts, personnel, etc.). Common for both profit and nonprofit organizations is that they can use marketing to better understand and satisfy their respective audiences with the goods or services that they offer.

Companies and organizations that are involved in marketing activities are frequently using external third parties in order to create and compose their marketing. The main reason for this is that marketing is a complex task. Studies show, for instance, that consumers are becoming more skeptical toward advertising (Rademaker, 2013), thus resulting in a need to manage the tension between consumers and the brand control better. Therefore, marketing communication needs to take on a broader approach to creativity, which requires profound corporate brand knowledge together with various communication skills (IPA, 2015).

With market conditions continuously changing there are many questions about the market that companies must answer in order to know what challenges are ahead. There are many different solutions to choose from, but the main challenge is that various marketing solutions must all fit together. The complexity requires a variety of expertise that must be coordinated effectively. It is simply too costly for most companies and organizations to have all the necessary experts in-house and to coordinate the work that all these different experts need to perform.

Examples of issues that companies are facing and that require coherent solutions are as follows: What are the needs and desires among both existing and potential customers and how do they want those satisfied (which products should we develop)? How much are different target customers willing to pay for our products and services and how do they want to pay (which price should we set and how should we get paid)? How do we reach our existing and potential customers, both communicatively and with the products themselves (how should we plan our marketing communications and how should our products be sold and distributed)? Who are our competitors? What is happening in the world and how should we adapt to these changes? How do we obtain the information we need about all this (data and analysis through marketing research)? How should we implement all the solutions we come up with, and how do we ensure that it all fits together?

This complexity has accelerated in recent decades, and it can be expected to continue to increase. There are several factors that have contributed to these changes, but the most important factor is the digitalization of our society. Within a short time frame, the digital revolution has contributed to new ways of conducting business and it has changed the functioning of many industries. Markets that were assumed to be stable have disappeared and new ones have emerged instead, where new products and services are exchanged via new channels. Some of the changes have been profound and also created new forms of social interaction.

Digitalization has affected marketing communications in a number of ways. For example, new types of digital advertising emerged that to a greater extent than before can be directed to the predestined user profiles on both ordinary web pages and through social media, based on the increased availability of consumer data and the development of new data analysis techniques of so-called *big data*. This way of doing advertising requires new expertise in programming of for instance systems design and predictive analytics.

Similarly, media planning and media selection for advertising campaigns have become increasingly complex and challenging as new digital media have had a faster diffusion than earlier new media, contributing to a much more fragmented media landscape (Nilsson, 2006; Svahn, Wahlund, Denward, Rademaker & Nilsson, 2016) to which consumers have responded by continuously changing their media behavior (Rademaker, Royne & Wahlund, 2015). Today marketers are thus facing more competition for consumer attention than ever before, and a new situation where consumers themselves can take command of communication, making companies more vulnerable.

The digitalization and the trend toward greater technology use, in connection with various marketing activities, have created skills-related challenges for companies and their marketing departments. Technology development has contributed to phenomena such as marketing automation, data and market modeling, data mining, big data analytics, interactive media, artificial intelligence and new types of advanced CRM systems (Svahn et al., 2016). Consequently, market, sales and IT are merging even more today into unique corporate CRM systems.

The rapid technological developments have made it more difficult for companies to have the necessary skills in-house. Those companies that have been striving to keep up with the rapid changes and always aim to adopt the latest skills, have simply been forced to seek help from specialists such as external consultants and partners. As a consequence, a plethora of companies have emerged specializing in various areas or niches in marketing. For example, new types of agencies have emerged offering not only creative expertise but also production while promising reach/frequency and distribution through, for instance, social media channels. Agencies are starting to combine advertising and PR (digital platforms) in order to create value for target markets. A recent study showed that in Sweden PR, advertising, and content agencies are increasingly redefining themselves as communication agencies. For example, while 56 percent of PR agencies prefer to remain to be called PR agencies, 33 percent now define themselves as communication agencies. In line with this, the interest among agencies to join associations that take a broader (communication) perspective is growing while other associations that have more narrow focus, are losing members (Dagens Opinion, 2016).

Education and Skills of Marketing Managers and Their Hired Consultants

Although the main reason for hiring marketing consultants is that they have skills that are too specific or up to date to be cost-effective enough to have in-house, a general understanding of how marketing works, with all its complexity, is of great importance because all activities must be integrated and coordinated toward the same aims. Table 6.1, based on surveys that the authors have carried out, shows the proportions of marketing managers and marketing consultants in Sweden with different levels of post-secondary educations.

According to Table 6.1, 63 percent of the marketing managers have post-secondary education with a major in marketing, while only 33 percent of the marketing consultants have such. Another 18 percent of the marketing managers have studied one or more subtopics in marketing within post-secondary education, while 25 percent of the consultants have such background. This level includes some form of education with a focus on for example advertising, marketing communications and media, or communications. Of the marketing managers, 17 percent have no post-secondary marketing education, but education in other fields. The corresponding proportion among consultants is 33 percent. These have studied, for example, law, information technology, history, culture or natural sciences. Finally, only two percent of the marketing managers and nine percent of the consultants are lacking post-secondary education. In total, 19 percent of the marketing managers

Table 6.1 Marketing managers' and consultants' post-secondary education

Education	Marketing managers		Consultants*	
	Frequency	*Percentage*	*Frequency*	*Percentage*
Post-secondary education with marketing as a major	66	63%	44	33%
Post-secondary education within subjects of marketing**	19	18%	33	25%
Post-secondary education within other majors or subjects than marketing***	18	17%	44	33%
No post-secondary education	2	2%	12	9%
Total	105	100%	133	100%

* Includes consultants at ad agencies, media agencies, web agencies, design agencies and the like. Eighty-eight percent of the respondents work at ad, communication or media agencies.
** For example sales, advertising, marketing communication, communication and media.
*** Among the respondents studied, majors are history, journalism, culture, operations analysis, optics, pedagogy, computer science, psychology, IT, political science, law, technical science and natural science.

and 42 percent of the consultants do not have marketing post-secondary education of any kind. The marketing managers are thus, in general, more highly educated than the marketing consultants they hire.

What, then, may explain the results? One self-evident reason for the lack of higher marketing education among some of the respondents, both marketing managers and consultants, is that individuals may acquire knowledge and skills in ways other than by formal education, primarily by experience or autodidactically, and then having been successful in some way, thus "proven" their competence. However, experiences are usually limited to specific issues and situations and may lead astray in other situations. Another explanation is that employment statistics as well as a number of recruitment companies' databases clearly show that there is a shortage of potential marketing managers with a higher educational background in marketing. This, in turn, results in a need for marketing consultants with such knowledge and skills, which one-third of them obviously have. This proportion corresponds quite well to the proportion of marketing managers lacking such education.

The remaining consultants are specialized to a greater extent than marketing managers, thus indicating that they possess some specific knowledge and skills needed and lacking in firms. It seems logical that people working for advertising and media agencies are more specialized in advertising and media. The many new digital media channels and availability of digitally generated consumer data (big data) also need a lot of technological and data analytic expertise. Still another explanation may be that one hires consultants to blame if things go wrong, thus not primarily because of their expertise. The lack of higher marketing education of quite a few marketing professionals may constitute risks or inefficiency for the companies they work for.

In order to test if there may be other explanations to why consultants are hired than the lack of some specific expertise a survey was conducted where a specific type of competence, namely media selection skills of advertising agencies, media agencies and market managers, was studied from the perspective of marketing managers. Marketing managers (n = 153) were asked how competent they perceive advertising agencies, media agencies, and themselves to be concerning media selection for marketing purposes.

Table 6.2 shows that marketing managers consider advertising agencies (M = 5.63) to have significantly lower media selection competence than themselves (M = 7.05) and media agencies (M = 7.10). The difference between the perceived skills of advertising and media agencies is quite logical, but why hire media agencies/consultants if one self-possesses about the same competence? From the marketing manager's perspective, it is perhaps not about hiring a media agency with more competence to fulfill the task better, but just not having enough need or demand for such competence in-house and being satisfied with having someone external, equally qualified, to perform the task, i.e. less costly in total. Use of media agencies, not being

Table 6.2 Marketing Managers' Perceptions of Media Selection Competence of Themselves and of External Consultants

	Ad agencies' competence	*Marketing managers' own competence*	*Media agencies' competence*	*Pairwise comparisons*
Mean (M)	5.63	7.05	7.10	t = 6.47; p < 0.001[a]
Standard deviation (SD)	(2.54)	(1.70)	(3.11)	t = −0.20; p > 0.10[b]
				t = −5.97; p < 0.001[c]

[a] Marketing managers vs Ad agencies [b] (Marketing managers vs Media agencies [c] (Ad agencies vs Media agencies)

*Scale: 0 = Has no competence, 10 = Has very high competence

perceived as more skilled than oneself, may also be explained by then having someone to blame. The advertising agencies wishing to offer their clients media selection competence are in any case clearly facing a greater challenge than media agencies.

Who Does What According to Whom?

Among the various types of agencies, companies tend to cooperate most frequently with advertising and media agencies (Rademaker, 2013). In today's competitive market, they work together to develop ways to effectively convey messages about the company, its products and other utilities. This task is sometimes straightforward but tends to become more complex the larger the company becomes, and the more markets and target groups to be reached. To examine the extent to which the various actors—marketing managers, advertising agencies and media agencies—are involved, data were collected whereby theses parties were asked to evaluate each others' participation in the various stages of planning and implementation of an advertising campaign.

The reason for choosing an advertising campaign for the study is that an advertising campaign involves several different tasks that include the various actors' areas of expertise. For example, the creative design of an advertising campaign is usually delegated to the advertising agency, while media decisions are delegated to the media agency. By asking the same questions to all three actors it is possible to explore whether they agree or disagree as to each other's competences and contributions.

First, the marketing managers' (n = 155) view of working with an advertising campaign is presented in Table 6.3. The results show that marketing managers consider all parties to be involved in all stages to some extent, but themselves to be more involved than their advertising and media agency

Table 6.3 Marketing managers' (N=155) perceptions of their own and the external consultants' participation in the different activities of an ad campaign

Level of Participation	Ad Agency M (SD)	Marketing Manager M (SD)	Media Agency M (SD)	Pairwise Comparisons
Definition of target group	3.56 (3.26)	8.72 (2.10)	3.87 (3.47)	t = 16.59; p < 0.001[a] t = 15.17; p < 0.001[b] t = −1.04; p > 0.10[c]
Overall message and goal	5.38 (3.37)	8.80 (1.98)	2.81 (2.68)	t = 11.07; p < 0.001[a] t = 22.21; p < 0.001[b] t = 11.08; p < 0.001[c]
Media strategy	4.31 (3.01)	8.28 (2.23)	6.01 (3.91)	t = 12.54; p < 0.001[a] t = 6.38; p < 0.001[b] t = −5.59; p < 0.001[c]
Media selection	4.02 (2.97)	8.01 (2.37)	6.11 (3.97)	t = 12.09; p < 0.001[a] t = 5.08; p < 0.001[b] t = 6.94; p < 0.001[c]
Campaign follow-up	3.78 (3.09)	7.91 (2.42)	5.20 (3.88)	t = 5.08; p < 0.001[a] t = 7.94; p < 0.001[b] t = −5.08; p < 0.001[c]
Communication objective	4.97 (3.17)	8.66 (2.03)	3.81 (3.23)	t = −4.74; p < 0.001[a] t = 16.00; p < 0.001[b] t = 4.74; p < 0.001[c]
Creative design	7.92 (3.32)	6.82 (2.99)	2.25 (2.88)	t = −2.89; p = 0.004[a] t = 13.72; p < 0.001[b] t = 18.41; p < 0.001[c]

[a] Ad agency vs Marketing manager [b] Media agency vs Marketing manager [c] (Ad agency vs Media agency)

*Scale: 0 = Not at all, 10 = To a very great extent

in six of the seven stages of the campaign process. The marketing managers thus consider themselves to be most involved in the development of the overall message and goals ($M_{marketing\ managers}$ = 8.80 vs $M_{ad\ agenies}$ = 5.38 and $M_{media\ agencies}$ =2.81), definition of target group ($M_{marketing\ managers}$ = 8.72 vs $M_{ad\ agencies}$ = 3.56 and $M_{media\ agencies}$ = 3.87), formulation of communication goals ($M_{marketing\ managers}$ = 8.66 vs $M_{ad\ agencies}$ = 4.97 and $M_{media\ agencies}$ = 3.81), formulation of media strategy ($M_{marketing\ managers}$ = 8.28 vs $M_{ad\ agencies}$ = 4.31 and $M_{media\ agencies}$ = 6.01), media selection ($M_{marketing\ managers}$ = 8.01 vs $M_{ad\ agencies}$ = 4.02 and $M_{media\ agencies}$ = 6.11) and campaign follow-up ($M_{marketing\ managers}$ = 7.91 vs $M_{ad\ agencies}$ = 3.78 and $M_{media\ agencies}$ = 5.20).

According to the marketing managers, advertising and media agencies are thus not as much involved in the planning and implementation of these stages of an advertising campaign. The only area where marketing managers consider themselves significantly less involved than any other actor is creative design ($M_{\text{marketing managers}} = 6.82$ vs $M_{\text{ad agencies}} = 7.92$). That marketing managers consider advertising agencies to be mostly involved in the planning and implementation of the creative design of an advertising campaign is logical because this type of work can be considered as one of the advertising agencies' main areas of expertise.

It should be noted that marketing managers believe that they participate significantly more than media agencies in the planning and implementation of both the media strategy ($M_{\text{marketing manager}} = 8.28$ vs $M_{\text{media agencies}} = 6.01$) and media selection ($M_{\text{marketing managers}} = 8.01$ vs $M_{\text{media agencies}} = 6.11$). This indicates that marketing managers do not delegate media strategy and media selection to the media agencies to the same extent as they delegate the creative design to advertising agencies. This result may be interpreted as marketing managers wanting to have greater control of an area they master, while leaving the creative design to advertising agencies because they have less or no competence within this area.

In Table 6.4, the perceptions of media, advertising and communication agencies as to their own and the marketing managers' involvement in the planning and implementation of the activities of an advertising campaign are compared. The first two columns of the table show advertising consultants' views on the extent of ad agencies' and marketing managers' participation in the different tasks of an ad campaign. Comparing these figures with Table 6.3 presenting the marketing managers' assessment, it is apparent that advertising consultants have a different view on the involvement in the work of advertising campaigns than the marketing managers. Advertising consultants believe that they participate more than marketing managers in all aspects of the work of an advertising campaign, while marketing managers believe that this applies only to creative design.

Advertising consultants further believe that the difference in participation is greatest when it comes to creative design ($M_{\text{ad agencies}} = 9.88$ vs $M_{\text{marketing managers}} = 4.96$), which is not entirely surprising. However, advertising consultants have the perception that they participate significantly more than the marketing managers when it comes to both the media strategy ($M_{\text{ad agencies}} = 7.83$ vs $M_{\text{marketing managers}} = 6.79$) and media selection ($M_{\text{ad agencies}} = 7.62$ vs $M_{\text{marketing managers}} = 6.54$), which are the media agencies' areas of expertise. The only result where there seems to be consensus between advertising agencies and marketing managers is creative design. In general, opinions thus seem to be divided.

In column three and four of Table 6.4, media consultants' perceptions on participation in ad campaigns are presented. Like the comparison between advertising consultants and marketing managers, there appears neither to be direct consensus between the media agency consultants and marketing managers, except when it comes to the creative design, which is the area where advertising agencies are mostly involved. Regarding media strategy, media agencies perceive that they participate significantly more than marketing managers ($M_{\text{media agencies}} = 9.43$ vs $M_{\text{marketing managers}} = 5.79$). The results are

Table 6.4 Consultants' perceptions of the marketing managers' and agencies' participation in the different activities of an ad campaign

	Ad agencies N = 51–52		Media agencies N=14		Communication agencies N=22–23		Pairwise comparisons
	Ad agency M (SD)	Marketing manager M (SD)	Media agency M (SD)	Marketing manager M (SD)	Communication agency M (SD)	Marketing manager M (SD)	
Definition of target group	8.62 (1.55)	8.40 (1.79)	8.93 (1.94)	6.43 (2.90)	8.77 (1.45)	8.13 (1.77)	t = -.69; p>0.10[a] t = -2.94; p=0.011[b] t = -1.09; p>0.05[c]
Overall message and goal	9.27 (1.14)	7.73 (2.40)	7.07 (1.73)	7.71 (2.16)	8.81 (1.92)	7.52 (2.35)	t = -4.30; p<0.001[a] t = 1.24; p>0.05[b] t = -1.74; p>0.05[c]
Media strategy	7.83 (2.10)	6.79 (2.30)	9.43 (1.87)	5.79 (2.12)	8.27 (1.96)	6.04 (2.64)	t = -2.76; p=0.008[a] t = -6.18; p<0.001[b] t = -4.02; p=0.001[c]
Media selection	7.62 (2.09)	6.54 (2.24)	9.43 (1.87)	5.57 (1.91)	8.18 (2.11)	6.17 (2.53)	t = -2.46; p=0.017[a] t = 6.97; p<0.001[b] t = -3.84; p=0.001[c]
Campaign follow-up	7.40 (2.15)	6.63 (2.63)	8.79 (1.97)	6.14 (2.32)	7.77 (2.31)	6.65 (2.55)	t = -1.10; p=0.051[a] t = -4.71; p<0.001[b] t = -1.74; p>0.05[c]
Communication objective	8.80 (1.37)	7.23 (2.44)	8.00 (2.04)	6.93 (2.67)	8.95 (1.50)	7.61 (1.88)	t = -5.20; p<0.001[a] t = -1.69; p>0.05[b] t = -3.58; p=0.002[c]
Creative design	9.88 (.32)	4.96 (3.15)	3.29 (2.05)	4.86 (3.03)	9.14 (2.21)	5.35 (2.96)	t = -11,12; p<0.001[a] t = 1.97; p>0.05[b] t = -4.52; p<0.001[c]

[a] Ad agencies vs Marketing managers [b] (Media agencies vs Marketing managers [c] (Communication agencies vs Marketing managers)
* Scale: 0 = Not at all, 10 = To a very great extent

similar as to media selection ($M_{media\ agencies}$ = 9.43 vs $M_{marketing\ managers}$ = 5.57), whereas marketing managers have an opposite view.

The last two columns of Table 6.4 show communication agencies' perception of the extent of marketing managers' and their own participation in campaign work. The reason for showing the results separately for communication agencies is that a number of advertising agencies in recent years have redefined themselves, taking a greater grip on the commercial communication services they offer and deliver. Instead of only focusing on the advertising services, they offer several other types of marketing communications services.

The results show that the response of communication agencies follows exactly the same pattern as the advertising agencies. Marginal insignificant differences confirm that communications agencies consider themselves more involved than marketing managers when it comes to all parts of an advertising campaign. Just as with advertising agencies, there is a consensus between the communications agencies and marketing managers only when it comes to the creative design of an advertising campaign. Again, in general, opinions are divided.

Management and Coordination of External Consultants

In the introduction of this chapter it was mentioned that several types of external consultants are often hired for a company's marketing efforts. Often, marketing managers perceive the number of collaborating agencies as being too many and wish for dealing with a less number of consultants or agencies. Marketing departments of most large companies therefore tend to organize cooperation with such consultants by appointing a strategic partner among the group of external consultants, a so-called main agency. The main agency takes on a leading role within the agency network and is responsible for entire projects. It is also responsible for ensuring that the cooperation between the agencies functions well. The main agency, most often the advertising agency, is considered being the company's closest contact and serves as the main link between the marketing manager/department and the rest of the network of external consultants/agencies.

Earlier in this chapter, it was discussed that especially those consultants/ agencies that have a leading or coordinating marketing function should have general marketing competence. We have also mentioned that this coordinating task is often given to an advertising agency, the main agency. At the same time, our data show that many consultants at advertising agencies lack higher marketing education. This means that the management and coordination of the various consulting services in marketing may in some cases be performed by consultants lacking needed knowledge or skills. This may in these cases result in less effective marketing of business and in society in general.

Working with a network of influential parties such as various types of agencies may itself create complexity and fragmentation (Grant & McLeod, 2007). At the same time, Grimes (2004) does not share the idea of companies appointing a main agency and argues that cooperation across a range of parties is central for successful marketing communication campaigns. This view is also supported by Grant & McLeod (2007) who argue that more democratic positions across the agency network will lead to better collaborating relationships. A consequence of appointing a main agency is that it could create a barrier for incorporating integrated marketing communication (IMC) when integration should be initiated and guided by the marketing manager (Schultz & Kitchen, 1997). Appointing a main agency may thus create a hierarchical structure in the network of agencies causing a barrier between the other agencies and the company. As a consequence, agencies may not be fully willing to share crucial knowledge that could benefit the company. This may include critical input on media selection. Whether this is true or not can only be resolved by further empirical investigations.

Company-Agency Cooperation: Based on Personal Chemistry or Performance?

It has been shown that marketing managers hire consultants they consider less knowledgeable or skilled than themselves. Does that mean that they care more about something else than performance?

Research among marketing managers in the US found that relationship factors were more crucial than measures of concrete agency performance (Wackman, Salmon & Salmon, 1987). In a similar study among marketing managers in the Netherlands, Verbeke (1988) found that evaluations of performance did not alter over time, personal relations were of no importance and that social bonding was not a concern. Among marketing managers in Sweden, personal chemistry is considered a crucial element for good collaboration between companies and external agencies/consultants rather than agency performance evaluation (Rademaker, 2013). Developing a good relationship is thus considered more important than being confident that the consultant can and will deliver what is needed by the company. Compared to earlier studies on company-agency cooperation, this phenomenon indicates that marketing managers in Sweden are more similar to American managers in the sense that they put social bonding before agency performance evaluations.

Furthermore, according to Rademaker (Rademaker, 2013) marketing managers in Sweden spend a great amount of time on selecting and building relationships with new agencies. It takes about one to one and a half year to get to know a new agency. Considering that Swedish agency collaborations last about two to three years, a great amount of the total collaboration time is spent on getting to know the agency. Main reasons given for switching agencies were primarily the lack of personal chemistry (tensions) and secondary a change of brand strategy. Blaming the agency for failures could also be a reason. In long-term relationships, all parties have clear expectations of each other.

The 1991 Nobel laureate Ronald Coase argues that it may cost more to obtain a good/service via the market than the price of the good/service itself. Assuming that switching agencies involves a number of transaction costs such as search and information costs, bargaining costs and keeping trade secrets, long-term agency collaborations could benefit companies over short-term collaborations. For example, when a company has decided to change its brand strategy, switching agencies may not be an optimal solution. Selecting and building relationships with new agencies demands a lot of time and other resources. Long-term agency collaborations would to a greater extent benefit the task at hand (for example when changing brand strategy).

Conclusions and Reflections

The purpose of this chapter has been to explore the rather extensive consulting industry in marketing. This was done by addressing the following questions: a) Why do companies hire various external consultants for their marketing tasks? b) What types of consultants are hired and what competences do they possess? c) What do these consultants actually deliver and how do they supplement the existing competences in companies? d) How is the coordination of internal and external marketing tasks organized?

One reason presented for hiring external marketing consultants is to help solve the increasingly complex tasks of marketing that require considerably more expertise than the existing in-house competence of a company. It was also pointed out that this complexity continues to increase, especially due to the digitalization of the society, leading to a growing need for even more specialized competences. On the other hand, when examining the contributions to the planning and implementation of ad campaigns according to the marketing managers—those hiring marketing consultants—they considered themselves in general contributing more to or being more involved in most such tasks than the consultants hired.

This paradox raises the question what other reasons there are for hiring consultants. The question is enhanced by the fact that marketing managers are in general better educated in marketing than the marketing consultants they hire, and that many marketing managers experience problems dealing with the growing number of external consultants whereby coordination does not always function as desired.

Some possible answers given to this question were that there is a general shortage of potential marketing managers with a higher educational background in marketing and thus, a general need for different supplementary marketing competences; that for individual companies there is not enough need or demand for specific in-house competences to build these internally (i.e. less costly to hire consultants); that the managers are more interested in the relations with agencies/consultants *per se* than in their performance; or that sometimes they just are in need of someone to blame for failures. Still another explanation is that they just do not want to admit that they are in great need of supplementary expertise in the present changing world, although recognizing it in practice. The fact is that the development of digital technology has contributed to the emergence of a mosaic of knowledge-based companies contributing to various aspects of corporate marketing work.

This leads to another paradox, the need for hiring more experts while wanting to deal with fewer. One solution applied by many larger companies is to appoint a so-called main agency, usually their advertising agency, given the role to lead and coordinate the other external consultants. One problem with this solution is that the company loses control of the implementation of the company's strategy, its marketing operations and policy fulfillment, tasks that are of crucial importance for a company. In addition, it was found that the external marketing consultants have less education and knowledge in marketing than the marketing managers that they are supposed to advise, help and provide their marketing expertise to. Thus, appointing a main agency would have the somewhat contradictory consequence that the marketing efforts and decisions may be made by consultants with less education-based knowledge in marketing than the clients they work for.

Another way is for businesses to simply force themselves to like the situation and try to deal with the increased number of consultants best they can, or to focus more on in-house competence. Still another possibility is for the consulting industry to organize itself into larger units, each including more and various skills. Some trends in this direction are already occurring. For example, several advertising agencies now call themselves communication agencies to indicate that they can take broader communication responsibilities. However, this chapter revealed only very small differences in the extent to which advertising and communications agencies are involved in various marketing activities.

It was also demonstrated that marketing managers and external consultants have widely different views about who is doing what and to what extent each of these actors are involved in various marketing tasks. The results suggest that there are ambiguities and differences in opinions on the division of roles. It could mean that marketing managers do not realize and/ or appreciate all the work that the external consultants do.

We also argue, in general, for the need of increased theoretical knowledge and insights in marketing among marketing experts, especially for the person responsible for the overall performance of a company's marketing and who coordinates and leads the parties involved. It was found that quite a few marketing managers and even more so external consultants have no post-secondary education in marketing. Such knowledge is necessary for successfully integrating and coordinating the many (new) marketing tasks and activities following the digitalization of the society, with increased fragmentation and competition and continuously changes consumer behavior.

As already mentioned, marketing managers were found to attach more importance to good personal chemistry as a key element for a successful cooperation than performance evaluation of consultants. This further compromises marketing effectiveness, partly because the relationship development itself takes a lot of time and lessening the focus on performance. It should be in the interest of companies to recruit marketing professionals with more relevant and adequate education, and to shift focus from personal chemistry to performance evaluation when hiring external consultants. From a stakeholder's point of view, it is most likely that investors and shareholders would dismiss the entire idea of having personal chemistry as the key factor and in favor of factors such as achievements and performance.

Finally, based on the discussions put forward earlier, one could wonder to what extent companies are aware about why they are hiring various external marketing consultants and what they are expecting to gain from it.

References

Dagens Opinion. (2016). Så vill byråerna bli kallade och organiserade. Veckans Brief nr. 10. http://www.dagensopinion.se/veckans-brief/2016/så-vill-byråerna-bli-kallade-och-organiserade Accessed March 28, 2016.

Drucker, P. F. (1999). *The Practice of Management*. London: Heinemann.

Grant, I. & McLeod, C. (2007). Advertising agency planning: Conceptualising network relationships. *Journal of Marketing Management, 23*(5–6), 425–442.

Grimes, J. (2004). *Creative Inspiration. The Communications Challenge: A Practical Guide to Account Planning, J. Saunders*. London: Account Planning Group.

IPA-The Institute of Practitioners in Advertising. (2015). The Future of Marketing and Agencies. The Next 10 Years for Consumer Engagement. http://www.ipa.co.uk/Framework/ContentDisplay.aspx?id=10904

Nilsson, P. (2006). *Attention to Advertising*. Dissertation. Umeå: Umeå School of Business and Economics.

Nilsson, P., Rademaker, C., Svahn, M. & Wahlund, R. (2013). Om medieutveckling—tillbaka till framtiden! In Andersson, P., Axelsson, B. & Rosenqvist, C. (eds.), *Det mogna tjänstesamhällets förnyelse*. Lund: Studentlitteratur, 253–274.

Rademaker, C. A. (2013). *Green Media: Exploring Green Media Selection and Its Impact on Communication Effectiveness*. Doctoral Dissertation. Stockholm: Stockholm School of Economics.

Rademaker, C. A., Royne, M. & Wahlund, R. (2015). Eco-harmful media perception and consumer response to advertising. *Journal of Cleaner Production, 108*, 799–807.

Schultz, D. E. & Kitchen, P. J. (1997). Integrated marketing communications in U.S. advertising agencies: An exploratory study. *Journal of Advertising Research, 37*(5), 7–18.

Statistics Sweden. (2001). http://www.statistikdatabasen.scb.se/pxweb/sv/ssd/START__NV__NV0109__NV0109E/ReklamKundkat/table/tableViewLayout1/?rxid=872c8d3f-626d-4025–96dd-f7aba4dcb1d6

Svahn, M., Wahlund, R., Denward, M., Rademaker, C. & Nilsson, P. (2016). A model for evaluating converging media for advertising purposes. In Lugmayr, A. (ed.), *Convergence-Divergence, Cross-Disciplinary Viewpoints on Media Convergence* (1st edition). Germany: Springer Verlag.

Verbeke, W. (1988). Developing an advertising agency-client relationship in the Netherlands. *Journal of Advertising Research*, *28(6)*, 19–27.

Wackman, D. B., Salmon, C. T. & Salmon, C. C. (1987). Developing an advertising agency-client relationship. *Journal of Advertising Research*, *26(6)*, 21–28.

Wahlund, R., Rademaker, C., Nilsson, P. & Svahn, M. (2013). Mediernas roll i marknadskommunikationen. In Nygren, G. & Wadbring, I. (eds.), *På väg mot medievärlden 2020*. Lund: Studentlitteratur, 159–184.

7 Organizing Counter-Expertise

Critical Professional Communities in Transnational Governance

Sigrid Quack[1]

Introduction

Many people think of expertise, as suggested by the contributions of this volume, as something that creates and maintains social order under conditions of complexity, uncertainty and ambiguity. That is certainly also the case in transnational governance. Expertise is considered an important currency in the manifold attempts to create and implement rules and standards aimed at influencing the behavior of actors across national borders (Djelic & Sahlin-Andersson, 2006). Much public and scholarly effort has gone into demonstrating how expertise is used in these settings to underwrite claims for authority of ruling elites at the cost of countervailing demands for broader participation of those affected. It has been shown that expertise in transnational governance arrangements, as in international organizations, supports claims for authority not only through guiding the "definition of problems, classification of social kinds, and the evaluation of social behaviors" (Miller, 2007, p. 331) but also through shaping the instruments and policies of governing (Voß & Freeman, 2016). Hence, expertise as a device to achieve legitimate ordering is often perceived as highly problematic from a democratic standpoint because it often tends to favor the materially powerful over the less powerful.

This, however, is only half of the story. Expertise plays an important part in legitimizing social order, but it can also be used to challenge such order. In this chapter I will show how certain groups of experts, henceforth referred to as critical professional communities, can seize opportunities arising from changing background conditions to challenge and disrupt established knowledge orders in transnational governance fields. By so doing, they open up new policy spaces for the articulation of a plurality of alternative views on governance problems and solutions by other actors that might transform the order of the field itself.

In order to demonstrate this argument, the paper will draw on two empirical case studies from transnational governance in copyright and accounting. These are paradigmatic cases of how expertise can be used to establish and challenge a monopolistic governance order. The results contribute to our understanding of how and when dominant ideas, which have been developed with the support of and partly administered by professional knowledge elites, become questioned and challenged by parts of these elites or other groups originating from the same professions or academic disciplines.

The Emergence of Critical Professional Communities

At the core of this paper stands the more specific question of how we can account for the emergence of alternative approaches in governance fields where epistemic authority has been monopolized in the past to the extent that it produced one dominant policy paradigm that was more or less taken for granted by a larger professional and knowledge community involved. To what extent and under what conditions can such alternative proposals arise from the closely knit professional and knowledge community that was supportive of the previous paradigm?

As professions typically span the domains of market, state and civil society (Halliday, Karpik & Feeley, 2007), they can serve as seedbeds for the emergence of competing and sometimes opposing knowledge communities. While the marketization and managerialization of professions may foster establishment-oriented professional communities (which might even be close to self-interested lobbying in some instances), their grounding in civic responsibilities entails the possibility to give birth to critical professional communities challenging predominant worldviews and opening policy spaces for less powerful actors. In struggles over the legitimacy of knowledge claims, professionals therefore draw not only on their recognized expertise (as opposed to lay knowledge) to distinguish themselves as groups or individuals but also use their public problem-solving mission as a reference frame to motivate and justify their involvement in face of high epistemic uncertainty and contested knowledge. In principle, professionals have a recognized base for claims to moral as well as to technical knowledge.

But when and why do parts of a profession mobilize to challenge the predominant organization of their own expertise? To answer this question, Thomas Rochon's (1998) analysis of the role of critical intellectuals in social movements is useful. According to Rochon, critical communities are formed by small groups of intellectuals who play an important role in the development of alternative worldviews, new theories and ideologies that often precede social movements. Tapping into countercultural currents in society, critical communities consist of people "whose experiences, reading, and interaction with each other help them to develop a set of cultural values that is out of step with the larger society" (Rochon, 1998, p. 8). Rather than thinking within existing frameworks, members of critical communities fundamentally "alter the conceptual categories with which we give meaning to reality" (Rochon, 1998, p. 15). Members of such critical communities are united by an overriding concern for an issue, but can be otherwise have quite diverging views, which they discuss through their own channels of communication such as journals, blogs, etc. Critical communities initially increase ambiguity and uncertainty about knowing by offering new and competing perspectives, rather than reducing it. In the terms used in this volume, they create—at least temporarily—disorder rather than order.

Yet, paradoxically, the members of such emerging critical professional communities need to organize their knowledge and themselves, both internally and in relation to other actors, in novel ways to achieve the leverage to challenge the pre-existing knowledge order in a particular field. Along both dimensions, organizing often occurs as an informal and gradual process during the formation period of such critical communities. Building on Fleck (1980 [1935]), it can be argued that it is the circulation of new but also slightly reformulated ideas, concepts and social practices in overlapping networks that can transform "collective thought styles" carried by "thought collectives." Finding other professionals who express skepticism about prevailing problem definitions and solutions and mutually recognizing each other's endeavors is therefore a crucial first step in organizing counter-expertise. At this stage, mutual recognition as like-minded professionals goes hand in hand with acts of demarcation from the dominant "thought style" and its supporters.

At later stages, organizing, both internally and externally, is likely to become more formalized. Critical professional communities may start to have their own publication outlets, associations and meetings to foster internal debate and coherence. At the same time, establishing linkages and coalitions with other actor groups in society, but also in government and governance institutions, is an important element for critical communities aiming to influence political developments. According to Rochon (1998), for example, critical communities become powerful because social and political movements pick up their ideas and mobilize for them. In other cases, critical communities have developed strategies to persuade key decision-makers with governments and public agencies to gain leverage.

All in all, multiple, complex and often distributed processes of social interaction and organizing are needed for a critical professional community to emerge, and its counter-expertise to become visible and publicly recognized as a distinct corpus of knowledge. Critical professional communities may travel along different routes throughout this process. These are, among other factors, shaped by their interactions with the dominant system of expertise and the opportunities that rise along the process for linking to other critical actor groups, as well as the more or less favorable political conditions in their environment.

In order to study empirically the process of organizing counter-expertise by critical communities, we turn now to the analysis of two transnational governance fields. Both of these fields, the international regulation of copyright and financial reporting had previously been strongly dominated by closed elites of professionals and their paradigmatic ideas of policy problems, instruments and solutions. In part, this established knowledge order is the result of different groups of professionals competing for jurisdictions in a newly evolving professional ecology of world politics with professionals arbitraging across different national and disciplinary boundaries (Seabrooke, 2014). The formation and development of counter-expertise by critical professional communities, however, cannot be solely explained by professionals' self-interested striving for jurisdictions and markets. As argued earlier, it is the combination of claims to moral and technical expertise that underlies the emergence of critical professional knowledge, not just the creation of new markets for selling their expertise. Critical communities develop civic rather than commercial epistemologies (Fischer, 2009).

Organizing Counter-Expertise on Copyright

Since the 1970s, the field of copyright regulation, like that of intellectual property rights as a whole, has developed from a very specialized intergovernmental field dominated by an elite of government officials and specialized lawyers, as well as by a small group of highly influential business lobbyists, into one of the most controversial areas in transnational governance. The Agreement on Trade-Related Aspects of Intellectual Property Rights (TRIPS) concluded in 1995, which created for the first time a regulatory regime legally binding on all 153 member states of the World Trade Organization (WTO) and contained enforcement mechanisms for intellectual property rights, was still negotiated behind closed doors. Drahos with Braithwaite (2002, p. 10) reports a senior US negotiator as stating, "Probably less than 50 people were responsible for TRIPS".

Yet matters have changed since then. In 2012, thousands of people took to the streets across Europe to protest against the Anti-Counterfeiting Trade Agreement (ACTA), which was then rejected by the European Parliament, while millions of people signed an online petition against SOPA and PIPA, two Internet piracy bills debated in US Congress (Sell, 2013). Underlying this politicization was that the hitherto dominant paradigm, according to which the expansion of intellectual property rights was necessary and beneficial for creativity, innovation and economic wealth in societies, came under increasing challenge from alternative ideas suggesting that in a digital world less protection could generate more of those outcomes. Who generated these ideas? How did they gain traction in a policy field dominated by technical expertise? How did apparently unintelligible issues become understandable for citizens, producers and users so that they could become a political issue at all?

All this required not only the production but also the *organization* of counter-expertise: a critical community of experts had to be formed, a corpus of counter-expertise consolidated, a practical template for change developed, and a coalition with other opposing groups built. There were many organizers and multiple organizing attempts at work over a period of more than 15 years to consolidate a group of critical copyright professionals and a corpus of critical copyright expertise. Organizing counter-expertise was an important, though not the only precondition for the politicization of intellectual property regulation during the 2010s.

Among the first to articulate skepticism about the existing copyright regime were critical lawyers, such as Laurence Lessig, Pamela Samuelson and others, from the academic sector in the US. Many of them held positions at well-known US law schools, but had also close links to practitioners from the digital economy, including Internet entrepreneurs and representatives of the open source and software community. These lawyers developed counter-expertise through two intertwined channels. On the one hand, they intervened from the beginning through public talks, testimonies in court proceedings, Internet blogs in public debates. On the other hand, they published critical academic work in recognized law journals. The emerging critical community of copyright lawyers was highly dynamic and expanded rapidly to include professionals and practitioners from Europe and other parts of the world. It was and remained a loose community with fuzzy boundaries, but that was to its benefit rather than its disadvantage. Situated at the intersection of academic and public debates, its members developed an amalgam of technical and moral legal arguments, translated into a multiplicity of applications, some of them addressing professional arenas (court pleadings), but many targeted at the broad public, such as popular science publications, opinion pieces and public talks, and statements on social platforms. The members of this critical professional community created catchy problem definitions and slogans. "Copyleft" instead of "copyright"; "free culture"; "Remix. Making art and commerce thrive in the hybrid economy" (Lessig, 2004, 2008) were only a few of the shorthands that made complex legal problems intuitively understandable to broader audiences.

Intellectual skepticism about the appropriateness of the dominant view of expansion of copyright as public interest in the digital area, as promoted by copyright industry, US and OECD governments, WIPO and WTO/TRIPS, provided a broad and flexible framework for a pluralistic debate within the widening critical community. Through transatlantic academic networks, critical voices from the US and Europe, and increasingly also from other continents became part of these debates. A very important mechanism for the stabilization and expansion of counter-expertise on copyright was the socialization of a younger generation of critical copyright lawyers through professional education at top US and European law schools, which restructured the beliefs and assumptions in the academic field itself (Morin, 2014).

Organizing counter-expertise had also an important practical dimension. In 2001, the nonprofit organization "Creative Commons" was founded in the United States by Lessig, Abelson and Eldred with the support of *Center for the Public Domain* to expand the digitally available commons of creative works. Developing a private license for sharing creative content in the Internet become soon a transnational endeavor with organizations from other countries joining the Creative Commons network (Dobusch & Quack,

2013). Under Creative Commons licenses, producers of content can determine which rights they reserve and which rights they waive for the benefit of users. While Creative Commons licenses built on existing copyright, they also transcended it in important ways. They provided an usable template of how an "intellectual commons" could be built in the absence of overly narrow copyright restrictions. The subsequent worldwide diffusion made Creative Commons licenses the leading standard for open content, thereby building a technical-legal infrastructure in which alternative ideas could be made practically working for a large number of producers and users of content around the world. Thus, standardization opened a powerful avenue for the implementation of counter-expertise by "positive example" on a large scale. The visibility and usability of "copyleft" licenses meant that they had a low behavioral threshold for participation, and once set in motion, produced considerable momentum by rapidly increasing the usage of Creative Commons licensed content. The network effects of Creative Commons licenses became an effective lever through which civil society coalitions could increase their influence on transnational rule setting.

Coalition building between critical academics, NGOs, parts of the digital economy and politicians, was another important dimension of organizing counter-expertise. From the beginning, the critical academic community of copyright lawyers addressed issues that were perceived as a "grievance" not only by Internet entrepreneurs, but also by growing numbers of Internet users in their everyday life practices. The mismatch between possible usages of creative content in the Internet and increasing legal and technical restrictions created a general climate among Internet users and the public that resonated with the framings of copyright problems provided by the critical epistemic community. Over time, loose coalitions between early founded digital rights NGOs, associations of public libraries, campaigns for access to knowledge and access to medicine, projects for peer-based production like Wikipedia formed within and across countries, each of them contributing to and further developing "a commons of counter-expertise" in the field of intellectual property rights. According to Sell (2013), brokerage, diffusion and mutual attribution of similarity contributed to horizontal scaling up of a social movement opposing further expansion of intellectual property rights by enrolling more members and keeping entry levels low. At the same time, there was also vertical scaling up of issues that were increasingly contested at a transnational level.

Organizing Counter-Expertise on Corporate Financial Reporting

International standard setting on financial reporting of companies, like the regulation of intellectual property, has been a domain of professional expertise for a long time. Since 1973, when the International Accounting Standards Committee (IASC) was founded, professionals have successfully upheld their claim that their certified expertise (as accountants and more recently also as finance professionals) and/or practical expertise (as partners and employees in international accounting firms, multinationals or financial institutions) qualify them to lead initiatives for cross-border harmonization (Botzem & Quack, 2009). International Financial Reporting Standards (IFRS), now produced by the IASC's successor, the IFRS Foundation and its International Accounting Standards Board (IASB), have been made legally binding for all consolidated accounts of listed companies within the European Union, and subsequently been made mandatory by the governments in many other countries worldwide. Still, in the 2000s standard-setting at the IASB remained very much in the hands of auditors and accountants, many of whom were related to the large international accounting firms (Botzem, 2012, p. 126f).

In accounting, a critical academic community had already emerged in the 1970s targeting the dominant positivist and microeconomic approach to accounting studies prevalent in US universities and business schools. Yet, this critical accounting community as a whole never built up strong traction in policy debates on international accounting standard setting, though individual members such as Anthony Hopwood, Prem Sikka and others took a stance on public issues. More recently, the IASB has been also criticized by governments and politicians for a lack of public oversight (Nölke, 2009). Furthermore, actors situated at the intersection of different regulatory communities, such as central bankers and financial regulators, have raised concerns about possible pro-cyclical effects of fair-value accounting which allegedly reinforced the crisis (Arnold, 2009; Lagneau-Ymonet & Quack, 2012).

In this chapter, however, we focus on the critical professional community that has proved most effective and successful in systematically building up counter-expertise toward the prevalent approach of IASB's global standard-setting. This is a small cross-professional group of academics and practitioners advocating a radically different approach toward the reporting of multinational companies to tax authorities. The emergence and development of this critical professional community provides an interesting case for comparison with the organization of counter-expertise on copyright. Therefore, the following section draws on the excellent analysis of the Tax Justice Network by Seabrooke & Wigan (2013, 2016). While the authors focus on professional competition, I will use their empirical findings to illustrate and support my argument that organizing counter-expertise is a gradual and protracted collective process that includes the establishment of a critical professional community, the establishment of a corpus of counter-expertise, usable templates to implement this professional knowledge and coalition building with other groups in society to broaden support. These two views are complementary rather than contradictory.

In the case of reporting cross-border economic activities to tax authorities in different countries, a small cross-disciplinary group of professionals with high-level academic, political and practical experience came together in the earlier 2000s to form the core of a critical community on tax justice. The foundation of the Tax Justice Network (TJN), a small NGO combining high-level advocacy, research and digital, easy-to-access popularized information on global taxation policy, in 2003 marked the beginning of a new dynamic phase of expansion and consolidation of this critical community. Seabrooke & Wigan (2016, 362f) identify John Christensen (previously a chief economic advisor to Jersey and trust and estate planner for UK financial institutions), Prem Sikka (a professor of accounting at Essex University), James Henry (an author who has widely published on money laundering, capital flight and other taxation issues), Sol Piciotto (emeritus professor of law) and Richard Murphy (chartered accountant, previously working with KPMG, and author of a template for country-by-country reporting) as key members the founding group of TJN. As can be seen from the professional backgrounds of these persons, they combine a plurality of academic and professional competences that have enabled them to intervene in debates that range from global policy forums, to accounting standard-setting, as well as broader public debates.

Through previous engagement in advising UN, OECD and NGOs like Oxfam on how to combat tax havens and tax evasion, each of these figures had wide networks to other actors active or interested in the production and consolidation of critical knowledge on global tax reporting. Prem Sikka, for example, was a member of the Association for Accountancy and Business Affairs in the United Kingdom, which had publicly scrutinized corporate and financial practices of UK institutions since the 1990s (AABA n.d.). Members of the founding team of TJN had also advised Oxfam International on its report "Tax Havens: Releasing the Hidden Billions for Poverty Eradication" published in 2000 (Seabrook & Wigan, 2013, p. 17). The UN Monterrey Consensus of 2002, which recognized the need to harness domestic resources in developing countries to combat poverty, provided a framework for advocacy initiatives seeking country-level disclosure of multinational companies about their tax payments to governments. Following the Asian financial crisis, there was also more public attention being given to the negative effects of competition between tax regimes, money laundering and tax havens on economic development.

The foundation of the Tax Justice Network as an internationally oriented NGO provided a platform for reaching out to other individuals and groups that were concerned about issues of fair taxation in the developing world. Campaigns like *Publish What You Pay* (PWYP), run by large NGOs such as Oxfam America, Human Rights Watch and others, initially focused on corruption as the main reason for low tax income in developing countries. So did the Extractive Industry Transparency Initiative (EITI), initiated in 2002 by UK Prime Minister Tony Blair.

It was through the advocacy by members of TJN that a linkage between accounting data, multinational company financial reporting behavior and low tax revenue in developing countries was established (Seabrooke &

Wigan, 2016, p. 366). Members of the critical inter-professional community evolving around the TJN platform challenged the previously prevailing view of the International Accounting Standards Board (IASB) that financial reporting of multinational companies should be primarily oriented toward investors and financial markets. The IASB considered company disclosure of financial information either according to business sectors or larger regions (such as South America) sufficient for investors. The critical TJN community, however, upheld the view that accounting was not only for investors, but should equally provide transparent information on company revenue to the governments of the countries in which these revenues had been obtained. Hence country-by-country financial reporting was promoted by TJN members as a necessary reform of IFRS.

As in the case of copyright, it was crucial for the successful organization of counter-expertise on financial reporting that it had a practical component from early on. In 2003, John Murphy, a member of the critical core group of professionals who soon after founded TJN, had published a proposal for an alternative accounting standard that would allow country-by-country reporting (CBCR) of corporate turnover and tax (Murphy, 2003). Like the Creative Commons license, the alternative standard for CBCR also became soon an essential instrument of advocacy and coalition building on issues of tax justice. Critical professionals associated with the TJN convinced the PWYP campaign leaders that country-by-country financial reporting was essential for developing countries to raise more taxes from the revenues that multinational companies generated on their territory. As a result, PWYP campaigned for CBCR to be introduced in International Financial Reporting Standards, and managed to get the issue on the agenda of the Board of the IASB in 2006 (IASB n.d.). Yet the IASB proved resistant and, while adjourning the issue to further consultation with the World Bank, IMF and other organizations, has not changed its position since then.

In many other forums, however, the NGOs of the PWYP campaign and the professionals of TJN have since used the alternative standard in manifold ways to inform political decision-makers and the public about its advantages, benefiting from the concreteness and ready-to-use character of the template. John Murphy, for example, was invited to present CBCR at the European Parliament, which subsequently passed a resolution in support of country-by-country disclosures in the extractive sector, and initiated a public consultation on CBCR requirements for EU companies. Other TJN members presented the proposals to the OECD, World Bank and other international organizations. As a result of this high-level advocacy, Seabrooke & Wigan (2016, p. 369) conclude that "CBCR has gone from an idea to a new international standard with the potential to address issues of corporate transparency and tax compliance".

Another parallel between TJN and Creative Commons is that members of both organizations merge technical and moral arguments with the aim to make complex issues comprehensible for everyone. The bilingual

English-French webpage of the Tax Justice Network is a very good example. It provides up-to-date blog posts on tax-related issues (a hashtag on the Lux-Leaks whistleblowers verdict became available only hours after the court sentence was released) and easy to understand background information on secrecy, race to the bottom, inequality and democracy. Furthermore, it offers *Taxcast*, the Tax Justice Network's monthly podcast with up to 30 minutes of the latest global news, scandal and analysis on tax havens and corruption. TJN has also initiated a journalist program *Finance Uncovered* which aims to equip "journalists and researchers from all over the world with practical skills to undertake complex investigations into tax abuse, corruption and money laundering" (TJN n.d.). By 2016, the team running the Tax Justice Network has globally expanded to include members and experts from Europe, North and Latin America, Africa and Australia. While originating from Britain, TJN has built a global network of like-minded authors, journalists and activists, which provides a solid infrastructure for organizing counter-expertise on a sustainable level.

Coalition building between critical academics, NGOs, investigative journalists and high-level political decision-makers was an important dimension of organizing counter-expertise on reporting on tax authorities in the very beginning of the movement, and it has remained so throughout. This was facilitated by the rising political salience of tax havens, circumvention of tax authorities and shadow financial markets following the global financial crisis. Issues of tax justice are still a matter for political activists rather than a broad social movement, but there can be little doubt that TJN since its establishment in 2003 has been able to broaden and expand the circle of like-minded activists. In addition to horizontal diffusion, TJN has also effectively scaled up issue awareness by promoting and proposing country-by-country corporate reporting in various global policy forums like the World Bank, IMF and OECD.

Comparing the Organization of Counter-Expertise across Cases

As varied as the two cases are, they allow for systematic comparison along five analytical dimensions: triggering events and favorable political conditions, emergence of a critical community of professional experts, assembly of a corpus of counter-expertise, design of a practical template for implementing alternatives and coalition building with other opposing groups (see Table 7.1). There is no natural sequence in this list, but all the elements were present in both cases at some time. It can also be argued that some of these elements were missing in other episodes of attempted critique of international accounting standards that turned out to be less transformative than the TJN's activism.

Triggering events and favorable political conditions: In both cases, copyright and financial reporting for tax, the emergence of critiques of existing

Table 7.1 Critical communities organizing counter-expertise

	Copyright	*Financial reporting*
Triggering events and favorable political conditions	*Technological change; grievances about open access in the digital age*	*Global inequality in development; Asian and financial crisis*
Critical community of professional experts	*Critical community of copyright lawyers*	*Critical cross-professional group establishing TJN*
Corpus of counter-expertise	*Combination of technical and moral legal arguments; translated into a multiplicity of applications, some of them addressing professional arenas (court pleadings), but many targeted at the broader public*	*Combination of technical and moral legal arguments; translated into widely understandable information as well as more specialized advice to high-level decision-makers*
Practical template for alternative problem solving	*Creative Commons license*	*Template for standard on country-by-country reporting to tax authorities*
Coalition building with other opposing groups	*Librarians, access to knowledge, open access movement*	*Development NGOs, investigative journalists*

forms of governance from professional and expert quarters was triggered by events that fell outside of what could be considered as "normal" under the prevailing paradigm. In the area of copyright, the triggering event was the rise of the Internet and the criminalization of opportunities for socially desirable ways of sharing under existing legal frameworks which were increasingly perceived as an illegitimate burden. In financial reporting, it was the combination of long-standing debates about how developing countries could retain more of their resources and the moral outcry about tax evasion in the developed world triggered by the global financial crises, which led groups of professionals and experts to formulate dissenting opinions, critiques and alternative proposals.

An emerging critical professional community: The cases differ as to whether critical voices arose from within a single profession or a closely knit group of professionals from different disciplines. In both cases, the evidence points to the emergence of a sizable critical professional community that shares a principled belief in and promotes an alternative paradigm of governance. The publicly minded critical community of intellectual property rights lawyers challenged the prevalent mantra of "intellectual property rights protection generates innovation and economic wealth" with its alternative paradigm of "sharing and open access foster innovation, well-being and economic wealth." The publicly minded group of critical accountants, lawyers and economists promoting global taxation justice was able to generate much more political traction than the more long-standing academic community of critical accountants. Both their critiques laid out an alternative paradigm for governance, understood in Hall's (1993, p. 279) terms as "a framework of ideas and standards that specifies not only the goals of policy and the kind of instruments that can be used to attain them, but also the very nature of the problems they are meant to be addressing."

Building a corpus of counter-expertise: In both cases, the critical professional community combined its technical knowledge with a moral "claim about how things should be" different—a capacity that Seabrooke & Wigan (2016, p. 360) rightly emphasize as not having received sufficient attention in the ideational literature. However, while Seabrooke and Wigan take knowledge and experience of professionals as given and focus on how it is fused with a moral claim and networked with other actors, the comparison of the copyright and financial reporting case pushes us to go one step further back and enter more deeply in the collective processes of knowledge production. The comparison suggests that, first of all, professionals need to revisit the assumptions of their own canonical knowledge and to collectively build their own critical knowing through repeated interactions within a small circle of like-minded people. This early stage of building counter-expertise has many features in common with the small group dynamics that Farrell (2001) analyzed in collaborative circles of avant-garde artists:

> At the core is a set of friends who, over a period of time working together, negotiate a shared version that guides their work. As the group evolves, the members develop their own rituals and jargon, and each member comes to play an expected role.

Critical professional communities in their early stages may not always go in hand with friendship, yet they provide a similarly sheltered small group environment in which peers can rethink and revise the hitherto taken for granted assumptions of their professional knowledge and through mutual interaction and social learning devise new lines of thinking. Critical professional communities need to revise the knowledge basis of their epistemic authority before they can claim alternative governance authority (Quack, 2016).

Designing a practical alternative: The creation of an open license for digital content, flanked by the catchy slogan "some rights reserved" instead of "all rights reserved", as well as the formation of a coalition with critical NGOs, has laid a foundation for subsequent broader protests against any further extension of IPRs and their enforcement. Based on its paradigmatic critique, its claim to (private) governance authority and the broad recognition of its leadership, this group might be considered a professional counter-elite to the predominant coalition of industry, political and some professional interests. Similarly, the design of a template for an alternative accounting standard that would provide for country-by-country reporting of corporate revenue and tax payments was a powerful advocacy instrument to mobilize high-level decision-makers and to inform the public (Seabrooke & Wigan, 2016). The contrasting example is the critical community of accountants, which despite having established itself as an institutionalized sub-discipline with its own academic journals, conferences and positions at British business schools, was unable to formulate a practical positive template for action. Nor did these critical academic accountants succeed in establishing a significant and sustainable linkage to broader publics or the critical professional communities operating from within existing governance institutions, such as the central bankers and financial regulators who promoted macro-prudential approaches (Baker, 2013).

Coalition building with other opposing groups: The copyright, like the financial reporting case, highlights the organizing and strategic capacities of experts, which according to Seabrooke & Wigan (2016, p. 260) have been hitherto neglected in the literature on ideas in transnational governance. The results of the comparison suggest to go even one step further by thinking about coalition building with other groups as a continuous collective process of knowledge formation and revision. As critical professional communities linked their criticisms to those of other professional groups, social protest movements and pressure groups, their professional knowledge and experience was not only expanded but partially also revised through interactions with these groups. Therefore, one might argue that a transdisciplinary expertise, including professional and practitioners' knowledge, emerged from such linkages. The positive effects of such linkages between what Fleck (1980 [1935]) referred to as the "the esoteric small circle" of an emerging thought-collective (here a critical group of professionals) and the "larger, exoteric cycle by which educated laymen" partake of scientific (in our case professional) knowledge (cited according to Cohen & Schnelle, 1986, p. xxv) are most obvious in the case of the critical community of intellectual property rights lawyers, but also visible in the case of the Tax Justice Network.

The further development of these critical professional communities—as embryonic some of them may be—depends among other factors on the ability of these groups to transmit their alternative paradigmatic ideas to junior colleagues through professional training institutions. In the field of intellectual property rights, leading figures of the critical community at US law schools have founded centers that fulfill such a function, such as the Berkman Center for Internet & Society at Harvard University and the Center for Internet and Society at Stanford Law School. In Europe, the Max Planck Institute for Intellectual Property, Competition and Tax Law in Munich and the Institute of Information Law at the University of Amsterdam among others are institutions where academics have signed critical declarations on issues of IPR in the digital age.

In addition to socialization through training, Fleck (1980 [1935]) mentions that over time peer relations among equals in newly emerging thought collectives can constrain its members into "a certain solidarity of thought in the service of a superindividual idea". Applied to emerging critical professional communities, this would suggest that their members might scrutinize each other for possible derivations from their shared ideas which in turn might reinforce its thought structure.

Conclusions

This chapter argues that in order to capture the dynamic nature of modern expert society, we should not exclusively focus on the organization of prevailing and dominant expertise, but equally encompass the less visible organizing processes through which critical professional communities emerge and develop their counter-expertise. The critical copyright and tax justice communities traveled along different routes throughout this process that were shaped by their interactions with the dominant system of expertise in their field and specific opportunities that opened and closed over time. However, the copyright and tax justice communities also show many similarities that support the argument that counter-expertise is something that needs to be organized over a protracted period of time.

The findings of this chapter contribute to our understanding of expert society in a globalized context in three ways. Firstly, the results highlight that we should be careful not to assume too much homogeneity of thought and practical engagement among experts at large, nor even among the members of a given profession. Professional knowledge elites—even when organized in small groups—tend to operate in a plurality of social settings which provide social experiences that might generate the seeds for dissenting and critical opinions or more far-reaching challenges to certain ways of governing or dominant ideational paradigms. Therefore, we should not take them as homogenous and unified groups *per se*. Instead, more research efforts should be directed toward studying the actual processes of formation, consolidation and expansion or shrinking of critical professional communities which share common ideational frameworks and are oriented toward a joint political agenda.

Secondly, the comparison of copyright and financial reporting for tax as two transnational governance fields that were previously characterized by the dominance of a rather small and unified professional knowledge elite and a taken-for-granted ideational paradigm, provided a starting point for the identification of preconditions and processes which facilitate the emergence of critical professional communities and foster their ideational and practical impact. The findings suggest that under conditions of complexity and uncertainty, claims to expertise-based rule are becoming increasingly contested—even in transnational governance fields that have a long-established trajectory of rule setting and rule-implementation monopolized by small groups of professionals, business people or technical diplomats. The results show significant variation in the triggers which led to the emergence of critical communities, but also indicate that such groups can emerge from within the professions.

Finally, the findings urge us to conceive social order as an evolving process rather than a static phenomenon. Hence, we are better advised to conceptualize the contribution of professional communities and other knowledge actors from a dynamic perspective which moves beyond prevailing (dis-) equilibrium models of social order and change. Whatever the social order is established with the help of experts, it is at best provisional and may well involve competing and conflicting elements.

Note

1 This author thanks the editors of this volume, Tiene Hanrieder, Dieter Plehwe, Len Seabrooke. Holger Strassheim, Jonathan Zeitlin and the participants of a panel discussion at the Berlin Social Science for very helpful comments on earlier versions of this chapter.

References

AABA (Association for Accountancy and Business Affairs). (n.d.). http://visar.csustan.edu/aaba/home.html [last access: 30.06.16]

Arnold, P. (2009). Global financial crisis: The challenge to accounting research. *Accounting, Organizations and Society, 34*(6), 803–809.

Baker, A. (2013). The new political economy of the macroprudential ideational shift. *New Political Economy, 18*(1), 112–139.

Botzem, S. (2012). *The Politics of Accounting Regulation.* Cheltenham: Edward Elgar Publishing.

Botzem, S. & Quack, S. (2009). (No) limits to Anglo-American accounting? Reconstructing the history of the International Accounting Standards Committee: A review article. *Accounting, Organizations and Society, 34*(8), 988–998.

Cohen, R. S. & Schnelle, T. (eds.). (1986). *Cognition and Fact: Materials on Ludwik Fleck* (Vol. 87). Dodrecht: Reidel Publishing.

Djelic, M. L. & Sahlin-Andersson, K. (2006). *Transnational Governance.* Cambridge: Cambridge University Press.

Dobusch, L. & Quack, S. (2013). Framing standards, mobilizing users: Copyright versus fair use in transnational regulation. *Review of International Political Economy, 20*(1), 52–88.

Drahos, P. & Braithwaite, J. (2002). *Information Feudalism.* New York: New Press.

Farrell, M. P. (2001). *Collaborative Circles.* Chicago: University of Chicago Press.

Fischer, F. (2009). *Democracy and Expertise.* Oxford: Oxford University Press.

Fleck, L. (1980 [1935]). *Entstehung und Entwicklung einer wissenschaftlichen Tatsache.* Frankfurt/Main: Suhrkamp.

Hall, P. A. (1993). Policy paradigms, social learning, and the state: The case of economic policymaking in Britain. *Comparative Politics, 25*(3), 275–296.

118   *Sigrid Quack*

Halliday, T. C., Karpik, L. & Feeley, M. M. (eds.). (2007). *Fighting for Political Freedom*. Oxford: Hart Publishing.
IASB (International Accounting Standards Board). (n.d.). http://www.ifrs.org/Current-Projects/IASB-Projects/Segment-Reporting/Meeting-Summaries-and-Observer-Notes/Pages/IASB-September-2006.aspx [last access: 30.06.16].
Lagneau-Ymonet, P. & Quack, S. (2012). What's the problem? Competing diagnoses and shifting coalitions in the reform of International Accounting Standards. In Mayntz, R. (ed.), *Crisis and Control*. Frankfurt/Main: Campus, 213–246.
Lessig, L. (2004). *Free Culture*. New York: Penguin Press.
Lessig, L. (2008). *Remix*. New York: Penguin Press.
Miller, C. A. (2007). Democratization, international knowledge institutions, and global governance. *Governance*, 20(2), 325–357.
Morin, J. F. (2014). Paradigm shift in the global IP regime. *Review of International Political Economy*, 21(2), 275–309.
Murphy, R. (2003). A Proposed International Accounting Standard: Reporting Turnover and Tax by Location. Basildon: Association for Accountancy & Business Affairs.
Nölke, A. (2009). The Politics of Accounting Regulation: Responses to the subprime crisis. In Helleiner, E., Pagliari, S. & Zimmerman, H. (eds.), *Global Finance in Crisis*. London: Routledge, 37–55.
Quack. S. (2016). Expertise and authority in transnational governance. In Cotterrell, R. & Del Mar, M. (eds.), *Authority in Transnational Legal Theory*. Cheltenham: Edward Elgar, 261–386.
Rochon, T. R. (1998). *Culture Moves*. Princeton: Princeton University Press.
Seabrooke, L. (2014). Epistemic arbitrage: Transnational professional knowledge in action. *Journal of Professions and Organization*, 1(1), 49–64.
Seabrooke, L. & Wigan, D. (2013). Emergent Entrepreneurs in Transnational Advocacy Networks: Professional Mobilization in the Fight for Global Tax Justice. GR:EEN Working Paper N. 41. Warwick: University of Warwick.
Seabrooke, L. & Wigan, D. (2016). Powering ideas through expertise: Professionals in global tax battles. *Journal of European Public Policy*, 23(3), 357–374.
Sell, S. K. (2013). Revenge of the "Nerds". *International Studies Review*, 15(1), 67–85.
TJN (Tax Justice Network). (n.d.). http://www.taxjustice.net/about/journalism-programme [last access: 30.06.16]
Voß, J.-P. & Freeman, R. (eds.). (2016). *Knowing Governance*. Houndmills: Palgrave-Macmillan.

8 Disembedding Expertise— The Shift from Relational to Formalized Purchasing Practices

Lovisa Näslund and Frida Pemer

Introduction

In this chapter, we will take the clients' perspective and discuss how their purchasing of expert services is undergoing major changes. As described in earlier chapters, expert services are characterized by being built on intangible and subjective qualities difficult to measure, such as creativity, trust, people skills and expertise. The projects the experts are hired for are often strategically important and expensive, where a mistake can have far-reaching consequences and be difficult to rectify. This creates a dilemma for the client, as it on the one hand is important to select the "right" expert and on the other is difficult to evaluate which expert is "right". To deal with this dilemma, clients have traditionally used relational purchasing practices (Axelsson & Wynstra, 2002) and hired experts they have good relations with, know well and trust (Werr & Pemer, 2007). Recently, however, a trend toward increased purchasing formalization has emerged, promoting the use of transactional purchasing practices (Axelsson & Wynstra, 2002), such as standardized purchasing processes, objective selection criteria, frame agreements and preferred suppliers. (Sieweke, Birkner & Mohe, 2012; Pemer, Werr & Bianchi, 2014). This trend has its roots in the increased societal demands on transparency, certifications, standardization, evaluations and rankings in both organizations, often referred to as the development of the audit society (Power, 1997; Power, 2000), and is observed both in Sweden and internationally (Pemer, Sieweke, Werr, Birkner & Mohe, 2014).

The emergence of such an audit society depends on the development and increasing prevalence of expert systems, which produce the audits and certifications. In the context of purchasing of expert services, the formalization trend challenges well-established relational purchasing practices, creates new demands on buyers and sellers, and might eventually lead to a reorganization of the market for expert services. This shift may be seen in terms of the development of expert systems, "systems of technical accomplishments or professional expertise that organize large areas of the material and social environments in which we live today" (Giddens, 1990, p. 27). Faith in these systems does not depend on a thorough understanding of the knowledge base they depend on or the processes they use, but moreover faith in the correctness of their principles, and the proper workings of the procedures used. It might be seen as a shift from interpersonal to impersonal relations, and part of a general tendency in modern society toward the impersonal relation, the dependency on abstract capacities of a disembedded system independent of the social context, rather than the interpersonal relation, where the perception of benevolence and good intentions in the other is vital (Giddens, 1990; Hedgecoe, 2012). Through the use of such expert systems, be it audits, certifications or other forms of formalized and organized expertise, social and spatial distances may be overcome, and thus interactions become possible that would otherwise not have been possible, either because the counterparts were not aware of each other, or, if they were, would have deemed interaction too uncertain and risky due to lack of knowledge of each other (Shapiro, 1987).

The shift from relational to formalized expert services may thus be seen as part of a larger trend toward the formalization of expertise, both in terms of purchasing expertise, but also in terms of the purchased expertise, as expectations of formalization from clients serves as one source of pressure to formalize knowledge and processes, transforming service providers from experts entangled in interpersonal ties, to abstract, disembedded expertise. Purchasing patterns and procedures thus serve as one arena of this formalization, which could bring insights into the effects of formalizing and systematizing knowledge.

To this purpose, this chapter will give a detailed description of the changed purchasing behavior among clients and the shift from relational to transactional purchasing practices. The chapter is primarily based on findings from the authors' earlier empirical studies of purchasing and selling professional services. In the following, we discuss the traditional relational purchasing practices and the importance of interpersonal trust in this context. We then move on to discussing the background to the emerging formalization trend and the increasing use of transactional purchasing practices. The chapter ends with a concluding discussion about the consequences of increased purchasing formalization for buyers and sellers of expert services. We argue that these consequences are to be seen in terms of what type of knowledge is used in relational versus transactional purchasing processes, what type of trust they depend on and where in the organization the purchases are performed. To illuminate the specificities of purchasing expert services we use management-consulting services as empirical example. We also delimit the discussion to only include private organizations as they, in contrast to public organizations, which in Sweden are regulated by public procurement legislation, are relatively free to decide how to organize their purchasing processes.

Relational Purchasing

When it comes to complex services, such as management consulting services, there are several reasons as to why a relational purchasing model would be put into practice. As stated earlier, following this model, clients choose experts that they know and trust, and often form long-term business relations. Apart from this being a convenient and thereby cost efficient way of purchasing, the prime advantage of relational purchasing would be in terms of uncertainty reduction. Because such consulting services are by nature co-produced with the client, a key factor for the potential success of the project is the ability of the client and consultant to work together. If it is already certain from the beginning that this is the case, possibly evidenced by successful projects in the past, this would significantly decrease the uncertainty of the project. The uncertainty would to some extent still be irreducible, if it is the type of service where each project is to some extent unique, and so there is no way, neither for the client nor for the consultant, to know for certain how the project will eventually turn out, or what the effects of it will be. Knowing the consultant you will work with, and knowing that they are able to work successfully within the client organization, is one way of decreasing this uncertainty to the level that is seems worth the risk to embark on the project.

Relational purchasing is thereby highly dependent on interpersonal trust (Näslund, 2012a). The client, the trustor in this case, faces uncertainty as to the outcome of the project and the future behavior of the consultant (the trustee), and furthermore is at risk and thereby vulnerable to the outcome of the project. As there is no way to know with certainty that the project will succeed, the purchasing will to a large extent rely on the client's assessment of the ability, integrity and benevolence of the consultants, in other words, their trustworthiness (Mayer, Davis & Schoorman, 1995; Rousseau, Sitkin, Burt & Camerer, 1998). A key way of assessing this trustworthiness is of course previous experience from working together, so new purchases will often follow the patterns of old relations. Even if another supplier were to offer the service at a lower cost, the risk involved in taking in an unknown, will in many cases surpass the gains to be had in financial terms. This risk is not only in terms of the money lost if the project were to fail but also the risk for the purchaser of losing face internally in the company if it were to happen that the consultant you vouched for delivered a substandard service. The purchaser, when it comes to management consulting in areas such as organizational change and development, will often be the HR-department, or, more specifically, the HR manager.

Being able to discern expertise, and choosing the right expert and the right consultant for the task at hand is often considered a key skill necessary for a successful HR manager. Therefore, poor judgment would reflect badly on the internal reputation of the HR manager, their standing in the company, and their ability to get approval for future projects (Näslund, 2012a).

Therefore, a failed consulting project, and a poor choice of consultant, puts not only the organization but also the HR manager at risk. Therefore, the "best" consultant is not necessarily the one offering the lowest price for a certain service quality, but moreover the consultant the HR manager and those involved in the project will be able to collaborate best with, to mutual benefit and satisfaction. For this reason, in the purchasing process, a third, independent party, such as the purchasing department, will oftentimes not be involved, as the base for the purchasing decision is the relationship between HR manager and consultant (Lian & Laing, 2007).

Thus, a consultant that the client has worked successfully with previously will often be the primary choice for a client company. Not surprisingly, an established consultant will often find most of their work in repeat customers. However, using established relationships, though efficient and risk minimizing, also has drawbacks, primarily in that there are only so many one would have that first-hand knowledge of. This approach thereby provides only a very limited number of possible suppliers. Going to the market, on the other hand, and relying on the public reputation, what is generally known about the company, while providing a vast array of alternatives, does little to provide detailed information on the trustworthiness of the consultants that will be working with the project, and moreover how they will fit with the client company. Not altogether surprising, clients often opt for a third option, if their personal network does not suffice, namely "networked reputation". That is, ask trusted friends and colleagues if they have experience from any suitable consultant that would fit the bill. This way, clients are provided with a wider range of consultants than solely their own acquaintances, but with a more trustworthy and detailed assessment than what is publically known (Glückler & Armbrüster, 2003). As could be expected, the most significant marketing techniques for management consultants are therefore to some extent relationship-based: using personal contacts to provide opportunities for making sales pitches and gaining information about upcoming solicitations for consulting services, taking part in consulting networks (formal or informal) as a way of getting referrals from other consultants, and finally subcontracting arrangements with other consultants, which enables even freelance consultants to take on larger projects (Ulvila, 2000). Consultants are often dependent on word of mouth as their primary method of finding new work, in the form of referrals of contented customers or consulting colleagues. Such third-party referrals from consulting colleagues who are trusted by their clients may of course be an effective way of gaining new clients, but similarly to when promoted by an internal advocate, such projects are especially damaging to fail, as it means losing not only the confidence of the new client but also of the person who recommended you (Kim, 2009). In other words, successful projects, in the sense that they leave the client satisfied with what they have received relative what it cost them, are essential to consultants who want to stay in business, not only because they lead to repeat business with that same client but also because it leads to positive word of mouth, and hence future business with other client organizations (Karmarkar & Pitbladdo, 1995). From a sales perspective, the ideal for a consultant will therefore be when relationships with clients are maintained and developed so that new customers become regular clients, regular clients becomes strong supporters for the consulting company and its services, and these supporters then show their support by becoming active and vocal advocates of the consulting company, which in turn generates positive word of mouth (Karantinou & Hogg, 2001).

The Client-Consultant Relationship

The significance of the client-consultant relationship in terms of knowledge transfer and the perceived success of the consulting project is well known, but, as we have seen, this relationship matters as much before the project has even begun, because it often is a precondition for the purchase and thereby the project coming about in the first place. Although the client-consultant relationship is ostensibly between the client and consultant organization, more often than not, it will primarily be an interpersonal rather than an inter-organizational relationship. As has been shown in earlier studies (Näslund, 2012a), interorganizational collaborations often tend to follow the interpersonal relationships, rather than the other way around. That is, when for example an HR manager changes company, chances are that he or she will take their consultants with them to their new company. For the consultant, having the manager you have worked with previously, especially if this has been your main contact with whom you have had a close relationship, leave the client company therefore poses a real risk to future business with that client. On the other hand, there are good chances of a new business at your contact's new employer. Consulting companies of course realize this, and may try to counteract this by forging a stronger tie with the client company, stronger in the sense that it does not depend solely on a good relationship with your main contact, the manager who signs the contract and gives you the project, but rather having ties to others within the company as well. Given, however, that trust is key to the client-consultant relationship, this requires tact. If your primary contact gets the impression that the consultant is going behind their backs in their own company, trying to woo others and thus getting too involved in internal politics, this may well have a deterring effect on trust building. A consultant you cannot trust is a consultant most managers would avoid working with, and therefore it often requires a good understanding of internal politics to forge new relationships within the client company without jeopardizing the existing ones. On the other hand, having a long collaboration and having worked together on numerous earlier projects will often give the consultants good opportunity to build such an understanding. If the multiple tie relationship with the client company is strong enough, it might well be that if the main contact leaves, the result is a new client, if the ties to the previous employer are strong enough that they remain as a client, while the manager's new employer then becomes a new client.

In this way, purchases may often be followed and explained by interpersonal relationships, and by taking note of existing relationships, it is often possible to explain why client-consultant relationships on the organizational level are created, maintained or discontinued. Given that this interpersonal relationship carries such weight, and that it requires a relatively high trust level, this means that the maintenance and creation of trust becomes a key asset in the client-consultant relationship, and the logic of trust thereby becomes the underlying logic to purchasing practices. Trust is not a stable construct, but might rather be seen as a continuous process, where the level of trust at any given point in time is given by previous events, and the assessment of future behavior based on these previous experiences. Trust might therefore be seen in terms of a sensemaking process, where the trustor continuously interprets cues so as to make sense of events that have passed, and based on this forms an assessment of the trustee (Adobor, 2005; Weick, Sutcliffe & Obstfeld, 2005; Fuglsang & Jagd, 2015). It should be noted that while trust-as-an-attitude (i.e., the trustor's assessment of the trustee) is thus a process, continuously shifting and evolving as events unfold, trust-as-choice (i.e. the actions the trustor choses to take as a result of this assessment) is in this context often binary (Li, 2007). This circumstance might give the trustee the false impression that, as the Dutch proverb goes, "trust arrives on foot but leaves on horseback"—that is, that trust is slow to build but quickly destroyed. While it may well be that if the client experiences a complete breach of trust, they might as a result re-assess the consultant completely, more likely transgressions will primarily be interpreted in the existing frame of reference. In other words, if the client trusts the consultant, transgressions will be interpreted from this frame of reference, as misunderstandings, bad luck, and so on, but not primarily as signs of malevolence, incompetence and opportunism, which would result in distrust, and the erosion of trust. For trust to be replaced by distrust, the clients frame of references would have to shift, which, as we have seen from previous studies of the sensemaking process, is avoided unless the discrepancy is so jarring that a shift of interpretative frames is perceived as necessary (Brown, Colville & Pye, 2014).However, this does not mean that trust is completely resilient: rather, transgressions, while given the benefit of the doubt and interpreted as misunderstandings, might still be remembered by the client, and might undermine trust, to the effect that if another transgression comes along, trust is more fragile, and will erode.

However, this sensemaking process, resulting in trust-as-an-attitude from the client, is often not visible to the consultant. To the consultant, it is when the attitude leads to trust-as-choice that it becomes visible, and trust-as-choice is binary. Either the client decides to go ahead with another collaboration, or they do not, put simply. If trust-as-attitude has slowly eroded during the course of previous interactions, it may well not become visible until the contract is not renewed. To the trustee, not necessarily being privy to the continuous process of assessment shifting as events evolve, it may therefore seem as though trust is quickly eroded and fragile (Näslund, 2012b).

The mechanisms of interpersonal trust, in terms of creating interpersonal ties, and in terms of the underlying sensemaking process that leads to the perception of the expert as trustworthy, based on an assessment the benevolence, integrity and ability of the other, and having an emotional as well as a cognitive aspect (Jones, 1996), will thereby, as we have seen, also be key to explaining the purchase of expertise, if this purchasing is made through a relations-based process. However, in later years, as we will see in the following, clients have increasingly replaced this model with a more formalized purchasing model. Shifting from an informal to a formal purchasing model will however have implications not only in terms of purchasing practices but also in terms of the construction of experts and expertise.

Toward an Increased Formalization of Purchasing

One central feature of the formalization trend is that the purchasing professionals, who previously tended to be excluded from the hiring of management consultants, now become increasingly involved and have more influence over the design and performance of the purchases (Werr & Pemer, 2007). An explanation for their increased presence is that purchasing has developed from a clerical function to a strategic one with responsibility for the organization's entire supply chains (Axelsson, 2005). Today purchasing professionals add to the organization's competitiveness both by securing access to the resources needed at the right time and price, and by engaging suppliers in innovation and the development of new offerings. As a result, purchasing has developed into a profession with its own certifications, professional associations and education programs. This has created a distinct knowledge base on how to organize purchasing and what processes, tools and methods to use. A key idea in this knowledge base is that purchases should be performed on a well-defined market with clear role descriptions for buyers and sellers, explicit specifications and contracts, competitive pricing, and objective supplier selection criteria. This is expected to enhance transparency in the market transactions, increase competition and lead to cost savings and better conditions for the buyers. As a result of the increased status of the purchasing professionals and the tangibility of their knowledge base, expressed as explicit processes with measurable outcomes, their knowledge has become more salient and valued in organizations.

Although the trend toward increased purchasing formalization is growing stronger, there is still a tendency in many organizations to continue to use relational purchasing practices. In a survey to the 500 largest organizations in Sweden performed by the authors, 53 percent of the responding organizations answered that they had not formalized their purchasing of management consulting services. Thirteen percent of the studied organizations were planning to formalize their purchasing practices and 34 percent had already formalized them. The most common formalization initiative was to set up guidelines for how to purchase management-consulting services. This was followed by defining selection criteria and policies for how and when to hire management consultants. The least common initiatives were to set up guidelines for how to evaluate the management consulting services after the project was finished, and how to document the activities performed by the consultants (Pemer & Werr, 2009). A possible interpretation of this is that when involved in the purchasing process, the purchasing professionals primarily implement tools close to their knowledge base, such as developing selection criteria and price lists. These tools can be regarded as explicit and objective measures that are used for creating a well-defined market for management consultants with clear directives on how to compare, price and purchase these services. The least common initiatives, however, are partly outside the purchasing professionals' knowledge base and have a more subjective character, because they deal with evaluation and documentation of the consulting projects. Managers have traditionally performed these tasks, because they collaborate with the consultants in the projects and make their own assessments of their performance.

Three Generic Purchasing Strategies

As illustrated earlier there is a variation between organizations in how they purchase management-consulting services. To investigate this further, an interview study was performed on how organizations in different industries organize their purchases of management consulting services and what reasons lay behind their choice of purchasing strategy. To get a rich picture of the purchasing processes and how they were perceived in the studied organizations, interviews were performed with managers, purchasing professionals and HR professionals. The study resulted in the identification of three generic purchasing strategies for management consulting services: decentralization, coordinated decentralization and centralization (Werr & Pemer, 2007).

Decentralization

In the first strategy, the purchases were performed by individual managers in the organizations using relational purchasing practices and their experience of different consultancies to select which one to hire. The purchasing professionals were only involved in case the managers needed help with contract writing. The decentralization strategy could be divided into two sub-strategies: forced and voluntary decentralization. In organizations using the *forced decentralization strategy* the purchasing professionals wished to formalize the purchasing processes, as it would enable the organization to make large cost savings and improve its control and transparency. However, as the purchasing professionals' status was weak, they felt they could not influence how the purchases were performed. They also feared that any attempt to formalize would be met with strong resistance from the managers. The purchasing of management consulting services was described as "a minefield where a mistake can lead to disastrous consequences". In organizations using the *voluntary decentralization strategy*, on the other hand, the managers and purchasing professionals agreed that it would be too costly and resource demanding to formalize the purchasing process, as management consultants were hired rather infrequently.

Coordinated Decentralization

In the second strategy, the purchasing professionals were involved in the purchasing process and had implemented formalization initiatives. This strategy too could be divided into two sub-strategies: partnership and coordinated variety. In organizations using the *partnership strategy* the purchasing professionals had a strong position and explicit support from top management for their formalization initiatives. To increase cost control and transparency the purchasing professionals had selected a few suppliers to become partners. The partner companies were supposed to work closely together with the organization and share both responsibilities and risks. The managers were not allowed to contact any other consultancies than the partner suppliers and had to follow the predefined purchasing process when they wished to hire consultants. Should none of the partner suppliers fit the manager's need another consultancy could be used, but then as a sub-consultant to one of the partners. The purchasing professionals had developed control mechanisms to track the managers' purchasing behavior and detect deviations. In case a manager did not follow the purchasing process, s/he was reported to top management "to explain her or his behavior". In organizations using the *coordinated variety strategy*, the purchasing professionals had chosen a different approach. Rather than trying to direct the managers purchasing behavior, they collected information from the managers on which suppliers they preferred to work with. The purchasing professionals then set up frame agreements with these suppliers to ensure that all necessary information about prices, conditions, etc., were in place. The managers were free to decide which supplier to hire, as long as s/he invited at least three suppliers to compete for the project before the final decision was made. According to the purchasing professionals, this solution fit well in organizations with a strong culture of delegated decision-making. It was also a way for the purchasing professionals to increase their control over the purchases without risking a conflict with the managers.

Centralization

The third strategy, centralization, was the least common of the three strategies and implied a clear division of responsibilities between different actors in the organization. In this strategy, the purchasing process was performed by an expert function specialized in management consulting. The expert function was responsible for creating a clear purchasing process as well as role descriptions for the involved actors and reported to the HR manager, as hiring consultants was regarded as temporary employment rather than a purchase. The purchasing process generally followed a number of clearly defined steps: first, the manager developed a specification of what kind of consultant and service s/he needed. The expert then scanned the consulting market and used her/his experience to create a short list of potential suppliers. These were invited to a meeting with the manager and the expert, in which they presented their services. After the presentation, the manager decided which consultant to hire while the expert took care of the contract negotiating and writing. This structure made it clear that the manager was responsible for understanding what needs the organization had, communicating them to the expert and ensuring that the hired consultant performed the project well. The expert, on the other hand, was responsible for keeping in contact with the consulting supplier before and after the project, for the purchasing process and for the contracts. Although both managers and experts agreed on the benefits of the centralization strategy, they also described it as very demanding to implement. To succeed, support from top management and a culture of centralized decision-making were needed.

Factors Influencing the Strategy Selection

As illustrated earlier, organizations use different strategies for how to purchase management-consulting services. When deciding how to organize the purchasing, it is important that organizations adapt the purchasing strategy to their unique characteristics and needs. As the study indicates, three factors are important to consider in this process. The first is the *purchasing professionals' status and influence in the organization*. The stronger status the purchasing professionals have, the more they can influence how management-consulting services are purchased. In case the purchasing professionals do not have enough status or influence to implement transactional purchasing practices, they need to seek support from top management. Otherwise, they risk meeting resistance from both managers and consultants wishing to maintain relational purchasing practices. The second factor is the *organizational culture*. In organizations with a strong culture of decentralization and delegation of decisions to local managers, it is likely be more cumbersome to implement transactional purchasing practices than in an organization with a culture of centralized decision-making and top-down control. The third factor is *how frequently management consultants are*

hired and how large sums of money are spent on their services. In organizations using management-consulting services seldom or only spending
very small amounts it might not be worthwhile implementing transactional
purchasing processes. On the other hand, organizations hiring management
consultants frequently and spending large sums on their services might benefit from increasing their control over the supplier base, establishing frame
agreements and invite suppliers to compete for projects (Pemer et al., 2014).

An interesting finding is that in all strategies but two, the organizations
had found ways of coordinating and integrating the knowledge bases of the
managers and the purchasing professionals. In these cases, there were no
reports of deviations from the chosen strategy. Rather, all parties seemed
content with how the purchases were performed. In the other two cases,
the forced decentralization strategy and the partnership strategy, it seemed
as if one of the parties had pushed through their ideas on how to organize
the purchasing process without acknowledging or trying to integrate the
other party's ideas. In organizations using the forced decentralization strategy the purchasing professionals expressed frustration as they saw many
benefits with using transactional purchasing practices, but felt forced to let
the managers continue to use relational purchasing practices, as they did
not have enough influence to change the managers' behavior. In organizations using the partnership strategy, the situation was reversed. There the
purchasing professionals had the mandate from top management to impose
transactional purchasing practices, whereas the managers had little room to
use their knowledge or influence which suppliers were hired. In both cases,
there was a widespread dissatisfaction among those whose knowledge had
not been integrated in the purchasing processes.

Consequences of Increased Formalization

The studies described earlier illustrate that purchasing professionals are
becoming increasingly involved in the purchasing of management consulting services, and that their knowledge base is winning more acceptance and
legitimacy. What then, are the consequences of this? A first consequence
is that the traditional dyadic relation between managers and consultants
is becoming increasingly replaced by a triadic relation, in which the purchasing professionals are also included. This creates new demands on how
the relation between the three parties should be organized, who should be
responsible for what, who has the decision power, etc. Well-established
communication patterns are also replaced by new ones when the managers
cannot contact a consultancy on their own but must follow the purchasing
process designed by the purchasing professionals, or select from a limited
list of preferred suppliers. For the managers, this means that their freedom
is somewhat delimited. It also means that they no longer need to carry the
responsibility for the supplier selection themselves. Should a consultant not
live up to the expectations or if the project fails, the manager can shift the

responsibility for this to the purchasing process and claim that s/he has followed it carefully and hired the supplier recommended by the system. Thereby the blame is transferred from the individual manager to the purchasing system. The purchasing of management consulting services thus transforms from building on client-consultant relationships, where the manager's skills and ability in making an accurate assessment of the trustworthiness of a consultant for a particular project, to a systems-based market transaction. By the development of such a system, relational aspects such as affect, interpersonal commensurability and assessment of benevolence will no longer come into play, and instead the assessment will be based on measurable aspects, making number of hours, price and number of consultants in the project key in the supplier selection. The interpersonal trust between consultant and client that is the cornerstone of relational purchasing is thereby replaced by system trust in the formal purchasing model, and the logic shifts from interpersonal trust to system trust. This is significant in two respects: the trustee is thereby no longer the consultant, but the system, and because systems are not generally perceived to have agency, affective aspects and perceptions of benevolence and intent lose significance.

The new triadic relation and division of roles between managers and purchasing professionals also pose new challenges for the management consultants. Who in the client organization are they allowed to contact? How should they adjust and organize their marketing and selling activities? Many consultants witness on feelings of frustration as they feel the purchasing professionals "focus on the wrong things", such as price rather than quality or value, and hinder them from being in frequent contact with the managers. They argue that the purchasing professionals should be more interested in adjusting the purchasing processes to the unique characteristics of management consulting services, than in trying to adjust the services to their models. There is also a widespread concern among the consultants that the increased formalization will change the perception of their services from being unique and strategically important to become standardized and commoditized (Pemer & Skjolsvik, 2012). In this sense, the shift in purchasing practices from informal and relational to formal and system based might, therefore, be seen as part of a larger development whereby local expertise is reconstructed as global. Thereby the focus of the user shifts from the expert as a trustworthy individual to the reliability of the expert system, and, to the supplier of expert knowledge, being perceived as an expert becomes less important than being able to construct expertise in a measurable way. The formalization of purchasing thereby serves to disembed the expert, replacing it with abstract expertise.

References

Adobor, H. (2005). Trust as sensemaking: The microdynamics of trust in interfirm alliances. *Journal of Business Research, 58*, 330–337.

Axelsson, B. (2005). Purchasing as supply management. In Furusten, S. & Werr, A. (eds.), *Dealing with Confidence: The Construction of Need and Trust in Management Advisory Services.* Copenhagen: Copenhagen Business School Press, 39–58.

Axelsson, B. & Wynstra, F. (2002). *Buying Business Services.* Chichester: John Wiley & Sons Ltd.

Brown, A. D., Colville, I. & Pye, A. (2014). Making sense of sensemaking in organization studies. *Perspectives of Organization Studies, 36*(2), 265–277.

Fuglsang, L. & Jagd, S. (2015). Making sense of institutional trust in organizations: Bridging institutional context and trust. *Organization, 22*(1), 23–39.

Giddens, A. (1990). *The Consequences of Modernity.* Stanford: Stanford University Press.

Glückler, J. & Armbrüster, T. (2003). Bridging uncertainty in management consulting: The mechanisms of trust and networked reputation. *Organization Studies, 24*(2), 269–297.

Hedgecoe, A. (2012). Trust and regulatory organizations: The role of local knowledge and facework in research ethics review. *Social Studies of Science, 42*(5), 662–683.

Jones, K. (1996). Trust as an affective attitude. *Ethics, 107*(1), 4–25.

Karantinou, K. M. & Hogg, M. K. (2001). Exploring relationship management in professional services: A study of management consultancy. *Journal of Marketing Management, 17*, 263–286.

Karmarkar, U. S. & Pitbladdo, R. (1995). Service markets and competition. *Journal of Operations Management, 12*, 397–411.

Kim, H. H. (2009). Market uncertainty and socially embedded reputation. *American Journal of Economics and Sociology, 68*(3), 679–701.

Li, P. P. (2007). Towards an interdisciplinary conceptualization of trust: A typological approach. *Management and Organization Review, 3*(3), 421–445.

Lian, P. C. S. & Laing, A. W. (2007). Relationships in the purchasing of business to business professional services: The role of personal relationships. *Industrial Marketing Management, 36*, 709–718.

Mayer, R. C., Davis, J. H. & Schoorman, F. D. (1995). An integrative model of organizational trust. *Academy of Management Review, 20*(3), 709–734.

Näslund, L. (2012a). *The Leap of Faith: Creating Trust on Professional Service Markets.* Stockholm: Stockholm School of Economics.

Näslund, L. (2012b). *Swift or Sluggish? The Influence of Sensemaking on the Volatility of Trust.* Paper Presented at the 6th EIASM Workshop on Trust within and between Organizations, Bocconi University, Milan.

Pemer, F., Sieweke, J., Werr, A., Birkner, S. & Mohe, M. (2014). The cultural embeddedness of professional service purchasing—A comparative study of German and Swedish companies. *Journal of Purchasing and Supply Management, 20*(4), 273–285.

Pemer, F. & Skjolsvik, T. (2012). Client and Consultant Logics on the Purchasing of Management Consulting Services. *Academy of Management Proceedings.*

Pemer, F. & Werr, A. (2009). *Professionalizing the Use of Management Consulting Services: An Investigation into Structures and Procedures for the Use of MC Services in Swedish Organizations.* Paper Presented at the 4th International Conference on Management Consulting. Management Consulting Division—Academy of Management.

Pemer, F., Werr, A. & Bianchi, M. (2014). Purchasing professional services: A transaction cost view of the antecedents and consequences of purchasing formalization. *Industrial Marketing Management, 43*(5), 840–849.

Power, M. (1997). *The Audit Society: Rituals of Verification*. Oxford: Oxford University Press.

Power, M. (2000). The audit society—Second thoughts. *International Journal of Auditing, 4*(1), 111–119.

Rousseau, D. M., Sitkin, S. B., Burt, R. S. & Camerer, C. (1998). Not so different after all: A cross-discipline view of trust. *Academy of Management Review, 23*(3), 393–404.

Shapiro, S. P. (1987). The social control of impersonal trust. *The American Journal of Sociology, 93*(3), 623–658.

Sieweke, J., Birkner, S. & Mohe, M. (2012). Preferred supplier programs for consulting services: An exploratory study of German client companies. *Journal of Purchasing and Supply Management, 18*(3), 123–136.

Ulvila, J. W. (2000). Building relationships between consultants and clients. *American Behavioral Scientist, 43*(10), 1667–1680.

Weick, K. E., Sutcliffe, K. M. & Obstfeld, D. (2005). Organizing and the process of sensemaking. *Organization Science, 16*(4), 409–421.

Werr, A. & Pemer, F. (2007). Purchasing management consulting services—From management autonomy to purchasing involvement. *Journal of Purchasing and Supply Management, 13*, 98–112.

9 Organizing Expertise through Improvising

Staffan Furusten

Management consultants are typical examples of the rise of experts in contemporary society, and Alexius has already shown in Chapter 2 that attempts to "professionalize" them have not been very successful, and Näslund and Pemer showed in Chapter 8 that interpersonal trust is a common way for management consultants to establish themselves as reliable service providers toward their clients. Such qualification of expertise and legitimization of experts is not transparent, and thereby difficult to assess for externals. Still, the qualifications are likely to contribute to order for those who have internalized them. Based on studies of how management consultants construct the services they deliver, this chapter will discuss what this order consists of.

The chapter is based on interviews with buyers and providers of management consulting services; in total, about 70 interviews, of which about 55 were with consultants and 15 with buyers. Most of the interviews were conducted with consultants representing small (less than 10 employees) and mid-sized (11–40 employees) consulting firms of local Swedish origin. The buyers interviewed represent organizations in the public sector. The consultants interviewed where mainly senior consultants. All interviews were seen as narratives from the field and have, as such, been interpreted and categorized qualitatively.

The chapter is structured in four main inductively constructed categories of characteristics relating to what the consultants do in order to produce themselves as trustworthy experts on the market. The four categories are systematic processes of: (1) building and maintaining relationships with clients, (2) being available, (3) representing relevant competence, and (4) differentiation. A small selection of quotations that clearly reflect the patterns that emerged from the analyses are used to illustrate the views of the interviewees.

Building and Maintaining Relationships through Versatility

In management consulting, as in any business situation, building and maintaining relationships with clients and potential clients is of great importance. Our data show that to succeed in this management consultants continuously struggle to be versatile. This means that they struggle to keep up with new developments in particular industries, management standards and fashions, and to carefully listen and adapt to the needs of their clients. The importance of versatility in building and maintaining relationships is demonstrated by the following quotation from an interview with a senior consultant who, at the time of the interview, was self-employed:

> It's not unusual to feel unsure of what you're going to do in a project, and the same goes for the client. Sometimes they're not sure what they want from me, if they're going to hire me, or what the project is going to look like. Sometimes they just want someone to talk to, but sometimes these discussions turn into projects.

This consultant made it very clear that the service he delivers is quite often defined in open discussions with the client. Therefore, he has to be open-minded and flexible, which means that the service he delivers may vary a great deal depending on the outcome of these discussions.

How open a project is, however, depends very much on how it is initiated. As the earlier quotation shows, the actual starting point of a business relationship can be unclear. The client wants a sounding board or wants to be brought up to date on modern management, or simply wants to meet the consultant because he or she is curious about what the consultant can do for them. The consultant also explains that clients may contact him because they have come across books or articles that he has written. When these are familiar to the client, the assignment is likely to be more clearly defined from the outset.

Although the consultant's projects may differ in many ways, he still points out that there are limits to what he can do. In order not to risk his reputation, he tries to avoid projects he feels he is not qualified for. However, to keep the relationship with the client, he might pass the client on to a colleague in another firm that he knows is more capable of providing that type of service. Sometimes several consultancies cooperate by systematically passing on potential projects to each other. This procedure may be based on agreements within groups of firms, whereby the firm that passes a project on to another firm receives a brokerage fee for this service. Hence, the idea is to build a system where the risk of not getting assignments regularly is reduced but also where everyone involved benefits from this form of cooperation. The fee is just one aspect, but the main goal is that the firms involved, in the long run, receive projects from each other.

Versatility, in terms of how best to help the client or decide whether to keep or pass on assignments, is a common strategy among consultants. However, it is not practiced by all. A senior and a junior consultant at one medium-sized consultancy reported that recommending someone else for a project could be very risky. Even though someone else is doing the work, in their view, they still carry part of the responsibility for the project, which could be problematic because it is virtually impossible to assure the quality of a service delivered by someone else. These two consultants work in a rather different mode compared to the senior consultant quoted earlier, and represent a category of firms that offer standardized services based on particular models. Their model (developed by the founder of the firm and published in books and articles in both the business press and in academic journals) is customized to suit growing firms. The business relationship begins when they inform a potential client that they have a solution (the model) to the kind of problems the client is likely to face as a growing organization. It is of crucial importance that the potential client matches the definition of a growing firm as defined by the consultancy. If it does not, the consultants say that they always turn down the potential assignment, because they believe that the service they offer would not suit firms that are not growing. Still, being versatile and understanding in their relationship with clients is important to them, but they do not apply these qualities in the same way as the self-employed consultant quoted earlier does. While they are not flexible in the service they deliver, they are naturally flexible in terms of starting dates and deadlines. They also offer a set of services that can be combined or purchased separately. In other words, although the content of the project is not negotiable, there may still be room for negotiating its size and form.

Being flexible about what types of projects one undertakes or offering relatively standardized models represent two extremes through which consultancies win projects. However, both strategies require versatility on the part of the consultants. To some extent, we would expect that the larger the firm, the less flexible and versatile it needs to be—or a firm may satisfy the need for versatility by having in-house specialists that can provide different types of services. It is also likely that larger firms have a reputation that sells projects more or less automatically. However, as the following quotation shows, they cannot rely too heavily on their reputation; they must also actively seek new business opportunities and build new and maintain old business relations. A senior consultant at one of the larger medium-sized and well-established Swedish consultancies describes how he and his colleagues do not just sit in their offices waiting for interesting projects to come along:

> I got the idea when I was working at the Central Student Support Agency (CSN). I realized that the model we were trying to implement there had greater potential to be successful at Sweden Post. So I went to Sweden Post and told them that I could help them develop a new area of business. I walked around their premises, walked up and down the stairs, popped in and out of offices, and talked to one person after another. It took about two years to convince them to give me an assignment. I see no limit to how many times this idea can be sold. We've sold it to two other public agencies and are about to sell it to a third.

The service he refers to here is a technical administrative routine, which is rather different from the more general services offered by the consultants discussed earlier. Still, considerable versatility was needed in the situation he described, although no negotiations regarding the content of the service took place. Nevertheless, the consultant fought long and hard to convince the client of the benefits of this routine for their organization. Finding economies of scale and commodifying services in this way is probably an opportunity that comes with the size of the consultancy. It is riskier for self-employed consultants or small firms to focus on one particular type of service. They need to be more flexible because they cannot rely on always winning projects of a particular kind. Sometimes, they just have to take whatever comes along. It is therefore important for them to be involved in a number of parallel relationships with former or potential clients.

These stories from the field reveal a core dimension of consultancy work: the constant search for new business opportunities. This involves successfully establishing and managing relationships with existing and potential clients. To do this the strategy that small and medium-sized firms in particular tend to use is to be versatile, which also involves a great deal of flexibility. We have, however, seen that larger firms (represented here by one of the larger medium-sized Swedish-owned firms) must also show some versatility in order to sell their specialized services. Whereas small firms, having less power to pick and choose, tend to be more likely to combine rather contrasting forms of consulting, larger firms are perhaps more likely to offer commodified and strictly standardized services. One reason for this is that the large firms have the capacity in their hierarchies to house different types of commodities run by different specialists. Another reason is that large firms house more senior consultants who can be involved in processes of establishing and maintaining relationships. Nevertheless, versatility is mainly a concept that represents the kind of activities consultants are involved in when struggling to build and maintain relationships, and is thereby one quality that everyone who wants to be accepted as a legitimate player in the consulting market needs to learn.

Being Available

It takes, however, more than versatility to win projects and survive in the consulting market. If clients know what they want and are looking for, for example, methods for improving service quality, they probably turn to consultancies that are regarded to have expertise in this area. On the other hand, if they have a good relationship with a consultant they like and consider competent, they might initiate a discussion about service quality in this already established relationship. In some cases, these discussions might reveal that someone else is a better choice for the project. Still, it is not unusual for one project to lead to other projects in the same company, if contact is maintained. A quality manager in a division of the Swedish telecom company TeliaSonera describes why he hired a particular self-employed senior consultant, the first time, and then once again:

> The division employed a new CEO from Ericsson. Some time later, the CEO hired me as his quality manager (QM). We used to be colleagues at Ericsson. I'm an engineer but have gradually moved from practical engineering to area-management positions. At that time, however, I had no experience of quality management. I thought the whole thing was a practical joke on the part of my former colleague, but it wasn't. So, in order to become informed in the area, I saw no other option than to hire a consultant, and I selected one from the pile of presentations I got in the mail from consulting firms.

For the consultant who was hired in this way, it was a question of lucky timing. His letter reached the QM at a time when he was receptive to quality management services. It was a "garbage can situation" (Cohen, March & Olsen, 1972), where the QM had a problem and the consultant a solution to the problem. The solution was in the market while the problem was experienced in the hierarchy. The QM continues his story:

> The first project was designed as an investigation of what kind of quality management system the division should go for. It was therefore rather technical in character. I felt, however, that we needed more than this. I therefore started discussing this with Sven-Goran[1] [the self-employed consultant] since he had rather eagerly and repeatedly expressed his interest in being involved in one way or another in the quality management project in the division. We met for lunch a couple of times and I thought he was a nice guy who had interesting and unusual ideas about quality management compared to the technical information I had received in the report from the first consultant. I hired him as a sounding board in order to bring more philosophical insight into the quality management project in the division. The first consultant's report suggested that ISO 9000 was the system the division should go with. Gradually, Sven-Goran's first assignment led to a situation where I asked him if he could act as a kind of undercover agent to very carefully underline the philosophy of quality management in the organization during the process of the division's struggle to attain ISO 9000 certification.

This story reveals how important it is for small and medium-sized consultancies to stay close to former and potential clients in order to be available when the client is ready to do business. If a consultant is not around at this point in time, it is very likely that the project will go to someone who is. One example of how this can be realized in practice is that once the consultant has established a good relationship with a client, they are likely to attempt to maintain this. This also comes through very clearly in the following quotation from the self-employed senior consultant (Sven-Goran) whom the QM hired twice:

> You have projects over the years and then after seven years you get: "Hey, can you help me with this?" But you already have a relationship, not just a personal one but also a relationship with this company, this industry or this organization and these people. . . . When you do a large project, it often leads to other projects, but after a while it is less and less. But then, after a year or so, they give you a call. Of course, you've been doing some type of relationship marketing the entire time. Sending a letter every now and then, a funny article and the like, though nothing vulgar. And you should be careful not to over-sell yourself, or they might get the impression that there's something wrong with you or your service!

The importance of being close-by and ready to act when the opportunity arises is an aspect of consultancy work most interviewees emphasize. Thus, how particular services are constructed is very much a matter of timing, i.e. catching the client when he is receptive, and then making a good first impression. The interviewees mentioned several strategies for achieving this. The client can be won on the spot in various ways: through letters and e-mail, telephone calls, lunch meetings, through recommendations from other clients or consulting firms, or with a combination of these. Many interviewees also emphasize that enthusiasm and eagerness is yet another strategy for winning clients. This was what characterized the work of the senior consultant of the larger medium-sized Swedish consultancy referred to earlier when he tried to convince Sweden Post of the brilliance of his administrative routine. His running up and down the stairs, popping in and out of offices, and chatting with different people for two years finally led to them hiring him as he was there so frequently and regularly that no other consulting firm could get a foot into this domain. Thus, a constant but not desperate presence among potential service buyers is another necessary component in trust building, and thereby another quality consultants need to acquire if they want acceptance as professionals in the market.

Representing Relevant Competence

Although versatility and availability are two core attributes for the construction of trust for the single consultant and certain consultancies in the market, this is not enough to win clients. If the consultant is not considered competent, it would seem that little will come of efforts to meet the other two attributes. Thus, potential clients have to believe that the consultant can in some way provide them with relevant services. This relevance has two dimensions: one social and one conceptual. When the QM referred to above hired the self-employed senior consultant, quality management and ISO 9000 formed the arena of competence where the quality manager and the consultant met. In that particular case, a fashionable management standard constituted this arena. The QM noted that he and his organization lacked expertise, while the consultant claimed that he had been working in quality management since the early 1980s, long before it had become fashionable. He also referred to a book he had written on the topic. However, the conceptual facts were not what first got the QM interested in the consultant: his social skills were more important. In the QM's opinion, the consultant was a pleasant and interesting fellow that he wanted to continue to talk to. In the discussions that would follow, the consultant's conceptual competence in quality management authorized him to act as somewhat of a quality management expert. If the consultant's social behaviour in the early, critical phase of the relationship was of great importance, his conceptual competence gradually grew in importance, ultimately leading to the first project and then the second, and possibly more after that.

In this particular situation, the consultant had extensive experience of the focal point of the project. Not all projects are of this kind. The same consultant explains, for example, that the management tool or technique he delivers depends on the particular circumstances of each individual project. This is a behavior he shares with most of the study informants, although this particular consultant was keen to point out that, when he chooses his tools, he does not turn to books or seminars. Instead, he says that he uses his intuition, his experience and his own analysis of all aspects of the client's organization to create the tools that are required. This therefore suggests that, when describing their know-how to potential clients, it is crucial that small-scale management consultants highlight learning as a fundamental component of their experience and expertise. However, it is difficult to link the learning that underlies a delivered service to particular events, books or management standards. Learning is a complex and continuous process, or as expressed by the same consultant:

> You're always learning—every time you do something you learn. But it is very difficult to know what it is you're learning and when or where you're learning. Hopefully you learn something every day.

Another senior consultant, a partner in a small consultancy, gave a similar account of how he learns in order to be regarded as competent by his clients. In his firm (as in many other small consultancies), all the consultants are senior consultants. In this case, the consultants are all over 40 years of age and have the relevant management skills for the kind of service they provide. This profile and approach to seniority does not characterize all small-scale consultancies, although they all agree that seniority can only be gained through long experience of both consulting and management positions. Assistant work, however, is still needed, but instead of employing junior consultants in their own firms, they often use young employees from the client organization who have a business degree. They also see this as an advantage because these people have greater insight into the organization than a junior consultant ever could. Regarding the competence of senior consultants, they claim that professionalism can only result from hands-on experience in the field. The senior consultant quoted earlier expresses his thoughts about professionalism and learning in the following way:

> I'm not conscious of everything I learn. An enormous amount of know-how is accumulated in your head, your body, in the bookshelves, on the wall, in your fingers, in your sensitivity, in your sense of smell, in your hearing. This type of knowledge is different from technical knowledge.

If these thoughts are representative of how senior consultants in small-scale consultancies reason, consulting skills are accumulated and constantly upgraded in every new situation. Learning takes place continuously, but it is difficult to define where it comes from. On the other hand, the situation is quite different with technical knowledge. As emphasized by many interviewees, technical knowledge can be learned from books, seminars and education. They also stress that technical knowledge is more easily commodified. This is implied in the following quotation, also from the senior consultant cited earlier, in which he also claims, however, that he and his colleagues do not sell technical knowledge.

> There are 17,000 management techniques out there to choose from. We use them in our services if the situation calls for them, but we don't sell them. We're not method consultants like the large US firms.[2]

Thus, what small-scale consultancies claim they do, as expressed by this senior consultant, is offer services based on management know-how, not on technical knowledge. Senior consultants believe that such services are difficult to sell and cannot be sold by their junior colleagues, because junior consultants do not have the know-how, or—as the same senior consultant explained:

> When I once said to a potential client "Well, I'm good at management, at understanding management situations", he replied, "OK, but what books have you read?" At that point, I decided to go home. This was someone who had never bought real management consulting services before. It's very difficult to put your finger on this type of knowledge since it isn't technical. You're trying to tell them what you know. It has a lot to do with intuition: to have the ability to relate things such as your experience, what you know, and the technical knowledge that's available.

What he means here is that this know-how cannot be specified in black and white and can, therefore, not be acquired from books. He believes that consultants with the right know-how intuitively know what to do in the consulting process. This is also emphasized by other interviewees. Thus, it is difficult to trace the origin of the knowledge and skills small-scale management consultancies gain through experience because, in the words of this consultant, "you learn new things all the time through constant work". He also adds,

> We read literature, of course, and try to keep up-to-date, but what we do explicitly in terms of learning to consult is to go to other industries. We go to the theatre but not to be on stage and talk about dogs and cows like the Boston Consulting Group. There are so many similarities between directing a play and being a consultant. You have a 7-month deadline. You have a cast you didn't choose. You're short of money and, when you start, you have absolutely no idea how it will all turn out.

What he is suggesting is that the kind of consulting he performs is more like an art than anything else. Relevant competence for small-scale management consultants would thus appear to involve possessing the skills and talent to perform the art, but the performance can never be only technical. The kind of service a small-scale consultant offers is therefore not exclusively based on particular methods. Or, as the consultant says earlier, methods are just tools that can be used when the problem is clearly defined.

Thus, the picture that emerges is that the relevant competence for a management consultant is non-specific. It consists of combinations of individually embodied know-how, international management standards and faddish management tools. The interviews show that seniority, generally presented in terms of "I'm good at management" is one capacity that can sell a service. For those who are not senior consultants and lack considerable experience of both management positions and consulting, it appears to be more important to be seen as specialists with extensive technical knowledge. Drawing on popular management standards may also be important to demonstrate relevant competence. Having said that, it can also be concluded that if social skills are lacking there will be no business—no matter how good the consultant may be at standardized management techniques and professional management consulting. Thus, it seems that, to be regarded as having the relevant competence, the small-scale consultant must possess a combination of conceptual and social skills, although the exact combination tends to vary between different forms of consulting. Learning to be relevant is therefore another quality necessary to become accepted as a professional in the consulting market.

Differentiation

As argued earlier, being versatile, available and representing relevant competence can be interpreted as crucial for the trust building of consultants, but perhaps less so once they become well established, have a good reputation in the market and have many connections and good relationships with clients and other consultancies. However, if this is not their reality, how they compare with other consultancies in the market becomes important.

This conclusion is drawn from senior consultants' tendency to emphasize that they are different from the others. Local consultancies in particular, in this case of Swedish origin, irrespective of size, appear to be anxious to define themselves as *not like* US firms, meaning that they claim they are not method or expert consultants. Instead, the consultants in this study say that they first offer a service that helps their clients to define their situation and problem and then help the clients to identify solutions. Sometimes they are also involved in implementation. They also say that the large global US or semi-US-based consultancies conduct comprehensive situation analyses but do not have the expertise to implement solutions. This is the expertise local consultancies claim to have. Thus if this is a fair description of the market, large consultancies, and in particular the US firms, provide standardized methods and solutions for standardized problems. Smaller, locally based consultancies, on the other hand, provide true process consulting without knowing the problems beforehand, and do not act as peddlers of particular methods. We must remember, however, that these are ideal market positions emphasized by locally operating consultants.

Smaller consultancies do not deny that they are familiar with particular methods or that the solutions they suggest may be based on popular and well-known management concepts or methods. Nevertheless, they claim that their proposed solutions are based to a larger extent on the clients' real problems than on a particular method they happen to have developed or adopted. This argument is common among the interviewees and is exemplified in the following quotation from the senior partner of the small consultancy referred to earlier (i.e. with only senior consultants, all of whom are over 40). He explains:

> There are consultancies that develop models and turn them into products—"this is our model"—and then try to fit all sorts of problems into that model. A model has one advantage, and many of the large US firms use them. That's why they can use young consultants, because they have a product: "Deliver this product! First you do this, and then that and that". We say: "That's nice, but we don't know the method until we know the situation".

Thus, smaller market actors clearly need to stress their uniqueness, while the situation is likely different for firms with a strong brand name, such as McKinsey & Co or Accenture. The local and smaller actors tend to work very hard to market themselves in terms of "I am this kind of consultant, not that kind. I am not like them". According to small-scale Swedish consultants, large firms are more likely to follow certain well-defined methods.

However, this should not be understood as small consultancies do not use methods. Rather, because the form of consulting they provide is more individual, they do not have the same need as larger actors do to formalize their methods in order to present a united front to their client.

The need of small consultancies to stress that their offering is different, if not unique, may derive from the complexity of the service they offer. If they cannot sell themselves by telling potential clients that they are good at management, a formalized mode for presenting their work, for example, one based on standards, may be more convincing. Presenting the service as clearly non-US, non-method and problem-driven, might make the difference, as may positioning oneself as complementary, or claiming to be as good as the US firms in every way, but much less expensive.

To recap, smaller and locally based consultancies emphasize that they are not like other firms. They all claim that their service is unique because they all have unique experience and know-how. However, a comparison of their services reveals many similarities. This means that, while claiming to be unique, they cannot risk being too different. Continuously dealing with this challenge is another quality needed for acceptance in the market as a professional.

Improvisation and Trust

Following from the previous discussion, and also emphasized by the consultants interviewed in this study, it seems that the most important mechanism for inclusion in the management consulting professions is acceptance by the market. If someone manages to sell his or her services on the market for management consulting, this person is accepted as a member of the occupation. However, not just any kind of behavior is likely to work. The main control mechanism is trust, meaning that there is a great chance that the buyers buy services from a particular consultant if trust has been established between them. Still, as shown earlier, there is also a pattern regarding the type of actions representatives of this occupation tend to employ as they endeavor to become accepted by the market and included as members of the community. They tend to make sure that they are versatile, available, relevant and different but not deviant.

This suggests that the management consultants' performance in any single business situation does not tend to be judged based on factors such as how well a management standard or a standard for management consulting is followed. Instead, performance tends to be evaluated on how well it satisfies the expectations of the members of the client organization and, most importantly, whether or not this leads to the establishment of trust in the business relation. The presence of a management consultant in a client organization may thus be evaluated primarily on the basis of how well the consultant manages to meet expectations and provide comfort and knowledge that give client organization members the confidence to deal with their daily toils.

This suggests that improvisation is a core mechanism for organizing expertise on the field of management consulting. Consultants strive to organize their activities in order to create space for them for versatility, availability, relevance and differentiation. Thus, the source for their expertise is not formal legitimacy, but local relevance, and this is a state of order that must be created over and over again in all assignments. Moreover, it also has to continuously be maintained and reconstructed at the local level because it is not a static order even in established relations with former, current and potential future clients.

The most common understanding of improvisation is that it represents a form of performance where rules are broken. This is, however, a too simple understanding. First, improvisation cannot be performed without thorough basic knowledge and skills (Barrett & Peplowski, 1998; Pasmore, 1998; Zack, 2000). The famous jazz base player Charlie Mingus expressed this as "you can't improvise on nothing, there got to be something" (Barrett & Peplowski, 1998). This means that improvisation is a concept that expresses that there is something that is established in a particular context and that this must be a point of departure for the improviser that he or she can build on, interpret and develop variations of. To be versatile, available, relevant and different at the same time means that one is not going with the wind all the time. For improvisation to work, the performance must be accepted as relevant in the context where it is performed. This means that it in this context also must be a something that is generally institutionalized.

Thus, improvisation is not an expression of something completely new being introduced in a specific context. It is rather a concept that reflects particular actors' capability to understand the institutionalized order on the market. It is also an expression for their ability to build on these structures and perform in ways that are likely to reach acceptance by other actors in a particular genre, and particularly the buyers. Consultants have developed a sense for how to improvise, to build on the institutionalized "something" and create something that is experienced as new and fresh while not deviant from the institutionalized something. It can be new combinations of already well-known models or ideas, or small complements added to well-established knowledge. To earn this sense for what kind of performance that is likely to be accepted cannot be taught in books, education or training programs, it takes time and practical experience. (Furusten, 2003, 2005, 2009).

This means that improvisation is not about taking chances, but to act from a well-known and established order. This order is, however, not clear-cut and the same in every consulting situation. This is why the expertise required from the consultants needs to be pragmatic and is locally assessed.

Order-Making through Improvising

In the field of management consulting, professionalism is not developed, maintained and guarded by a superior body. It is a continuously ongoing institutionalization of appropriate performance by consultants in different situations, and this institutionalization is best understood as result of constant ongoing actions. Thus, actions are taken by consultants in order to fit with other actions, such as when they adjust their proposals of services to actions they believe potential buyers of consulting services are in need of. The buyers, on the other hand, refrain from taking actions that they think that consultants are better prepared to take. In this way, actions are taken from both consultants and clients in order to create interfaces where the expertise delivered by consultants is defined. Through this action-based organizing, order is created on the market between providers and buyers of consulting services, but the order is local, non-transparent for outsiders and consolidated between particular clients and consultants.

Notes

1 The names of individual interviewees have been changed to protect their privacy.
2 Whether or not this view of the large US firms is justified is not addressed here. It is, however, a view shared by most of the interviewees in this study. Swedish firms that claim they are not like US firms may do so as part of their marketing strategy.

References

Barrett, F. & Peplowski, K. (1998). Minimal structures within a song: An analysis of "All of Me". *Organization Science*, 9(September/October), 558–560.

Cohen, M. D., March, J. G. & Olsen, J. P. (1972). A garbage can model of organizational choice. *Administrative Science Quarterly*, 17(1), 1–25.

Furusten, S. (2003). *God managementkonsultation—Reglerad expertis eller improviserat artisteri?* Lund: Studentlitteratur.

Furusten, S. (2005). Reglering utan regler—normer för managementkonsultation. In Fernler, K., Henning, R. & Svedberg-Nilsson, K. (eds.), *En illusion av frihet*. Lund: Studentlitteratur, 163–184.

Furusten, Staffan. (2009). Management consultants as improvising agents of stability. *Scandinavian Journal of Management*, 25(3), 264–274.

Pasmore, W. A. (1998). Organizing for jazz. *Organization Science*, 9(5), 562–568.

Zack, M. (2000). Jazz improvisation and organizing: Once more from the top. *Organization Science*, 11(2), 227–234.

10 Expertise in the Selection of Employees

Pernilla Bolander

This chapter focuses on employee selection and touches on expertise in two different ways. First, employee selection is an important organizational process for assessing individuals and their attributes. In the selection context, expertise is, in other words, subject to assessment. Second, selectors make use of their expertise to assess candidates and make decisions about whom to hire. This expertise is not uniform and may be based on different domains of knowledge. Therefore, it becomes interesting to explore how selection experts legitimize their expertise and thus also their working methods and decisions.

In my studies of employee selection, I have interviewed a number of people engaged in their organizations' selection processes and asked them how they assess candidates and how they know that they have found the right person (Bolander, 2002). A common response is "gut feeling". You know it is the right person because it feels right. Others, on the other hand, answer that they have a selection process that is well thought through and proven. They work in a methodical and structured manner, and use tools that are technically rigorous. In this chapter, we will take a closer look at these two dominant ideas of how to find the right person—through gut feeling or formal methods. We will consider them as legitimization grounds and explore the consequences of their use. Based on a study of the everyday practice of selection, a third possible ground for legitimation is introduced—namely, contextual knowledge.

Research on Employee Selection

Human Resource Management (HRM) had a wide breakthrough in the 1980s and is today often used as a broad term for "activities associated with the management of work and people in organizations" (Boxall & Purcell, 2011, p. 1). Key activities include, in addition to recruitment and selection, developing, evaluating and rewarding employees at all levels. Today these activities are often presented as critical to organizational performance and competitive advantage, especially in knowledge-intensive organizations (Storey, 2007; Purcell, Kinnie, Swart, Rayton & Hutchinson, 2008).

Although HRM is therefore often said to be strategically important for organizations, HR functions and specialists have long fought an uphill battle to achieve higher status and legitimacy and establish a professional identity (Pritchard, 2010; Ulrich, Younger, Brockbank & Ulrich, 2013). One way of putting this is to state that they wish to assert their expertise of people and of different strategies and principles for how employees can be managed and work organized in a way that leads to desired organizational outcomes. Different approaches are applied to accentuate this expertise, e.g., to use "business" language, to evaluate the effects of HR processes using economic measures, and to categories and quantify the "human resources" (Bolander, 2011). Another way to build expert status and professionalism is to use the models and tools generated in research (Iles, 1999). The latter method is used not least in the context of employee selection.

Research on employee selection has been conducted for around a century, making it one of the most widely researched HR processes (Anderson, 1992; Schmidt & Hunter, 1998; Salgado, 2001; Sackett & Lievens, 2008). Most of the research has been based on the underlying assumption that every job consists of a number of discrete tasks, that individuals possess stable attributes and that job and person can be assessed and measured independently (McCourt, 1999). It has focused on developing and testing selection models and tools that can be used to identify those candidates whose attributes best match the job and organizational requirements.

In 2011, another tool was launched: an international ISO standard for assessment services, which has been highlighted in Sweden as something of a "silver bullet" for assessment work. The standard covers the entire assessment process and contains requirements and recommendations for procedures and methods to assess people in work and organizational settings.[1] The standard can be described as an attempt to formalize the selection process.

Formalization of the Selection Process

In the context of selection, formalization means that the selection criteria used are defined and weighted in advance, that assessment takes place only on the basis of these criteria, that the candidates' qualities are measured in a standardized way with the help of technically rigorous tools, and that the selection process is carefully documented (Jenkins, 1986). The promise of formalization is to transform selection from an informal process in which decisions are made on unspoken grounds and where subjectivity is likely to dominate, into a formal process in which there are clear rules and where objectivity prevails (Newton, 1994).

The main arguments that are put forward for formalization are increased efficiency, objectivity and fairness. Formalization facilitates employee selection by giving structure to the assessment process. Proponents also argue that it creates conditions for higher quality in assessment and decision-making.

Moreover, the basic assumption of meritocracy leads to less arbitrary assessment procedures, and the transparency principle counteracts discrimination.

As a concept, formalization is based on a number of ideals. One is that the job market is an open and competitive market that everyone has access to, and where all can compete on meritocratic grounds (Jewson & Mason, 1986). Another concerns the organization and its work processes; formalization is based on a bureaucratic ideal. Weber (1922/1983, p. 153) wrote of the ideal-typical bureaucracy as dominated by a "spirit of formalistic impersonality" where decisions are taken "without hatred and passion". A central idea of formalization is that it should not matter who is being assessed or who is doing the assessment. It is not the individuals involved, but rather the working method—the model or standard—that is crucial. The principle aim is an objective selection process, and objectivity is achieved by the assessment taking place without regard to the context in which it occurs. Good practice is universal and impersonal rather than situated and personal, as McCourt (1999, p. 1011) observes. In other words, formalization makes decontextualization a key objective.

How Does Assessment and Decision-Making Take Place in Practice?

Because there are a number of different models for how selection should be carried out, it may seem as if we have a fairly good idea of how assessment and decision-making actually takes place. The models, however, provide what might be called an indirect description (Sandberg, 2000). They focus on the steps leading up to assessment, such as the definition of criteria, the choice of selection tools and how to gather information, rather than assessment itself. The selection decision is seen as an outcome of the earlier steps, almost as if it were taken by itself. Thus, the given descriptions only provide a "partial account" of selection (Ramsay & Scholarios, 1999, p. 64). In addition, most empirical studies of selection decision-making are based on post hoc interviews, or simulated situations such as experiments. There are only a few studies of decision-making "in real life situations with real life candidates" (Zysberg & Nevo, 2004, p. 118). Therefore, there is reason to study closely such situations where the candidate is assessed and selection decisions are taken.

In one such study, decision meetings in two organizations in the IT industry were observed (Bolander & Sandberg, 2013). At these meetings, different people gathered together—HR specialists, managers, colleagues—to discuss candidates that had already been interviewed a number of times. The purpose was to decide if the candidates should be offered employment. Eight meetings were observed, audio-recorded and analyzed using a combined ethnomethodological-discourse analytical approach.

The results of our analysis showed that assessment and decision-making are, in many ways, local work. This means that the meeting participants constantly took into account situation-specific conditions when they assessed candidates and made selection decisions. To briefly exemplify, we can focus on how they handled the selection criteria. Although the meeting participants had defined and weighted the selection criteria in advance, they always had to determine the following: "What does this criterion actually mean in this context?" If we start with a relatively unambiguous criterion such as previous work experience, it was rare that a candidate had exactly the experience that had previously been set up as a requirement. The questions that arose among the meeting participants were therefore manifold. Is four and a half years of experience so close to five years that the requirement can count as fulfilled? Does ten years of experience mean that the candidate is over-qualified and therefore less suited? How should you assess seven years of experience in a related field, but one that is not exactly what you asked for? The questions became even more numerous when the criteria were more difficult to define, e.g., "good analytical ability", "able to work independently" and "good teamwork skills".

To resolve these types of questions, the meeting participants discussed specific details of the candidate, the working group and the organization. You could say that they assembled an ethnographic context that made interpretation possible (Leiter, 1980). Was the candidate nervous during the interview? Then maybe it's a mitigating circumstance. How did the candidate talk about their current job? It may say something about their ability to work independently. Is this a job position that we know, from experience, that we will have a hard time finding good candidates for? Then we maybe need to be generous in the interpretation of certain criteria. What skills and personal qualities do the employees have that already work in the working group? It says something about the relative importance that we should apply to various criteria. Is there already a great deal of conflict in the working group? Perhaps then, we should not bring in someone who may be perceived as controversial. By using this type of knowledge of the specific situation, what Garfinkel (1967) termed background knowledge, the meeting participants reasoned their way to local versions of the candidates and their attributes, based upon which they could make decisions.

This says something about how the rules work. The selection criteria (and other selection tools) represent a set of rules in the sense that they "speak of" how decision-makers should act: "if x, do y". However, as the early ethnomethodological studies of decision-making so illustratively demonstrated, even those rules which are most evident require interpretation when applied in actual and practical situations (Garfinkel, 1967; Wieder, 1970, 1974; Zimmerman, 1970; Cicourel, 1974; Leiter, 1974; Sudnow, 1974). Rules are indexical, i.e. context-bound, and simply do not automatically lead to decisions (Leiter, 1980; Heritage, 2013). No situation is exactly the same as another one, which means that rules are always applied "for another first time" (Garfinkel, 1967). To elaborate how a rule should be understood in a particular situation thus requires that the actor reads the context. At the same time, the actor uses the rule as an interpretive scheme to define the situation. The rule has, for example, a decisive influence on which of all details that actually characterize a situation that the actor observes and makes relevant. Indeed, these details are perceived as facts that are "out there", but it is rather that the actor actively mobilizes them. Taken together, this is what is meant by reflexivity: the rule and situation constitute one another. Contextualization is therefore an essential part of assessment and decision-making.

Implications of Formalization

As we have seen, formalization through the use of models, standards and tools is presented as an answer to how employee selection can become more efficient and fair. The benefits of formalization have been discussed earlier in this chapter but based on the aforementioned study, it also seems relevant to discuss what is likely to be lost with increased formalization.

An important question is what kind of knowledge about the candidate, the position, the working group, and the organization can be considered as legitimate. If formalization is taken to extremes, it means that the kind of knowledge that selectors in the aforementioned study used in order to make sense of and make decisions about candidates, should either be made completely explicit or not used at all. Making it completely explicit is practically impossible because each situation is unique and it is impossible to specify beforehand exactly what knowledge will be needed to make the decision or to specify it in every detail. Not using that knowledge at all, if it is even possible, would perhaps be unfortunate. One could argue that the conditions for taking reasonable and appropriate decisions will be better if one uses the knowledge to which one actually has access, for example, to evaluate information (jfr. Leiter, 1980).

A further reasoning about the risks of increased formalization relates to the "best practice versus best fit" debate that has raged within the HRM literature in recent years (see for example Boxall & Purcell, 2011). In this context, "best practice" asserts that there is a best way to conduct selection processes. It does not, for example, matter in what industry the recruiting organization operates, how big the organization is, what skills are to be recruited or how quickly the vacancy has to be filled. Large parts of the traditional selection research are based on such a "best practice" view of the selection process. However, there are others who advocate the "best fit" approach, i.e. that the selection process is adapted to, for example, institutional and economic conditions. They have shown that there are circumstances in which the selection process is perceived as less effective when it is standardized and formalized (e.g., Jewson & Mason, 1986; Scholarios & Lockyer, 1999; Lockyer & Scholarios, 2004, 2007; Nickson, Warhurst, Hurrell & Dutton, 2008). We can take the choice of selection tools as an example. Traditional selection research evaluates tools using primarily validity; and with formalization, the requirements for the use of valid tools are increased. However, it is necessary that there are many applicants for each vacancy, that it is costly to select the wrong people and that the person who is offered the job ("the best") also accepts it, for valid tools to also have high utility (Scholarios, 2009). These assumptions are far from always met, and thus it is not always the most valid tools that are the most useful ones. Instead, more informal tools such as interviews and references are more highly valued, as shown in the earlier study and in numerous others (see for example Highhouse, 2008). In these organizations, formalization is often seen as an obstacle, even if it is a politically correct one, which makes it difficult to manage the selection process in a successful way and do what's best for the business.

A third question has to do with the view on selectors. Formalization puts the focus on selection models and tools. Such a one-sided focus easily gives the impression that it is these methods that make selection decisions and that the responsibility for decisions made should be assigned to them (Newton, 1994). Perhaps that is sometimes even an argument that makes it attractive to use them. In other words, there is a risk that formalization takes the selectors out from selection decision-making. However, it is they who use the selection tools and actively assess the results and make the decisions; and to understand how decisions are made, we must focus on their sensemaking and their knowledge (Bolander & Sandberg, 2013).

In sum, there are some risks associated with an increased formalization; that selectors cannot use certain types of knowledge, that they cannot follow selection methods that they know, from experience, to work, and that they are not seen by others or do not see themselves as actors. I argue that these risks point to a simplification that is often made in the selection context.

Legitimization Grounds for Expertise in the Selection of Employees

The simplification consists in seeing formalization, including systematization and objectification, as the only alternative to the selection process as being subjective, unpredictable and shaped by coincidences, emotional whims or politically charged motives. Either selection is based on formal methods, or it relies on gut feelings. In addition, there seems to be a tendency to disparage gut feeling and perceive it as unfounded and unknowledgeable, especially in comparison with more structured approaches (Scholarios & Lockyer, 1999; Miles & Sadler-Smith, 2014).

On the basis of my studies, I would like to argue that what is widely dismissed as a gut feeling does not only include just a feeling but also professional assessment based on the knowledge of local circumstances and many years of practical experience of assessment and decision-making (Bolander & Sandberg, 2013). In other words, it is not unfounded or unknowledgeable but instead based on contextual and local, rather than theoretical and generic, knowledge (Hislop, 2008). Thus, there exist at least three different grounds for legitimization. The first is driven by formalization and is based on a theoretical and generic knowledge base. The second is driven by gut feeling and is based on a local and emotional knowledge. The third and last is driven by professional judgment and is based on a local and contextual knowledge. The latter, however, is much more difficult to make explicit than the first one, and thus harder to trust. It might seem easier to formalize and put trust in the system.

Formalization and Selection—Where Are We Today?

Formalization is by no means a new idea in the selection context. As described earlier, research on selection has been conducted for a long time, and much of the research has been based on the idea of formalization. However, it seems that it has recently gained more attention, not least due to the introduction of the ISO standard and the increasingly widespread use of scientifically validated tools. Two factors that lead to increased formalization and standardization can be highlighted. First, it seems that the tendency to formalize increases when more external actors show an interest in what is happening in the business. Second, the tendency is greater when it comes to socially important issues. A part of the answer to the question of why the interest is increasing in formalizing the selection process can be found here. Discrimination at work is probably higher up on the agenda today than ever before. In addition, the audit society causes us to set goals and document for preventive purposes, so that we can show that "all the paperwork is in place" if the decisions taken would to be questioned.

How far has the formalization of selection actually reached by this stage? Two observations may be made with regard to this question. Firstly, it is not certain that the introduction of formal methods and tools affects actual practice to any great extent. Because assessment and decision-making are elusive processes, it is still possible for those who principally wish to continue in the same way as before. The "tracks" that decision-making processes leave behind, in the form of documentation and justified decisions, can often easily be constructed ex post facto to meet requirements. Even with increased formalization, it is difficult for outsiders to determine what criteria "actually" were applied in a certain selection decision or to assess whether or not the process was properly carried out. Newton's (1994) analysis of the use of assessment centers is a good example of how the use of formal methods can cover up an informal practice, but still emphasize objectivity and fairness.

Secondly, there are domains where formalization is not increasing but where informal tools and criteria are still used. Some of them could be characterized as "pockets" where formalization tendencies have not yet reached, while others can be seen as the expression of some sort of "resistance" to formalization. A considerable number of sectors, particularly professional services, today place a greater emphasis on general and immeasurable moral criteria close to the informal, relative to the importance given to specific and measurable technical and functional criteria (Scholarios & Lockyer, 1999;

Kumra & Vinnicombe, 2008). Assessments are not only limited to criteria such as education, specific skills or specific experience but also increasingly include what is termed personal acceptability, i.e. that the person is the "right" kind of person, motivated and fits into the organization. In addition, executive search firms do not seem to be significantly affected. They do not build trust primarily by being able to show off a formalized and transparent working method; instead, other confidence mechanisms tend to be more important (Finlay & Coverdill, 2000). Another example is companies that choose unorthodox methods as being (as they consider it) more suitable to achieve their objectives by, for example, selecting from a broader recruitment base. One such method that has recently attracted considerable attention is the "auditions" or competitions that are judged by selection juries.

In this chapter, we have explored the nuances of the idea of formalization in the selection context. We have looked at the ideals on which it is based, its advantages and disadvantages and the conditions for introducing it in practice. We have seen that formalization does not always lead to the intended effects and that it may also have some unintended ones. Nevertheless, there are probably few who would argue for leaving the playing field completely open for an informal selection process, considering how it can demonstrably be abused. Rather, the point is that neither formalization, gut feeling nor the use of what we have termed contextual knowledge, does, in itself, ensure that one succeeds in selecting the expertise one is looking for. Employee selection is a fundamentally uncertain process in which important decisions are made on the basis of ambiguous and scarce information. In practice, it is probable that formal and informal selection practices exist side by side, and should do so (jfr. Boden, 1994).

Note

1 See Swedish Standards Institute, www.sis.se; International Organization for Standardization, www.iso.org.

References

Anderson, N. R. (1992). Eight decades of employment interview research: A retrospective meta-review and prospective commentary. *European Work and Organizational Psychologist*, 2, 1–32.

Boden, D. (1994). *The Business of Talk*. Cambridge: Polity Press.

Bolander, P. (2002). *Anställningsbilder och rekryteringsbeslut*. Stockholm: EFI.

Bolander, P. (2011). *Measuring Competence: A Case Study*. Paper Presented at EGOS Colloquium in Gothenburg July 6–9.

Bolander, P. & Sandberg, J. (2013). How employee selection decisions are made in practice. *Organization Studies*, 34(3), 285–311.

Boxall, P. & Purcell, J. (2011). *Strategy and Human Resource Management*. Basingstoke: Palgrave-Macmillan.

Cicourel, A. (1974). Police practices and official records. In Turner, R. (ed.), *Ethnomethodology: Selected Readings*. Harmondsworth: Penguin, 85–95.

Finlay, W. & Coverdill, J. E. (2000). Risk, opportunism, and structural holes: How headhunters manage clients and earn fees. *Work and Occupations, 27*(3), 377–405.

Garfinkel, H. (1967). *Studies in Ethnomethodology.* Engelwood Cliffs, NJ: Prentice-Hall.

Heritage, J. (2013). *Garfinkel and Ethnomethodology*: Cambridge: Polity Press.

Highhouse, S. (2008). Stubborn reliance on intuition and subjectivity in employee selection. *Industrial and Organizational Psychology, 1*(3), 333–342.

Hislop, D. (2008). Conceptualizing knowledge work utilizing skill and knowledge-based concepts. *Management Learning, 39*(5), 579–596.

Iles, P. (1999). *Managing Staff Selection and Assessment.* Buckingham: Open University Press.

Jenkins, R. (1986). *Racism and Recruitment: Managers, Organisations and Equal Opportunity in the Labour Market.* Cambridge: Cambridge University Press.

Jewson, N. & Mason, D. (1986). Modes of discrimination in the recruitment process. *Sociology, 20,* 43–63.

Kumra, S. & Vinnicombe, S. (2008). A study of the promotion to partner process in a professional services firm: How women are disadvantaged. *British Journal of Management, 19*(1), 65–74.

Leiter, K. (1974). Adhocing in the schools: A study of placement practices in the kindergartens of two schools. In Cicourel, A. (ed.), *Language Use and School Performance.* New York: Academic Press, 17–75.

Leiter, K. (1980). *A Primer on Ethnomethodology.* New York: Oxford University Press.

Lockyer, C. & Scholarios, D. (2004). Selecting hotel staff: Why best practice does not always work. *International Journal of Contemporary Hospitality Management, 16*(2), 125–135.

Lockyer, C. & Scholarios, D. (2007). The 'rain dance' of selection in construction: Rationality as ritual and the logic of informality. *Personnel Review, 36*(4), 528–548.

McCourt, W. (1999). Paradigms and their development: The psychometric paradigm of personnel selection as a case study of paradigm diversity and consensus. *Organization Studies, 20*(6), 1011–1033.

Miles, A. & Sadler-Smith, E. (2014). "With recruitment I always feel I need to listen to my gut": The role of intuition in employee selection. *Personnel Review, 43*(4), 606–627.

Newton, T. J. (1994). Discourse and agencey: The example of personnel psychology and 'assessment centres'. *Organization Studies, 15*(6), 879–902.

Nickson, D., Warhurst, C., Hurrell, S. & Dutton, E. (2008). A job to believe in: Recruitment in the Scottish volutary sector. *Human Resource Management Journal, 18*(1), 18–33.

Pritchard, K. (2010). Becoming an HR strategic partner: Tales of transition. *Human Resource Management Journal, 20*(2), 175–188.

Purcell, J., Kinnie, N., Swart, J., Rayton, B. & Hutchinson, S. (2008). *People Management and Performance*: Routledge.

Ramsay, H. & Scholarios, D. (1999). Selective decisions: Challenging orthodox analyses of the hiring process. *International Journal of Management Reviews, 1*(1), 63–69.

Sackett, P. R. & Lievens, F. (2008). Personnel selection. *Annual Review of Psychology, 59*(1), 419–450.

Salgado, J. F. (2001). Some landmarks of 100 years of scientific personnel selection at the beginning of a new century. *International Journal of Selection and Assessment, 9*(1–2), 3–8.

Sandberg, J. (2000). Understanding human competence at work: An interpretative perspective. *Academy of Management Journal, 43*(1), 9–25.

Schmidt, F. L. & Hunter, J. E. (1998). The validity and utility of selection methods in personnel psychology: Practical and theoretical implications of 85 years of research findings. *Psychological Bulletin, 124*, 262–274.

Scholarios, D. (2009). Selection. In Redman, T. & Wilkinson, A. (eds.), *Contemporary Human Resource Management*. Harlow: Financial Times/Prentice Hall, 89–116.

Scholarios, D. & Lockyer, C. (1999). Recruiting and selecting professionals: Context, qualities and methods. *International Journal of Selection and Assessment, 7*(3), 142–156.

Storey, J. (2007). *Human Resource Management: A Critical Text*: London: Thomson Learning.

Sudnow, D. (1974). Counting deaths. In Turner, R. (ed.), *Ethnomethodology: Selected Readings*. Harmondsworth: Penguin, 102–108.

Ulrich, D., Younger, J., Brockbank, W. & Ulrich, M. D. (2013). The state of the HR profession. *Human Resource Management, 52*(3), 457–471.

Weber, M. (1922/1983). *Ekonomi och samhälle: Förståendepsykologins grunder, del 1*. Lund: Argos.

Wieder, D. L. (1970). On meaning by a rule. In Douglas, J. D. (ed.), *Understanding Everyday Life: Toward the Reconstruction of Sociological Knowledge*. Chicago: Aldine, 107–135.

Wieder, D. L. (1974). *Language and Social Reality: The Case of Telling the Convict Code*. The Hauge: Mouton.

Zimmerman, D. H. (1970). The practicalities of rule use. In Douglas, J. D. (ed.), *Understanding Everyday Life: Toward the Reconstruction of Sociological Knowledge*. Chicago: Aldine, 221–238.

Zysberg, L. & Nevo, B. (2004). 'The smarts that counts?': Psychologists' decision-making in personnel selection. *Journal of Business and Psychology, 19*(1), 117–124.

11 Expressions of Expertise

Annika Schilling

In today's modern society peoples' choice of occupation is often an integrated part of their view of who they are and their place in society (Giddens, 1991). In expert occupations in particular the individual experts have often made a great investment, not least in time, to acquire the education, experience and knowledge needed in order to be allowed to enter the occupation. A lot of effort and intellectual work is needed, which also includes working on changing ones view of the world and of oneself. As a result of all this effort the choice of occupation becomes an investment in who we are. It's an investment in an identity. We can see this particularly in profession-based occupations such as architecture, law and accounting which all have in common that the practitioners have completed a specific educational program, have passed some specific knowledge tests and acquired some specific values and beliefs associated with the occupation. But also within business advisory occupations, with a less clearly defined knowledge base, the individuals' work with their self-image is a significant part of the role and crucial for being perceived as competent.

Identities in expert occupations have an extra dimension if the experts are employed or hope to be employed in so-called elite firms—those expert firms that have the best reputation and highest status within its specific field of expertise. A typical example of such an elite firm is the management-consulting firm McKinsey & Co, which for many business students is perceived as the dream employer after graduating and therefore can hand-pick the "best" individuals around the world in their recruitment. To be a part of McKinsey and to follow the development and promotion paths they prescribe becomes a life project for the consultants. In order to fit the image of the McKinsey consultant, an individual with superior personal characteristics and an elite level of competence, they need to work on shaping both their mind and their body.

The identity as an expert is thus closely intertwined with competence and expertise. Research that has looked at what competence means in the knowledge-intensive work of experts has found that formal knowledge only makes up a small part of the competence needed (Alvesson, 2001; Sandberg & Pinnington, 2009). To be and be perceived as competent for expert work the experts also need to show skills in for example analytical, social and rhetoric abilities. These skills are largely of a rather vague character and imply that the individuals use their judgment in the right way. This indicates a more complex image of what expert knowledge is and we could rather speak of people *being* competent rather than *having* competence (Sandberg & Pinnington, 2009). Competence becomes a specific way of being—to have acquired a certain identity.

In this chapter, I will portrait four expert roles: the management consultant, the IT consultant, the business lawyer and the communication consultant. The purpose with these portraits is to explore how these experts, in the context of elite firms operating in Sweden, construct different expert identities with specific characteristics and how these could contribute to a convincing image of valuable and legitimate expertise.

Identity and Image among Experts

Within organization studies, identity has been recognized as a variable that effects how people conduct their work and thus contribute to the operation of organizations. Identity can in these contexts be seen as a social product, which means that identity is created in the interaction between people in which similarities and differences are constructed (Jenkins, 2004). In work life, identity is shaped by belongingness to an organization, a particular profession or occupation or the employment in a specific hierarchical position. These make up points of comparison with others based on which the individual creates an understanding of herself and her role in the context she participates in. Through these processes the employees identify themselves with the company, their professional role and their occupation (Ashforth & Mael, 1989; Alvesson, 2000).

Both on an individual level and in organizational contexts, identity has been given an internal as well as external dimension (Mead, 1934; Hatch & Schultz, 2002). The internal dimension of identity is about the need to reflect on ones place in the world and to deal with the existential need of a stable and positive self-image. In his renounced book *Modernity and Self-Identity*, Anthony Giddens (1991) argues that in today's society in which the possible choices of who one is and can become is larger than ever before the work with the self-identity is a constant project for the individual.

In the external dimension, identity is instead about expressing one's belongingness and creating an image of oneself in the interaction with other people. Already in 1959, in his book *The Presentation of Self in Everyday Life*, Ervin Goffman wrote about how the interaction between people in their daily lives is driven by a more or less unconscious wish to present ourselves in a certain way. We do this partly through what we communicate; the words we use, tone of voice and body language; and through how we act. Goffman shows us that in the social interactions a set of social roles exist that are connected with specific expectations on how an individual in this role expresses him or herself. Through life, we take on multiple such roles that we unconsciously enact. Research illustrates that consultants manage their expressions in interactions with clients in order to convince the clients of the relevance of their expertise (Clark & Salaman, 1998).

These two dimensions of identity are also found in different studies of the professional identity of experts, in which the results show that in expert firms' identity is an important resource both for internal control and external image creation (Kärreman & Alvesson, 2004). Professional identity gives the experts instructions for how they should think, act and be in ambiguous situations and as a result contribute to reduce the uncertainty associated with expert work. Ibarra (1999) has shown how young consultants and investment bankers experiment with their professional identity in their pursuit for promotion. An important resource in this experimentation is to mimic senior colleagues. Further, in his study of the large global auditing firms Grey (1998) have found that when experts talked about being experts they rather talked about how to *be* in the professional role rather than about technical knowledge and certificates. Most noticeably, they talked about the importance of looking like you fit the part. Similar results have been found by Haynes (2011) who shows how looks, appearance and attire is closely related to professionalism both among auditors and lawyers and that the expert role therefor can be seen as having an embodied dimension. In my own studies, I have found that experts tend to have a strong tie to their professional identity through the connection to a specific way of working (Schilling, 2008). These results show us that the identity of the experts, and how they express their expert roles, contributes to defining their expertise.

Expressions of Expert Identities

Expert identity refers to the experts' understanding of self as being a part of an expert role or occupation in which work is based on specific area of expertise. The expert identities are expressed in ideas about who the experts are in terms of education and experience background, values in life in general and in relation to work, and how the specific expert role is reflected in expectations on clothes, look, attitude, personality and other embodied elements of what characterizes belongingness to a specific expert role. In order to make the identity concept more concrete I here divide expert identity into three parts: background, values and embodied expressions. These should not be seen as all-inclusive in order to define professional identity in all contexts but are chosen with the purpose to bring focus on the features highlighted by the experts themselves.

Background

The entry into most expert roles presupposes some specific education or experience base. The homogeneity of the education and experience background can however vary between expert roles, as can the degree to which these expectations are espoused. Within more established professions, such as law, auditing and architecture, there are institutionalized requirements on those who are allowed to practice the profession. For other expert occupations, there are several possible ways to acquire the competence believed to be needed for its practice. The portraits that follow are, therefore, guided by the following questions: Which education and experience background is associated with the expert role? At what point in life do individuals typically enter the expert role? What other demands are expressed for entering into the expert role?

Values

The second part that distinguishes an expert identity is the values seen as typical among the experts in the particular expert area. These values have different bases such as in institutionalized norms for the expert role in the industry at large or in more local ideas within a specific expert firm about what type of individuals fit and are attracted by the work of the particular expert role. These ideas can encompass both expressed values as well as what motivates individuals who work as this kind of expert. The portraits that follow are guided by the following questions: What is considered attractive with the work? What types of individuals are attracted to enter the expert role? How can experts reach success within the expert role?

Embodied Expressions

Embodied expressions of an expert role, such a specific appearance, attire and specific manners, can be used by the experts to convince the world that they are legitimate as experts within their specific area of expertise. Embodied expressions can both be driven by expectations in the world at large about how a specific type of expert should look and act, as well as by the experience of self-confidence and status that can derive from dressing for a high status role. The embodied expression of expertise can here be divided into two parts. First, there could be expectations on the experts' physical appearance and the views on dress codes within the expert role. Second, there could be expectations on the experts to act in accordance with specific values and thus to express a specific attitude. The portraits that follow are guided by the following additional questions: What is the espoused dress code within the profession? What attitude should the experts express in their way of acting?

Portraits of Four Expert Identities

During my studies of management consultants, IT consultants, communication consultants and business lawyers I have observed how experts describe how an individual ought to be to fit into the expert role and how that differed between the four types. The empirical material for these studies consists of interviews with representatives from these four expert roles. These representatives are or have been employed at the Stockholm offices of elite firms within these expert areas. The interviews took place over a time period between fall 2001 and spring 2012. All in all, I have interviewed 73 experts: 20 management consultants, 20 IT consultants, 18 communication consultants and 15 business lawyers.

Next, the portraits of four expert identities are drawn. These portraits are based on the words of the experts themselves. A summary of the expressions of expertise in the four expert identities can be found in Table 11.1.

The Management Consultant

Management consultant is a term with a wide meaning and thus is not easily defined. In broad terms, the management consultant is in the business of giving advice to other companies on their business, organization and strategy.

The *background* of the management consultants is typically heterogeneous with a rater un-specific experience base and without formal barriers of entry. Even if business administration tends to be the main academic training associated with management consultants, other educational backgrounds, such as in engineering, psychology or behavioral science, are also possible. The entry into the expert role does not necessarily take place at a specific age, but instead one can see both new graduates and more experienced individuals who have recently entered the field. There is, however, a tendency that large international management consulting firms, and specifically the elite firms, mainly hire young, formable individuals while the smaller firms hire more experienced and independent individuals.

The main *values* expressed among the management consultants in elite firms are to a large extent based on career focus and status. The prospect of pursuing a high status career and working with high status assignments is what is attracting individuals to the expert role. This expert role attracts ambitious and driven individuals who like the challenge of competing with others striving to climb the career ladder. The competitiveness also unites the employees internally through an emphasis on "a war" with the competing elite firms to win the clients. A successful management consultant claims to be confident and to have a wide and solid network. This is how one management consultant describes the people in the industry:

> This industry is filled with prima donnas. This is, sort of, how things work. Most people are here to boost their own ego and they think they are so damn good. And some even are. But that is the foundation of it all. You have to want it, I think. What drives this type of people is not always self-evident. It is money, it is status and appreciation or what ever.
>
> *(Management consultant)*

Table 11.1 Expressions of expertise in four expert identities

	The management consultant	The IT consultant	The business lawyer	The communication consultant
Background	Heterogeneous educational and experience background / Entry into the occupation at different ages / The organization-specific culture determines the entry barriers.	Heterogeneous experience within a limited framework. / Education in IT with possible specialization. / Business knowledge relevant in strategy, sales and project management roles. / Entry into occupation at different ages.	Homogenous educational background from (Swedish) law schools. / Almost exclusively recruitment of young, newly graduated. / Further experience besides education a merit.	Heterogeneous experience and educational background. / Politics, journalism and financial analysis/communication common fields of experience. / Entry into occupation mainly later in life. / The recruitment of younger individuals increasingly common.
Values	Career and high status assignments attract. / The expert role attracts ambitious, driven and competitive individuals. / Road to success: self-confidence, ability to sell oneself and build strong networks.	Learning and the interest in IT attract. / The expert role attracts individuals who are both interested in details and in the context. / Road to success: become skilled in IT and in cooperating with colleagues in large projects.	Career and professional development attract. / The expert role attracts high achievers who want to be acknowledged. / Road to success: ability to create trust among the clients, combined with a good analytical ability.	Interest in media and communication and the opportunity to leverage unique competence attract. / The expert role attracts individuals interested in the public debate and who want to promote communication. / Road to success: to have a large network, including key players in public opinion, and have a good understanding of the media landscape.
Embodiment	Dress code: suit and tie, but still adjust to client. / Attitude: driven, "on", charismatic and somewhat of a diva.	Dress code: unspecified, jeans, shirt and a jacket common in client meetings. / Attitude: interested in IT and in the client.	Dress code: proper, formal and conservative (dark suit for both men and women), although still adjust to client. / Attitude: social, driven and analytical.	Dress code: unspecified, as in previous occupational field. Adjust to client. / Attitude: interested in social issues and social and political awareness.

The *embodiment* of the management consultant role is dominated by the need to give clients and colleagues a trustworthy impression. The dress code is defined in terms of a suit, a tie and "neatly filed finger nails", that is, proper and well groomed. However, it is also important to adjust to the level of formality of the client. The dress code is formulated in relation to what is typical for men within the expert occupation, while it is less clear what this means for women. The attitude management consultants should have is said to be one of drive, to be "on", being charismatic and to have a demanding presence in terms of "being somewhat of a diva".

The IT Consultant

The IT consultant gives advice to companies on the use of information technology to support and develop their business. The focus of this advice can vary from integration of IT in the client company's strategic thinking to implementation and management of different technological systems and solutions. A specific feature of this expert role is the close link to the material technology that makes the service/product and it's delivery less ambiguous (Bloomfield & Danieli, 1995).

The *background* of the IT consultant is a typically heterogeneous experience base, but limited within a specific framework where both IT and business experience is a merit. The IT consultant typically has an education within IT, but it is also possible to have acquired an equivalent knowledge base through practical experience. In this expert role, the possibility to specialize within a narrow knowledge field is larger than in the other three expert roles. For example, not all IT consultants do with time learn to take on a selling or project management role. Therefor a background in business may be relevant for some who want to focus on strategic IT or project management, but it is not necessary for everyone. The entry into the expert role can take place either when young, right after university, or later in life as second career.

The *values* expressed among the IT consultants can be summarized as the joy of learning new things. The opportunity of constant learning attracts individuals with knowledge in IT to the consulting role in particular through the opportunity to face different types of issues and problems in different client organizations. Additionally IT consultants claim that they are thorough and detail-oriented in their work. Mistakes are costly and getting it right is a matter of honor. The consultant role in combination with a focus on technology attracts individuals with both an interest in the details of the technology itself, in working with IT more strategically and in working in many different contexts. A successful IT consultant is skilled in working with IT as well as having a good ability to cooperate with people with other types of knowledge in large projects. In the quote that follows, one IT consultant expresses how cooperation and trust in the competence of colleagues is valued among IT consultants.

In other types of consulting firms they spend their morning coffee break bragging about the great work they are doing stealing each other's assignments, and such. Those kinds of things don't happen here. It's amazing when it is assumed that everyone is good and competent. It is possible to work together with anyone.

(IT consultant)

The *embodiment* of the IT consultant was not mentioned much. There is no specific dress code, even though it is said to be common that people dress in jeans, a shirt and maybe a jacket. The jacket is mainly used in meetings with the clients. There is also no discussion on differences of attire between men and women, even though the description of the typical attire is based on the way men dress. The attitude IT consultants should have is to be interested, that is, interested in IT and in the clients and their problems.

The Business Lawyer

The business lawyer offers advice and assistance in legal matters to companies and organizations. Business law is one of the more standardized expert areas and it is the only expert group discussed here who is formally classified as a profession in the classical sense.

The *background* of the business lawyers is characterized by the highly regulated barriers of entry into the expert role. Business lawyers typically have a homogenous education and experience background where a degree from a law school is mandatory. Because legal work in a Swedish context largely means dealing with issues concerning Swedish law, the prime focus when recruiting is on degrees from Swedish law schools. New hires are almost exclusively made from the pool of young newly graduated law students, as individuals who have attended law school later in life are rare. Transfers between law firms have so far been less common and the main reason an employed business lawyer choses to leave the law firm is to seek employment as a corporate lawyer in a client organization. Besides the mandatory law degree, extra-curricular experiences during law school are seen as a merit for the candidates in the recruiting process. Candidates who have a double degree in law and business are of particular interest. Overall, the competition to be recruited by an elite law firm is tough.

The *values* expressed among the business lawyers focus mainly on achievement. The high competition in recruitment to the most prestigious firms make it possible for these firms to have high expectations on the candidates both in terms of academic achievements and in terms of social competence. Those who have succeeded in winning a position as a business lawyer have through this achievement proven that they can perform in accordance to the high standards and as a result, they are allowed to work with other individuals with the same abilities. Achievement therefor becomes something that defines the expert role. Career prospects and the opportunity to develop through working with increasingly challenging assignments and work tasks is said to be what attracts individuals to this expert role. Maybe not surprisingly, the interest in corporations and business issues is said to distinguish those law students who are attracted to the business law firms from the group of law students in general. The challenge of the high entry demands further targets those students who are or see themselves as high achievers and who want to prove it. It is mainly these students who are attracted by the elite business law firms. A successful business lawyer has both an excellent analytical ability and an excellent social competence because it is the combination of the two that is said to create trust with the clients. This is how one business lawyer describes how a lawyer ought to be in order to fit in the expert role.

> We, as many other business law firms, have rather high demands on our employees. Because this is the type of services we sell. It is important to have good grades and it is important to be ambitious and a driven person. We need a combination of people who are good lawyers with the ability to dig deep into things and people who are very driven to be service minded and who are willing to deliver the kind of availability our clients expect.
>
> *(Business lawyer)*

The *embodiment* of business lawyers is to a large extent marked by the expectations and perception in the world of what business lawyers are and how they look. The wish among the experts is not to deviate too much from what is expected from a business lawyer. The dress code is defined as proper, formal and conservative where a dark suit works both for men and women. For a more casual day at the desk with no client meetings, it is recommended to have more formal attire available in case an unexpected client meeting pops up. The attitude of the business lawyer should be to be social, driven and analytical.

The Communication Consultant

Communication consulting is a rather young occupation that has grown in size the last 10–20 years. A specific characteristic of the communication consultant in Sweden is the close link to the political sphere (Tyllström, 2010). The link to politics and thus also to the public debate shapes the expert identity of the communication consultant as it enables an image of civic participation.

The *background* of communication consultants can vary widely. However, there are a couple of typical background profiles. Most communication consultants have a background in either politics (for example as active in a Swedish political party or nonprofit organization), journalism (for example an experienced journalist who has made an acknowledged contribution to the field of journalism) or financial analysis or financial communication (for example someone who has realized it would be more meaningful to help companies communicate effectively instead of continuing on the financial treadmill). The entry into the expert role has so far mainly been made later in life after the individuals has acquired experience within one of these communicational occupations. Academic degrees within communication studies are increasingly common, and as a consequence, the recruitment of newly graduated persons is increasing.

The *values* of the communication consultants focus on an interest in media, communication and the public debate and public opinion. Because communication consulting often is entered into as a second career many of the individual experts have built up strong personal profiles, a good reputation and a wide network with actors in their old field. To change to a communication consultant role can be seen as a way to get a wider leverage of a unique experience and competence. To enter this expert role is also described as a way to settle down, get more freedom and improve the quality of life in general. The expert role attracts individuals who are interested in the public debate and who want to make a difference for the clients in their attempts to make themselves heard. A successful communication consultant has a wide network that includes key players for Swedish public opinion and has a good understanding of the media landscape. In the quote that follows, one communication consultant describes what is attractive with this expert role.

> One factor is that you grow through working together with extremely competent and engaged colleagues. Another factor is that you can influence. It's a really effective way to influence organizations, companies and the social development.
>
> *(Communication consultant)*

The communication consultants do not talk much about the *embodiment* of the expert role. The dress code is said to be to adjust to the client, but what this means is not developed further. It is however common that the individuals embody the position they had in their old field, as this is what in the past has contributed to their personal profile and reputation. The attitude of the communication consultants should, according to them, be to show an interest in social issues and to be socially and politically aware.

Different Ways to Convince of Expertise

If we look at the four portraits, we can see that they have a few characteristics in common. Within all four expert roles emphasis is put on the importance of hiring smart and driven individuals with a strong educational and experience base, or who, alternatively, have the potential to over time acquire the kind of experience and knowledge needed to be considered an expert under the roof of the expert firm. We can also see that the right values and attitudes toward the expert role are something that is stressed across the roles. To be considered an expert does not only require having the right factual knowledge but also to act and express oneself in a specific way. The experts' attire and what attitude they express are seen as important to win legitimacy as an expert. However, what is considered the right background and appropriate values and attitudes differs between the four expert roles. These differences are relevant for understanding how the experts within these four expert roles try to convince the world of their expertise.

The Immateriality of the Service

Experts typically work with services that are characterized by a high *level of immateriality,* as there is little to see or touch for the client because of the service having been delivered. The intended change from the advice the experts give is rather a change in the clients understanding of their own business or of the environment than in anything tangible. This specific characteristic of expert advice services implies a challenge for the experts to prove beforehand that they have expertise that will bring value to the clients if they buy their services. This is a challenge the experts need to deal with and they do this by, in the terminology of Goffman, presenting themselves in a specific way.

The level of materiality varies between the expert services discussed in this chapter. Through the link to the tangible technology IT consultants have a more concrete service than for example the management consultants whose services rather focus on changing the client's business as well as how people work and see their role in the organization. In the latter case, the most tangible element of the service might be a written report. A consequence for the management consultants' clients is that it often is hard to see what the results of the consultants' advise was and if the change was a success. In order to convince current and possible future clients of their expertise the management consultants to a higher extent than the IT consultants resort to using their external attributes to create the impression that they possess the competence of an expert. This also explains why the management consultants put more focus on how they dress and act, and being charismatic and driven in comparison to the IT consultants. It also explains why the management consultants stress the importance of high barriers to entry into the expert role as these internal processes also signal externally that the individual experts within the management consulting firms are of high quality.

We can also see how the level of immateriality plays a part in the other two expert areas. Business lawyers emphasize the importance of high grades among their new recruits partly in order to show that they have good individuals employed. It is also expected that the business lawyers adjust the way they dress to what is expected by a professional business lawyer. Successful or unsuccessful legal procedures might be less problematic to spot than the impact of management consultants' advice, but still there might be a challenge in determining what part of success or failure that depended on the competence of the lawyer or the nature of the situation. Through their link to different types of communication media, the communication consultants might have a higher level of materiality than both management consultants and business lawyers but still they emphasize the individual consultant's personal story in their efforts to convince of expertise. Recruiting individuals who have developed a good reputation already before entering this expert role is a great shortcut to convincing the world of legitimacy of communication consultants as experts.

Mirroring the Client

A second characteristic of expert services is that they are relation and interaction centered. This means that the service and the experience of its value are created in the interaction between the expert and the client. The interaction between expert and client also trigger identity work among the experts in which both their self-identity and image is defined. A central process in this identity work is what Hatch & Schultz (2002) call *mirroring*. Mirroring means that the image others have of an individual or an organization (in this case an expert role) become a mirror in which they confirm their self-identity. The image in the mirror informs the experts of their role and status in relation to others. The relationship with the clients becomes important here as the demand for the expert services confirms the value of what the experts have to offer. In order to get the image and self-identity to match mirroring also means adjusting self-expressions to what the clients expect and are familiar with. The identity the experts express is therefore both a reflection and a result of the myth about the expert and of the identity of the client.

Representatives of the four expert identities interact with different roles in the client organizations, which means that the mirror they face in these relationships differs. In management consulting and business law, the business is built on longer client relationships where happy clients create opportunities for further assignments and for word-of-mouth recommendations to new clients. To build and nurture relationships with "the business elite", individuals in top positions in the larger corporations in Sweden, is a central part of the expert role and the responsibility of this task is given to more senior experts as they climb the career ladder and develop professionally. As a result, the more senior management consultants and business lawyers often work in close cooperation with CEOs or individuals on other high positions in the client organizations. One part of nurturing these relationships is to build trust through fellowship and solidarity between expert and client representative. The experience of fellowship and solidarity in the relationship could be created through emulating the client both in terms of expressed values and in embodiment, such as in attire and manners. In the identity of the management consultants and the business lawyers, we can see results of this process in a more formal dress code, a self-confident lingo, career focus and an elite life style. Business lawyers deviate from the management consultants as their legal services, with a unique formalized knowledge base, give them a power advantage over the client that could be experienced as intimidating for the clients. To compensate for the risk of the clients feeling hostile in these situations the business lawyers emphasize the importance of being sympathetic and socially competent.

IT consultants have a different relationship to their clients. The different roles in IT consulting tend to be more specialized, and far from all consultants meet representatives from the client on a day-to-day basis. Only individuals with a role in sales or in project management in larger projects interact with people on top positions in the client organizations. For others it is more common to interact with individuals on operational or middle management level and specifically with people in the clients' IT departments. Therefor IT consultants do in general not have the same need to constantly relate to the client in everything they do. When they do interact with the client it is with individuals who express different attitudes and lifestyles than the business elite. In the identity of the IT consultants, this relationship is expressed in a more relaxed relationship to style and dress codes where an adjustment is made only in certain situations. We can also see how this relationship mirrors an interest in the technology as the focus of work rather than in career advancement.

Just as management consultants and business lawyers, communication consultants build their business on relationships with individuals in top positions in the Swedish society. However, unlike the other expert roles the relationship with the clients is only one in a network of relationships that is central to the work of the communication consultants. The relationships with opinion leaders, such as journalists, newspaper editors and politicians, are part of the communication consultants' service offering. The social network has been accumulated over a long career and the communication consultants can use them to help their clients reach out with their message. While the clients may come and go, the relationships within the broader network are more long term. For these reasons, the mirror the communication consultants face is rather in the interaction with the opinion leaders. In the identity of the communication consultants we can see how this is expressed in how the consultants often have a background in another communication field and in how they have an attitude, style of dress and a lifestyle that is common within this previous field. We can also see how the interest in social and political issues and the social and political awareness of these experts reflect the relationship with opinion leaders.

Expertise, Image and Identity

In this chapter, I have tried to show how expertise, image and identity are closely linked in the work of experts. To have expertise and to be considered competent do not only entail possessing the formal knowledge associated with the field of expertise but also to a high extent to be able to take on the identity an expert within a specific field is expected to have. To be an expert is a project in which the individual adjusts his or her values and embodied expressions to convince the world that he or she has expertise and is a legitimate member of the expert role. Relationships are also part of this project as they mirror the identity made possible for the expert.

To be an expert thus also includes involving oneself personally and to present oneself in alignment with what is considered right and proper for the specific expert role. Even though some commonalities can be seen between the experts we have seen how what is considered right in terms of background, values and embodiment differs between the expert roles. My argument is here that these differences to some extent can be explained by differences between the expert areas in terms of the immateriality of the service and the mirroring of the client.

References

Alvesson, M. (2001). Knowledge work: Ambiguity, image and identity. *Human Relations*, *54*(7), 863–886.

Alvesson, M. (2000). Social identity and the problem of loyalty in knowledge intensive companies. *Journal of Management Studies*, *37*(8), 1101–1123.

Ashforth, B. & Mael, F. (1989). Social identity theory and the organization. *Academy of Management Review*, *14*(1), 20–39.

Bloomfield, B. & Danieli, A. (1995). The role of management consultants in the development of information technology: The indissoluble nature of socio-political and technical skills. *Journal of Management Studies*, *32*(1), 23–46.

Clark, T. & Salaman, G. (1998). Creating the "right" impression: Towards a dramaturgy of management consultancy. *The Service Industries Journal*, *18*(1), 18–38.

Giddens, A. (1991). *Modernity and Self-Identity: Self and Society in the Late Modern Age*. Stanford: Stanford University Press.

Goffman, E. (1959). *The Presentation of Self in Everyday Life*. London: Penguin.

Grey, C. (1998). On being a professional in a "Big Six" firm. *Accounting, Organizations and Society*, *23*(5/6), 569–587.

Hatch, M. J. & Schultz, M. (2002). The dynamics of organizational identity. *Human Relations*, *55*(8), 989–1018.

Haynes, K. (2011). Body beautiful? Gender, identity and the body in professional service firms. *Gender, Work and Organization*, *19*(5), 489–507.

Ibarra, H. (1999). Provisional selves: Experimenting with image and identity in professional adaptation. *Administrative Science Quarterly*, *44*, 764–791.

Jenkins, R. (2004). *Social Identity*. London: Routledge.

Kärreman, D. & Alvesson, M. (2004). Cages in tandem: Management control, social identity, and identification in a knowledge intensive firm. *Organization*, *11*(1), 149–175.

Mead, G. H. (1934). *Mind, Self, & Society: From the Standpoint of a Social Behaviorist*. Chicago: University of Chicago Press.

Sandberg, J. & Pinnington, A. (2009). Professional competence as ways of being: An existential ontological perspective. *Journal of Management Studies*, *46*(7), 1138–1170.

Schilling, A. (2008). *Kan konsulter fusionera? En studie av betydelse av identitet vid en fusion mellan konsultföretag.* Stockholm: EFI.

Tyllström, Anna. (2010). PR-konsultbranschens framväxt i Sverige. In Pallas, J. & Strannegård, L. (eds.), *Företag och medier.* Malmö: Liber, 169–191.

12 Career Factory and Expert House—Two Development Environments for Experts

Andreas Werr and Annika Schilling

Introduction

The expert organization is built and developed in a field of tension between two distinct markets—the client market and the labor market. On the client market the organization offers the expertise of its employees in competition with other expert organizations, and often also in competition with experts within the client organization. On the labor market, the expert organization competes with other expert organizations and with client organizations for the most attractive experts. They also compete with the experts' ability and often desire to start their own business.

On the client market the main means of competition include the employees' collective competence, experience and skill to live up to the clients' expectations and to some extent price. On the labor market, the main means of competition are instead the opportunities for development, prestige and to some extent remuneration (Maister, 1993). For many expert organizations within for example management and engineering consulting it is the labor market rather than the client market that restricts their growth.

In this context, the expert organization's strategic challenge is to find a sustainable mix of offerings to the customer and labor markets. An organization, that for example, competes by offering creative expert services that can be standardized only to a limited extent, will require more creativity, motivation and competence from its employees than an organization offering a more standardized service (Løwendahl, 2005). In order to be attractive to such experts, the organization must be able to offer them an attractive and competitive environment in terms of prestige, remuneration, professional challenges, development opportunities, etc. (Maister, 1993)

Because professional development in expert organizations is usually closely linked to the work itself—the client projects—the customer and labor markets become even more closely linked together. It is the expert organization's client projects that determine its ability to attract and develop experts, while, at the same time, it is the experts that create the conditions for the successful delivery of these projects (Fosstenløkken, Løwendahl & Revang, 2003).

To develop experts is thus a key challenge for the expert organization—both as a means of developing their ability to deliver assignments that produce satisfied customers but also in order to create an environment that current and future employees find stimulating and attractive, that helps the organizations attract and retain key experts. In this chapter, we will therefore look at the development environments that expert organizations offer to their experts. More specifically, we will focus on expert organizations' personnel concepts (Alvesson, 2004), i.e. organizations' perceptions of the kind of experts one wants to attract and how to design the organization, and especially the HR practices, to fit those individuals. The chapter is based on a study of Human Resource Management practices in 23 expert organizations in eight different industries: auditing, architecture, communications consulting, IT consulting, law, marketing, management consulting and engineering consulting. In each industry, the individual responsible for HR was interviewed in a, relative to the industry, small, medium and large company. On some occasions, especially in large companies, the responsible person for HR was an HR specialist, sometimes it was an expert in the respective field (e.g., architect or consultant), and sometimes a CEO.

The Expertise That Is to be Developed

A discussion about how experts develop in organizations requires both an understanding of what and who is to be developed. We will begin with the first aspect. The nature of expert knowledge has been discussed in detail in previous chapters. A common denominator in these discussions has been the complex nature of expert knowledge. Expert knowledge is more than a clearly definable body of knowledge. The explicit knowledge base can be more or less well defined. In the "classic" professions, law or audit, you find well-defined requirements for what an expert should be able to do, and to some extent how one should behave. If one does not comply with these requirements, one cannot call oneself "attorney" or "auditor". However, it is not this knowledge that makes someone an "expert". This is more about abilities and skills that are difficult to define. Furusten (Chapter 9), for example, focuses on the experts' ability to improvise when faced with a specific problem. Näslund and Pemer (Chapter 8) emphasize the ability to create confidence as key to the experts' ability to establish themselves as experts; and Schilling (Chapter 11) notes their ability to build an image and identity as experts.

Although experts often have a formal knowledge base (which, however, can be more or less well defined), it is thus their ability to apply this knowledge in solving complex problems in practice, often in social interaction with other experts and representatives of the client organization, that makes them successful experts (Schön, 1983). This is an ability that is primarily reached through experience. It is through one's own mistakes and successes, and by observing and discussing actual cases with colleagues, that the experts build this ability. To develop experts in organizations is thus largely about creating opportunities for new experiences, to observe and collaborate with colleagues in different contexts and to discuss actual challenges with other experts (Schön, 1983; Brown & Duguid, 1991).

The Expert That Is to Be Developed

In order to understand how experts in organizations are developed we also need to understand something about the nature of the expert. What is it that drives experts to develop (or not develop) themselves? To seek new experiences, conversations with other experts and other new knowledge?

A common denominator in much of the literature on experts is that they are driven by the pursuit of development and learning. It is the professional challenges that attract: the intractable problems, the larger, more complex projects with the more prestigious clients, etc. The literature, however, provides two rather different images of the drivers behind this strive to develop.

The Classic Expert

A first image of the expert, which is provided by the sociology of professions (Freidson, 1984; Abbott, 1988) focuses on the expert's interest and identification with a particular area of knowledge. The expert is depicted as passionate about their (often specialized) knowledge area and strongly motivated by the opportunity to work with the challenges in this area. This often also means contributing to society as the classical professions all fulfill important societal functions such as upholding the judicial system (for the lawyer) or contributing to a sound business environment (for the auditor). It is the satisfaction of working with these problems rather than any other (monetary or career-related) reward that drives them (Løwendahl, 2005; Gorman & Sandefur, 2011). They keep up to date with the development of knowledge in the field through extensive professional networks that can go beyond organizational boundaries and strive to be part of the development of knowledge in their field. Gaining recognition as an expert in a particular area is a major driving force. The organization where they are employed is, in this context, of secondary importance. It becomes a vehicle for the experts in the construction of their expertise, but if they are offered better opportunities elsewhere, they happily accept them. Gouldner (1957) makes a distinction in this respect between professionals of various kinds—"cosmopolitans" and "locals". Cosmopolitans are characterized by having a low level of loyalty to the organization in which they are employed, a great commitment to their specific professional knowledge and skills and that they compare themselves with, and orient toward, other professionals within their guild. Locals, on the other hand, primarily identify themselves with the organization they work for, have less commitment to their professional knowledge and skills, and orient toward individuals within the organization.

The classical professional is a cosmopolitan. In view of the earlier discussed orientation and focus on expert knowledge, this type of expert has a great need for independence and autonomy. Only other experts have the legitimacy to judge the expert's work in connection with managerial control and evaluation and the only legitimate evaluation criteria are those that derive from the norms and criteria of the profession (Alvesson, 2004)

The Career Expert

As an alternative to the classic (and according to some, romantic) image of the professional expert, it has been suggested that the expert's motivation to develop is less about a commitment to contributing to society or a deep loyalty to a particular field of knowledge and more about a way to maintain a positive self-image. Based on studies of large, global professional service firms such as management consultancies, law firms and investment banking firms, that have a reputation for recruiting the most intelligent and hard-working elite on the labor market, Maister (1993) suggests that people in these organizations are driven by a need for continuous challenges in order to maintain their self-image. The challenges are being sought out for the satisfaction gained from mastering them, to once again prove to oneself and the environment that they can do it. Maister (1993) refers to such people, who he claims typically are attracted to the elite kind of expert organizations as "insecure overachievers". For these experts, it is not primarily the satisfaction of working with a challenging task that is sought but rather the satisfaction of having mastered it successfully. Signals that show that the expert is on the "right" path are key here. Clear goals to evaluate this against, as well as frequent and clear feedback, are therefore requested and appreciated. What these goals actually are is less important. They can, of course, relate directly to the profession and area of expertise (the quality of work), but might also be more commercially oriented (such as utilization or sales targets). The employees orient themselves toward targets set up by the organization (rather than the profession). Loyalty is directed toward the organization. The career expert is a "local" rather than a "cosmopolitan" in Gouldner's (1957) terms.

While the traditional image of the expert assumes a tension between bureaucratic/organizational goals and professional goals (Alvesson, 2004), the relationship between these objectives is, according to the alternative view of the expert, unproblematic, because the professional goals have weakened. This is supported by research that shows that the professional values of the classic professions have lost ground over a long period of time in favor of a more commercial orientation (Gorman & Sandefur, 2011).

This orientation to other than professional goals is also shown in studies of why students choose to study, for example, business or law. It appears that it is not primarily the subject itself, the expert area, which attracts. Instead, especially of business students, career motives were central (Schleef, 2000).

Two Development Environments for Expertise and Experts

Although experts also develop through training programs, courses, seminars and other formal development initiatives, their main development takes place by being confronted with challenging tasks and by discussing and solving them with others. Thus, expertise and experts are primarily cultivated in day-to-day work. Consequently, we need to understand how work is organized and managed in order to create a sustainable mix of offerings to the customer and labor markets. Subsequently we will call such a combination "personnel concept" (Alvesson, 2004). A personnel concept captures an organization's idea of what kind of people it intends to attract and how the organization is designed to meet their specific characteristics in ways that make the organization attractive to them, while at the same time motivating them to contribute to the organization's objectives. Central aspects of the personnel concept comprise both the nature of the work and its organization and the central HR processes recruitment, competence development, evaluation/performance management, reward systems, and the career system.

Our study of 23 expert organizations in eight industries shows that there appear to be two personnel concepts that provide different environments to cultivate expertise and experts. These two environments represent different ways of looking at both the expertise and the expert. The first of these environments we call the Career Factory. It provides an integrated approach to the development of the expert with a clear career and feedback structure. The second environment, the Expert House, offers experts a context for qualified problem solving and the personal development of its expertise. These two environments are summarized in Table 12.1 and are described further next.

Table 12.1 Two personnel concepts in expert organizations—Career Factory and Expert House

	Career Factory	*The Expert House*
Recruitment	*Directly from education* "hungry" "ambitious" "driven" *Focus on "the best" (grades)* "Career expert"	*Experienced experts* *Recruitment through networks* *Focus on commitment to and position in the "profession"/expert area* *The traditional expert*
Competence development	*Formal; well-defined package* *In assignments*	*In assignments; challenging projects* *Training according to need*
Performance management	*Frequent* *Formal* *Multidimensional (focusing on contributions to the organization)*	*Yearly* *Informal* *Customers' and colleagues' feedback most important*
Reward system	*Fixed wage* *Performance-based bonuses*	*Fixed wage* *Profit sharing*
Career path	*Well-defined career ladder* "Up or Out"	*Flat structure, changing positions of authority* *Hierarchy of projects* *Career across organizations*
Work organization	*Hierarchically organized projects; mix of experienced and less experienced people*	*Multidisciplinary projects, often only one person/discipline*
Examples	*Large law firms* *Large management consulting firms* *Large auditing firms*	*Large and small architect firms* *Large and small engineering consultancies* *Large and small advertising agencies* *Smaller management consulting firms*

The Career Factory

The Career Factory is a development environment that develops its experts "from scratch". *Recruitment* primarily focuses on young, newly educated individuals, preferably from reputable schools where the firms attempt to establish an image among students of only recruiting "the best". What the organizations look for is good grades, but emphasis is also placed on personal qualities, where "ambition" to be "hungry" and "driven" are emphasized qualities. What is offered to these people, who represent what was described earlier as "career experts", is an environment where they can find an outlet for their ambition in a clear and well-defined career development. It is precisely the well-defined career ladder which is seen as a key to motivation and development in this environment:

> Those who start out as consultants at [MC (L)] are extremely development-oriented and want to do well. Basically, they have always been the best ones in school and they want to be the best also when they enter the business world. Of course, they want to make a career. They want to advance—either to get the experience in order to be promoted and move on or to become a partner, get more responsibility and all those things. [. . .] The biggest motivation is to be promoted. No one knows what your pay check is, but everyone can see that you got promoted and have more responsibility.
>
> *(Large management consultancy)*

> For us, this career and competence model is important. Because, the reason that you want to work at [IT (M)] is development. And if we do not manage to give all employees development, then they leave us. Consultants are usually quite ambitious people who are driven by this opportunity for development.
>
> *(Medium-sized IT consultancy)*

> One is rewarded by developing and advancing on the career ladder, that one is part of a career path. A type of promotion is climbing the ladder.
>
> *(Large law firm)*

To support the experts' rapid development, they are usually offered well-defined *competence development programs* in which the prospective experts are given a toolbox for development in the current role or as preparation for new roles. These education programs are usually delivered internally by the more experienced people in the organization. A large part of competence development also takes place in the day-to-day work, in which the Career Factory is organized in relatively large, hierarchically organized projects, where more experienced experts are responsible for the management and supervision, while the less experienced act in apprentice roles, where they are continually given more responsibility.

Performance management is typically performed after each project where the experts receive detailed feedback on their performance in the project and on a more general level at least every 6 months. This feedback is well structured and linked to the requirements of each career level. Development needs for promotion are also discussed in this context. The evaluation criteria are often wide-ranging and cover, in addition to the activities in customer projects, aspects such as skills, attitudes, participation in the organization's social activities and contributions to colleagues. It is, to a great extent, the expert as an "organizational member" rather than independent professional that is being evaluated. Several sources of information are used, including the manager, colleagues and customers.

The reward system in the Career Factory is closely linked to the evaluation of the individual, with the variable part of remuneration being linked to the results of the evaluations. The higher up you go in the organization, the greater the variable part in remuneration. Typically, it was also commercially (rather than professionally) oriented criteria that formed the basis for the variable remuneration such as sales goals or utilization rates.

To clarify the development paths for its employees, organizations that represent the Career Factory model have well-defined *career paths* with up to six different steps. The time between one career step and the next is also well defined and communicated and normally comprises two-three years. Also, criteria for promotion are well defined and relate to the organization's performance management system.

Although none of the studied organizations representing the Career Factory development environment had an explicit "up-or-out" career policy, there appeared to be limited possibilities to stay on a certain level of the career ladder. There were possibilities to take a "break" in connection with, for example, parental leave or illness, but not advancing without such reasons was implicitly perceived as a signal to find a job elsewhere. This was clearly illustrated in large law firms where the decision not to promote someone to partner usually led to that person leaving the organization:

> Some already have external offers when talks about partnerships take place and there are those who thrive and develop in the firm about a year after a negative partnership decision. [. . .] But most usually quit within a year after such a decision.
>
> *(Large law firm).*

Those who quit usually move to a position in a client organization. Nevertheless, it also happens that they start their own firm or go to a competitor. The Career Factory model was primarily found among management consultants, law firms and PR consultants.

The Expert House

The Expert House is a development environment that targets a different kind of individual—the kind of person we described earlier as the "classic expert". In the Expert House, *recruitment* focuses on experts with various levels of experience that show a strong commitment to their field of expertise. The networks and the current employees' knowledge of the industry were important channels to identify potential new recruits. Among the architect firms, it was, for example described how they identified and kept track of talents for future recruitment already among students in architecture school. The individuals being sought were described as being motivated by an environment that gave them the opportunity to work on interesting and challenging assignments in which they could both demonstrate and gain appreciation for their expertise, but also further develop this:

> The standard architect or the common man in the architectural profession is motivated by being part of a development. To constantly develop. To try out new things and learn new things and to do good work. It means that we need . . . we cannot put someone in a corner and have them draw doors for five years. That does not work. Then they are soon gone. They must feel that they are becoming better and better architects.
> *(Small architectural office)*

> I would probably prefer that you are motivated by the customer base you have, that you want to create great stuff for the client. That this is what motivates you.
> *(Large advertising company).*

Even if organizations here focus on "development" as a central aspect of the personnel concept, like in the Career Factory environment, it is a different kind of development—a development toward a better "expert" rather than a move toward the next notch in the career ladder. To enhance the ability as "experts" is again seen as closely linked to the actual work performed, where the projects worked on are seen as the central vehicle to skills development as well as the experts' motivation. Unlike in the Career Factory, projects in Expert Houses were often smaller and contained several different skills rather than varying levels of similar skills. This reduced the opportunities for less experienced employees to take an assistant or apprentice role to develop their skills. Instead, they were responsible for smaller projects and gradually worked their way up to the larger and more important projects.

Formal competence *development programs* are rare in Expert Houses. Competence development beyond on the job training is often described as driven by the individual's own initiative. The financial resources to take an education outside the organization are usually made available if an employee wants to develop him or herself in a specific field.

Performance management in the Expert House is usually more informal and evaluation less frequent than in the Career Factory. Typically, performance reviews are held annually (at least according to plan—it's not always they are actually carried out, which is not perceived as a major problem). The criteria used are often less clear and well thought through than in the Career Factory. They are dominated by qualitative aspects of the experts' work and their skills. What is instead more important is customer appreciation and colleagues' reviews both from within and outside the organization. In line with the aforementioned "classical" experts' more cosmopolitan orientation, employees in the Expert House seek appreciation within the expert field. This is what gives satisfaction.

As with the performance management system in the Expert House, the formal *reward system* is generally less well developed. Variable elements of remuneration are rare. Profit sharing exists in the employee-owned organizations, but is rarely related to any performance criteria.

Well-defined *career paths* are often absent in the organizations that represent the Expert House. The organizations are flat and the experts can have different roles in different projects depending on their scope and the expert's relationship with the customer. An expert can thus be the project manager of one project and subordinate project staff in another. Typically, the more senior employees work on the larger and more important projects. This is not, however, something that is reflected in any formal roles or titles. There are also opportunities to develop in different directions within the organization. Within an engineering consulting company, employees were offered the choice to develop toward technological specialization, project management or general management. For most, however, the driving force is to strengthen their position in the expert field and win the appreciation of colleagues (both within and outside their own organization) rather than have a "career" in a traditional sense.

> It's pretty flat, [. . .] but it is of course much about, I think, that you become more knowledgeable, that should be the kick, that I get bigger assignments or get to manage assignments or something like that. I would probably say that is the driving force for most.
>
> *(Section manager, large engineering consultancy)*

> There is no career here. Ha-ha! The only thing there is, is that you get responsibility for more interesting and larger projects. It is a kind of career. There are no titles or so.
>
> *(CEO small architect firm)*

Motivation in the Expert House is less about climbing a well-defined career ladder and more about moving between increasingly challenging projects and, through this, achieving the respect of colleagues. In order to achieve this, staff are often willing to change employers. Mobility between Expert

Houses in the same industry is therefore greater than between Career Factories.

We primarily found the Expert House model among the more aesthetically oriented industries such as architecture and advertising. In addition, the Expert House model was found among engineering consultants.

The Distribution and Consequences of the Development Contexts

It has often been argued that knowledge workers, or experts, as we have called them in this book, have special properties as employees. In order to make experts thrive, develop, and be productive, organizations need to adapt to these characteristics. The starting point of this chapter has been that the expert organizations' ability to make these adaptations is an important condition for their survival. Meanwhile, the understanding of the experts' specific characteristics has often been simplistic, as well as the understanding of how organizations best address these characteristics.

The point of departure for this chapter was that expert knowledge is a kind of knowledge that has a formal and explicit dimension, the importance of which varies between fields of expertise, but which to a large extent is tacit and experience based. This means, that if we want to understand how expertise is developed, we must understand in what way the experts are given the opportunity and are motivated to develop their expertise in their daily work. As a basis for this, we identified two images of the "expert"— the classic expert and the career expert who were found to thrive in two distinct personnel concepts found in expert organizations.

The Career Factory and the Expert House represent two, internally consistent personnel concepts that offer a stimulating and challenging environment for experts, but do so in very different ways. We explained this earlier as that they target different types of experts with different motivations. While the Career Factory is an attractive and stimulating environment for the career expert, the Expert House offers an attractive environment for the classic expert. So, in which organizations can we find the respective personnel concepts?

If we take a closer look at the 23 companies in eight industries that formed the basis for the current study, we find that both the expertise and the size of the organization appear to affect the incidence of the different personnel concepts (see Figure 12.1). In terms of expertise, it appears that there is a predominance of the Expert House in the more aesthetic and technical areas. We found the Expert House personnel concept in both architect firms and advertising agencies, regardless of size. However, also among engineering consultants the Expert House personnel concept was dominant. Within the larger organizations, in these areas of expertise, there were constant discussions about adopting more of the Career Factory concept with clearer

Expert Area

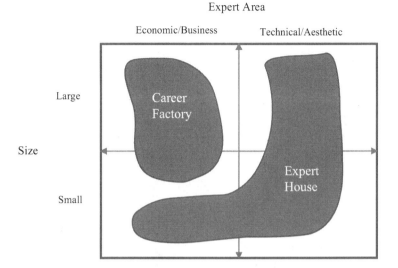

Figure 12.1 Prevalence of different personnel concepts.

performance management and more well-defined career paths, but the spread of these initiatives was still limited.

The Career Factory, on the other hand, we primarily found in connection to what could be called the "economic/business" expert areas, i.e. management consultants, PR consultants, IT consultants, accounting firms and law firms. The large organizations in these areas of expertise all applied a clear Career Factory personnel concept.

However, the personnel concepts were not only linked to the area of expertise but also to the size of the organization, where smaller organizations in the economic/business areas of expertise tended to follow more the Expert House personnel concept. In these cases, this was often marketed actively as an alternative to the Career Factory personnel concept to attract experts with a more traditional rather than career oriented focus.

This suggests certain types of experts dominate in different areas of expertise. The classic expert seems to dominate the aesthetic and technical areas of expertise while there is room for both types of experts in the economic/business areas of expertise. In the latter case, however, with a certain dominance of the career expert, who is common in the most prestigious, large organizations in the market which have also grown the most in recent decades (FEACO, 2009).

The increasing dominance of the Career Factory model, particularly in the economic/business domain of expertise, indicates a changing view of the expert and expert knowledge. Less emphasis is placed on traditional values such as the experts' autonomy and their loyalty to the expert area and more emphasis is placed on the experts' ability to sell their expertise—both internally to colleagues in the organization and externally to customers. The ability to create satisfied customers is what is in focus, skills that relate to social skills and an ability to "improvise" (see Chapter 9) rather than any deep expertise. In the Career Factory, expertise has become a means rather than an end in itself. Expertise is a means for the organization to generate an economic surplus (Teece, 1998) and for the individual expert to reach a certain status and standard of living (Schleef, 2000).

There has long been a debate within the sociology of professions where this development has been described as *de-professionalization* (Gorman & Sandefur, 2011), where professional autonomy is replaced by administrative control and policy instruments, and where professional goals are replaced by economic objectives and restrictions. This de-professionalization is seen as a threat to the professions and their unique role and position in society, and is expected to be actively counteracted by the experts. However, the increasing popularity of the Career Factory among at least some experts shows that for some—the career experts—this constitutes an attractive environment that is actively being sought out. Thus, it is by no means self-evident that experts oppose attempts at structuring, monitoring and performance management (Gorman & Sandefur, 2011).

Furthermore, we cannot escape the fact that the de-professionalization which is considered to follow from a Career Factory personnel concept has enabled global expert organizations' capacity to exploit the combined experience of thousands of experts all over the world in the solution of their (global) clients' problems. The organizational structures and systems here create the ability to coordinate expertise and problem solving across geographical distances and the ability to deliver this problem solving around the world to global clients (Werr & Stjernberg, 2003).

The global Career Factories have also developed a very attractive offer to the labor market, where they usually top the list of the most attractive employers for students at various elite educations, especially in business, but also in different engineering educations. They offer a well-defined career path that fosters students to good employees, viable in not only their own but also other organizations. It is the ability to translate expertise to business rather than the expertise itself that is rewarded by the career system, which means that their skills will have a wide scope. It is, for example, shown in a study of students at the Stockholm School of Economics, that the large management consulting organizations—with the typical Career Factory personnel concepts—are the most popular employers among students, but they are also those employers students expect to stay with the shortest time. They are thus seen as a stepping-stone for other careers rather than a career in itself.

The Career Factory is thus an effective delivery system of expertise, which attracts an elite in the labor market. At the same time, important characteristics, which have long been associated with expertise and expert organizations and represented in the Expert House, have moved out of focus. It seems that the Career Factory personnel concept is the one that increasingly dominates expert organizations. This does not mean that the Expert House model will disappear—it will always be attractive to some experts, and there will always be customers who prefer their genuine loyalty to expertise. Nonetheless, the spread of the model, especially among smaller organizations, as well as organizations in the more aesthetic areas of expertise which often act quite locally, suggests that this personnel concept is under some pressure from the Career Factory, which appears better equipped to meet the increased demands for efficiency, large-scale operations, explicit quality assurance, global knowledge sharing and monitoring, requirements that are becoming increasingly important as the buyers of experts becomes professionalized (cf. Chapter 8). We will conclude with some reflections on the implications of this increasing dominance of the Career Factory model.

The classic expert organization, which shares many characteristics with the Expert House, was organized as a partnership with experts as owners and solidary liability for their colleagues' professional practice. External ownership of legal firms was for example long banned in England. The purpose of this form of ownership was to place the interest of the expertise at the forefront and highlight the experts' societal function (Greenwood & Empson, 2003). The experts' advice should not be clouded by some short-term profit interests or career ambitions and be genuinely "impartial".

The Career Factory personnel concept could lead to a depletion of expertise in two dimensions—one more cognitive and ethical. Related to the cognitive dimension, the Career Factory attracts individuals with high ambitions and rewards them for their ability to apply their skills to make the customer happy—because a satisfied customer will come back and further recommend the expert, creating financial success. Too much specialization in a field of knowledge is, however, often counterproductive, because that is not something that the customer is willing to pay for. In contrast, success depends on the expert's social skills to interact and build trust with the customer (Näslund, 2012; see also Chapter 7) rather than their deep expertise in a particular field (although this obviously helps to a certain degree). The Career Factory thus rewards other abilities than in-depth expertise in the own field of expertise.

The Career Factory, with its focus on economic viability and individual career success, further risks eroding the ethical dimension of expertise. What is "true" or "false" is less interesting than what the customer wants to hear in order to buy a specific service—or extend it. We would in no way suggest that Career Factories systematically act unethically, but scandals such as Enron, where accountants and consultants systematically concealed maladministration in the organization to protect their business interests, give reason to reflect on the ethical implications of the Career Factory personnel concept.

Career Factories, with their focus on the organization as the experts' primary source of identification, weaken experts' identification with the expert field and the collegial control mechanisms that have been identified as central to the traditional experts. The loosening of traditionally well-defined areas of expertise (such as law) and the lack of clear boundaries around newer areas of expertise (e.g., management consulting) as well as the globalization of many sectors of expertise, lead to an increasing lack of uniform standards for ethical behavior of experts and difficulties to follow these up. The Career Factories, with their control and monitoring systems have attempted to take on the role as the guarantor of expertise, particularly in the areas of expertise where clear quality standards are missing (e.g., management consulting; see Chapter 2), often with success, but as the example of Enron in the beginning of the 21st century with the auditor/consultant Arthur Andersen demonstrates, not always. Here, the auditors' unprofessional audit led to one of USAs largest corporate scandals and the disappearance of one of the world's largest auditing firms.

References

Abbott, A. (1988). *The System of Professions.* Chicago: University of Chicago Press.

Alvesson, M. (2004). *Kunskapsarbete och kunskapsföretag.* Malmö: Liber.

Brown, J. S. & Duguid, P. (1991). Organizational learning and communities-of-practice: Toward a unified view of working, learning and innovation. *Organization Science, 2*(1), 40–57.

FEACO. (2009). *Survey of the European Management Consultancy Market 2009/2010.* Brussels: FEACO.

Fosstenløkken, S. M., Løwendahl, B. R. & Revang, Ö. (2003). Knowledge development through client interaction: A comparative study. *Organization Studies, 24*(6), 859–879.

Freidson, E. (1984). The changing nature of professional control. *Annual Review of Sociology, 10*, 1–20.

Gorman, E. H. & Sandefur, R. L. (2011). "Golden Age," quiescence, and revival: How the sociology of professions became the study of knowledge-based work. *Work and Occupations, 38*(3), 275–302.

Gouldner, A. W. (1957). Cosmopolitans and locals: Toward an analysis of latent social roles I. *Administrative Science Quarterly, 2*(3), 281–306.

Greenwood, R. & Empson, L. (2003). The professional partnership: Relic or exemplary form of governance? *Organization Studies, 24*(6), 909–933.

Løwendahl, B. R. (2005). *Strategic Management of Professional Service Firms* (3rd edition). Copenhagen: Copenhagen Business School Press.

Maister, D. (1993). *Managing the Professional Service Firm.* New York: Free Press.

Näslund, L. (2012). *The Leap of Faith.* Stockholm: Stockholm School of Economics.

Schleef, D. (2000). "That's a good question!" Exploring motivations for law and business school choice. *Sociology of Education, 73*(3), 155–174.

Schön, D. (1983). *The Reflective Practitioner—How Professionals Think in Action.* New York: Basic Books.

Teece, D. J. (1998). Capturing value from knowledge assets: The new economy, markets for know-how, and intangible assets. *California Management Review, 40*(3), 55–79.

Werr, A. & Stjernberg, T. (2003). Exploring management consulting firms as knowledge systems. *Organization Studies, 24*(6), 881–908.

13 Organizing Expertise in the Professional Service Firm— Meritocracy in Theory and Practice

Savita Kumra and Andreas Werr

The Meritocratic Ideal of Organizing Expertise

A key organizing principle of expertise in the contemporary expert society is the principle of meritocracy. The meritocratic ideal is defined by Farber & Sherry (1995) as

> positions in society should be based on the abilities and achievements of the individual rather than on characteristics such as family background, race, religion, or wealth. This ideal requires that merit be objective in the sense of being definable without reference to those personal characteristics.
>
> (1995, p. 856)

The concept of merit underpins many HRM systems, e.g., recruitment and selection, performance management, talent management, reward and career development. For merit to be an operative social contract a number of conditions must apply. These are articulated by Young (1990) as: qualifications, technical skills, performance and competence. Applying Young's conditions to HRM processes, Van Buren (2002) observes qualifications must be assessed in respect of their ability to provide the holder with technical skills and competence to produce specified results. Organizations seeking to use merit as a criterion for recruitment and promotion are required to determine the results required from each employee and establish which qualifications and technical skills are consistent with achieving these requirements. Performance and competence must be capable of individual assessment; it cannot be assumed that certain competencies or aptitudes are distributed unequally within identifiable groups (e.g., ethnic minorities, males, females). Performance must be evaluated and individuals ranked through the utilization of value and culture neutral measures.

Merit is thus presented as a measure of individual ability and achievement, based upon objectively measured qualifications and the ability of the individual to apply them to job-related tasks. It is a social system in which 'merit or talent is the basis for sorting people into positions and distributing rewards' (Scully, 1997, p. 413). Popularized by Young in 1958 (1994), the concept has received much attention. Key concepts embedded within the meritocratic principle are objectivity, fairness and reward for hard work (Farber & Sherry, 1995); personal responsibility and ownership of one's progression (Brennan & Naidoo, 2008) and equality of access to key career enhancing opportunities, (Tomei, 2003). The notions of meritocracy are appealing. A number of survey studies in the US have shown support for the approach believing not only that meritocracy is the way the system ought to work, but is in fact the way it does work (Kluegel & Smith, 1986; Ladd, 1994; Ladd & Bowman, 1998). Thus meritocracy has been culturally endorsed and accepted as a fair and legitimate approach to the distribution of rewards and resources and thus the organizing of expertise within society by many capitalist countries and organizations (Scully, 1997, 2002; McNamee & Miller, 2004).

However, as we will elaborate on in the next section, the realization of this ideal in organizations is not without challenges. Establishing HR systems that adequately assess merit has in much previous research been shown to be difficult, creating a discrepancy between the meritocratic ideals on the one hand and assessment and promotion practices through which expertise is organized on the other. How knowledge workers in an expert organization deal with these discrepancies, and what the consequences of their different approaches may be is the focus of the current chapter.

Challenges to Meritocracy in Practice

A key mechanism in the organization of expertise in contemporary organizations is the organizational hierarchy, where career advancement is viewed as a signal of superior knowledge in comparison to those at lower organizational ranks (see also Chapter 12). Organizational advancement is highly desirable in modern liberal democracies. Individuals enter organizations having progressed through a number of hurdles anticipating it will be necessary to negotiate many more to progress further. The main criterion determining progression; viewed as practically and morally acceptable within a liberal democracy, is merit. However, merit, far from being a purely objective measure, has uncertainty embedded within it, as it requires predictions about future performance based on the past (Knights & Richards, 2003; Thornton, 2007; Sommerlad, 2011).

Appointing a candidate to a new position, requiring them to perform tasks they have no experience of involves risk. There is also clearly an element of subjectivity in determining the factors to take into account, i.e. what aspects of an individual's past performance do we use to determine their likely future performance and how are they to be evaluated? For example, Sommerlad (2011) contends in the legal profession, the explanation for the skewed and unrepresentative nature of the senior ranks does not rest with objective job-related criteria, but rather in "...common sense understandings of, for instance, appropriate gender roles, ways of conducting business in the profession, and relatedly, what constitutes merit and professionalism" (2011, p. 2496). Assessing academic promotions, Brink & Benschop (2012) though not arguing against the notion of meritocracy itself, take issue with one of its core contentions, i.e. those in power are there because they are the most meritorious. Along with Williams (1991), Roithmayr (1997) and Sommerlad (2011) they argue the constitution of merit is constructed and endorsed by prevailing power elites who stand to gain most from maintaining the status quo. By presenting the processes enabling them to advance to their positions of seniority and power as precise, objective and unequivocal, these processes are rendered beyond reproach and responsibility for those who do not succeed within the prevailing system is laid squarely on their own shoulders (Brink & Benschop, 2012).

Closer examination of the concept thus reveals it has no meaning without reference to the social context to which it is applied. Williams (1991) contends merit standards represent socially acceptable preferences developed by members of social groups in power at a particular time and place in history whose descendants gain advantage from decisions made under those standards. The subjective history of the standards has been conveniently forgotten (or suppressed) and they are represented as 'ahistorical', objective measures of ability. By separating the standards from their history, the notion is rejected that the constitution of ability itself is subjective, leading Roithmayr (1997) to argue that rather than protecting against 'bias', the concept of merit is inscribed with subjective, hierarchically-based social bias. From this perspective, merit can be viewed as historically inscribed socially acceptable bias for particular qualities. These apparently opposing concepts are thus unable to reveal when a preference is an illegitimate 'bias' or legitimate 'merit' (Roithmayr, 1997).

Merit is thus presented as fair to the extent it ensures individual hard work and abilities/competencies are rewarded (Van Buren, 2002). For these reasons, the discourse of merit is appealing. Organizations are unlikely to claim legitimacy for processes which are unfair, subjective and inconsistent. However, in practice meeting the conditions outlined earlier is not a straightforward matter as there are a number of issues involved in moving from merit as a theoretical construct to its application in everyday usage, as we will see in this chapter. For example, comparing performance between individuals is not empirically unproblematic as our evaluative processes cannot separate individual performance from the individual themselves.

We thus see that within organizations, employment policies and processes aimed at linking employees' abilities to their career outcomes are presented as embodying the principles of meritocracy (Scully, 1997). The aim is to develop systems which reward performance alone, free from consideration of ascriptive characteristics (Heneman & Werner, 2006). Many studies have, however, indicated the difficulties associated with objective evaluation, and a number, controlling for employee performance, even challenge the contention that merit-based reward practices overcome disparities in wages in respect of gender and race (e.g., Elvira & Graham, 2002; Castilla, 2008).

Experts' Approaches to the Tension between Meritocratic Ideals and Practices

The empirical context of the current chapter is the performance management process in an international management consulting firm, 'Consultco' (pseudonym). Consultco is a global management consulting firm, operating in over 50 countries and employing more than 30,000 people. It is one of the world's leading providers of management consulting and technology services and works with high prestige clients. The study was located in the UK practice.

The focus of data collection was the Global Competency Framework (GCF), the performance management process within the firm. The GCF requires consultants in light of their experience during the past year to assess their attainment level in respect of key, pre-determined competencies. Only when they are able to evidence that they have achieved a certain level of competence in each of the required areas, will they be deemed ready to advance to the next level within the firm. The process operates with individuals making a personal assessment of their attainment against each of the specified competences which is then verified by their line manager. Line managers have a role in recommending which level of competence the individual should aim for in the process and also in ratifying the self-assessment made. To ensure parity across managers and business divisions a moderation/ratification process is conducted whereby samples are taken from across the business and assessed independently. As a result of this process, assessments as a whole may be revised up or down.

The principal method of data collection was 1:1 semi-structured interviews with 34 consultants (15 male and 19 female) drawn from across the UK practice. Interviewees represented three grades within the UK practice, Consultant 3, Principal Consultant and Director (the level just below partner). The interviews averaged between 60–90 minutes in length. All interviews were tape recorded (with participants' permission) and later transcribed. The interviews sought to establish participants' understanding and structuring of their world (Basit, 2003) and thus the interview questions were kept as broad as possible so as not to direct interviewees to particular themes or issues. Based on the interviews, three ways of relating to the GCF process were identified

Conformists

Conformists generally displayed an acceptance of the GCF system as a system creating transparency as to what is required to advance and support the view that progression through The Global Competency Framework (GCF)

can only be gained by those able to understand the requirements and willing to put in the effort to meet them. The rigidity of the system is made clear; endorsing the objectivity and fairness of decisions made.

> Up until a few years ago we had grades, now we don't have grades we just have a GCF. It's an annual process and you're reviewed in terms of your effort against the stated criteria and certainly the view; the widely held perception is the way you progress is to literally tick the boxes until you make the grade. So you have to make sure you understand exactly where you are in terms of your GCF and make sure that the work that you're doing keeps building on that and adding to it and brings you forward
>
> *(Joanna)*

In the extract, several references to the basic ideas of the meritocracy are made. Firstly by reference to 'effort'; which is related to clearly stated and universally-applied 'criteria', defined by the system and applied consistently and objectively to all. Progression is attained by individuals able to 'literally tick the boxes', with the implication this is regardless of ascriptive characteristics they possess and thus meritocratic. She also invokes another key idea associated with the meritocratic ideology; that of an individual's personal responsibility for their progression (Brennan & Naidoo, 2008; Brink & Benschop, 2012). Emphasis on individual agency in shaping career outcomes creates space for exercising personal control over one's career path and enables individuals to feel empowered and in control within the meritocratic structure in the firm which requires individuals to understand 'exactly' where they are in terms of their GCF and ensures they engage in work which enables them to add to their present GCF-related capabilities and thus go 'forward'. The implications of this process for those who do not take ownership of the system in this way; who simply work hard, do a good job and obtain high levels of performance, is that they may not have their contributions recognized through the system. However, the responsibility for this is placed squarely on their shoulders.

> I think basically if you want to get on you have got to prove that you have the capability to be doing the next stage whether that is two years or whatever and that you really are working towards it; it is almost I mean, you are not playing a game, but there are these things that you will need to tick off and if you're not prepared to do those 'tick-offs', then you are not going to be able to do it. It didn't used to be like that, but it certainly is now.
>
> *(Julia)*

Julia echoes some of the sentiments expressed by Joanna. She also indicates that the GCF is a system that requires advancement through evidencing of capability and as such is fair and objective. However, she then begins to question some of the underlying principles of the process, but hesitates to do so as she says 'it is almost I mean, you are not playing a game'. She realizes that the process is rigid and requires evidence of performance on a narrow range of competencies which she also realizes can become mechanistic and 'like a game'. She further emphasizes the rigidity of the system in the extent that unless the 'tick-offs' are made, advancement will not be achieved. Her faith in a change in process and a departure from the past where perhaps the process was not as rigid or formal is evidenced by her final sentence, 'It didn't used to be like that, but it certainly is now'. Here we see some regret that those unwilling or unable to conform to the present 'tick-off,' process-oriented approach to advancement will see their progress halted in a way that would not have been the case previously.

Both Joanna and Julia have adopted largely 'accepting' subject positions in relation to the meritocratic discourse evident within the firm and its practice through the GCF. However, within both accounts we see some sense that there is a certain tension. In the next quote, we see an example that some individuals adopt a more cynical version of the conforming view, making the tension between the intentions of the CGF and its practices more explicit:

> [How do you get promoted?] It depends where you are, but if you are at a level where I am or a bit further up, it's about how to play the numbers in GCF and about how to make your own good PR . . . it's far more important that your manager thinks you're doing a good job than you actually are and it's far more important that you can link what you're doing to GCF than it's of value to the client if you want to get promoted.
>
> *(Mark)*

In Mark's quote we see that once again, there is a view that the GCF is viewed as a 'numbers' game, a process which requires individuals to systematically work through the requirements for each level, satisfy them and move to the next. However, in Mark's extract we do not see any acceptance that the GCF process is reflective of meritocratic ideals or principles. In his view, there is the possibility for individuals to cynically exploit the space provided by the failure of both the GCF and other organizational practices, i.e. staff management and client satisfaction; for their own advancement. When Mark says, 'It's far more important that you can link what you're doing to GCF than it's of value to the client', what he is referencing is that the system and the work do not always align and thus it is important to recognize this and take control of the process in order that you do not miss out on advancement because you were side-tracked doing work that was of importance to the client, but not your own advancement. Here again, we see a space open up between regulatory processes operating within the firm to ensure that client work is the focus, and an individual's ability to 'play' the system, such that they ensure they do not miss out on promotion because they have failed to gain some knowledge/experience required for the GCF.

This is a highly individualistic position putting the individuals' career advancement first, and one which runs contrary to the key principles of objectivity and fairness underpinning the meritocratic ideal. However, from Mark's perspective it is the system itself which creates these problems and leads individuals to behave contrary to the meritocratic ideal. As Mark indicates, the system is viewed as "given" and it is thus important for individuals to take control of the process personally and 'play' the system, so that advancement is gained, but it may be at the expense of the client as work is being done which is not of 'value to the client'.

Challengers

Challengers have a clear recognition that the key tenets of the meritocratic ideal are not represented in organizational work reality in respect of their experience of the GCF. As both the meritocratic ideal and effective performance management processes are seen as important, we see a degree of frustration expressed by organizational members and a wish to fix the system such that it aligns with meritocratic principles and works in practice as it purports to rhetorically.

> I have an appeal outstanding in GCF which actually I've been quite upfront about the fact that I didn't really care about the result one way or the other; I'm really pursuing it as a point of principle. I'm doing it in quite a light-hearted nice way, but I have asked that my appeal considers my relations with 3 or 4 other people, because I think the results are 'knocked up'. I've seen these people at work, I know what they do and I know what I do. Now, they may have had more time to write it up and they may have more support, or they may have been able to write a more persuasive case, but I know what they do and I flagged that and I asked them to consider that because I think that's very unfair. It encourages self-promotion, there are no; despite what people say, the moderation processes are not robust and ultimately nobody knows what everyone's doing. There is no true accountability.
>
> *(Jenny)*

In this quote, we see that Jenny raises a number of issues in relation to the way in which the system is 'supposed' to work and the way it actually works. In doing so, she indicates that a number of the tenets of the meritocratic ideal are not reflected in the day-to-day functioning of the system and that these are in her view going undetected. By calling attention to these issues through a formal appeal, Jenny could be viewed as someone interested in only her own outcomes in the GCF process. However, she distances herself from this by establishing that she is simply appealing the decision made in respect of her performance in a 'light-hearted, nice way', and that 'I didn't really care about the result one way or the other'. She wishes to be clear that her motivation is 'a point of principle' and thus goes beyond her own self-interest to the interests of the firm itself and others who may have been negatively impacted through the process.

In terms of the tenets of meritocracy that Jenny seeks to defend we see a repetition of 'I know what they do', signaling that in her view, the objective performance of those she is comparing herself with is in some way lacking and thus should not be rewarded through a performance management process which purports to uphold meritocratic principles of objectivity, fairness and reward for hard work (Farber & Sherry, 1995). By listing non-meritocratic processes that may enable those Jenny compares her performance with to succeed within the system, i.e. 'they may have had more time to write it up and they may have more support, or they may have been able to write a more persuasive case, . . . It encourages self-promotion' she identifies clearly the disconnects between the meritocratic ideal and practices which not only run contrary to this ideal, but which appear to thrive and remain unchallenged. She thus sees her only course of action as drawing attention to these issues by appealing her own rating within the system and in this way ensure the system itself is called to account and decisions made within it attain additional scrutiny, as in her view at present 'despite what people say, the moderation processes are not robust and ultimately nobody knows what everyone's doing. There is no true accountability'.

The inherent tensions between discourses of objectivity, hard work and fairness and the actual experience of the GCF process are further reflected on by Jackie.

> I think the GCF is fair because it's based on experience, but I think it's grossly unfair when people aren't given the opportunity to have those experiences. For example, you could end up working on a project where all you have done is testing for 2 years and therefore you're not going to progress, but how do you move onto another role in order to progress? It's great because it comes over as this well balanced perception of somebody, therefore, if you achieve certain goals you will get promoted. So it appears to be based on experience and knowledge, but if you're not given the roles to develop those skills then you won't get promoted, and that's not your fault; it's very competitive.
>
> *(Jackie)*

In this quote Jackie clearly identifies with much of the meritocratic discourse, accepting that 'the GCF is fair because it's based on experience', however she then goes on to challenge her initial assertion, noting that access to the required experiences is not equally available to all making the system as it operates 'grossly unfair'. Jackie's observation that the process is 'competitive' and her belief that subjectivity exists within the system because the 'right' type of assignments are allocated to some, but not others further problematizes abstractly defined merit.

While Jenny actively opposed the GCF, Jackie adopts a more passive version of the 'challenging' subject position. She voices her concerns privately and offers no solution in respect of how the dilemma is to be resolved. Her recognition that the process is 'competitive' may provide a clue that for Jackie, the likely approach she will adopt in the future will be to adopt some of these 'competitive' behaviors herself and thus progress within the system; there is little indication that she will seek to challenge the system or highlight the tensions she has identified.

Rejecters

The rejecters recognize that the key tenets of the meritocratic ideal are neither represented in organizational work reality nor in respect of their experience of the GCF. However, for this group the problem lies with the system (rather than its practices) and it is the system that needs to be changed to better reflect reality:

> It's not the people necessarily who would be best placed to do them, it's the people who are trying to put the right ticks in the right boxes for promotion and this was obvious even more through the GCF. You get people volunteering to do stuff and they get a score of X on their particular parts and you get people who are the worst people managers agreeing to be mentors or staff advisors, just to tick the GCF box. I really wanted to be a staff manager because I felt that I could add value to the business by performing that role, but what really irked me was that they thought I was doing the same as them; just ticking boxes.
>
> *(Philip)*

For Philip, we see that a number of doubts are apparent in respect of the way in which the process works and the results it produces. He begins by expressing concern that roles are being undertaken by people who are 'not necessarily . . . best placed to do them' and who are only 'volunteering' for them to 'put the right ticks in the right boxes for promotion'. This causes two problems; the first is that the necessity to 'get the right ticks in the right boxes' means there is an incentive to undertake roles regardless of the competency to perform them. The second concern evident in Philip's extract is the broader worry of the kind of behavior likely to be observed and endorsed in the firm and the impact this will have on future staff development and the performance of the firm. If individuals who are 'the worst people managers' are gaining positions as 'mentors or staff advisors' a message is sent to those aspiring to future roles themselves. Philip also indicates a concern with what this practice of promotion may do to the business when 'the worst people managers' are appointed to management or mentoring positions.

Among rejecters, we see a wish to be distanced from the 'tick box' approach; 'I really wanted to be a staff manager because I felt that I could add value to the business by performing that role'. We see expressed here a justification as to why he wanted to be a staff manager which was different to those volunteering for the role with no real interest in it. What Philip wants to make clear is that he is not 'the same as them' (the conformists). 'They' may be acting from a self-interested position; he is not. He wishes to add value to the business. The ability of the GCF to create a meritocracy and thus business value is further questioned by Trevor:

> We have put a veneer of objectivity over something that still has huge amounts of subjectivity in it and rather than being honest about it and building that into the system we have put a huge infrastructure in place called the GCF, which soaks up a lot of time and enables old patterns of behaviour to continue unchallenged and unchecked as before . . . I think we are putting in place systems that are designed for stability, for a world that has gone away already, where people are thinking in three to five years. I am not saying that people should not have clear goals etc., but do you really have to support those goals with like 14 pages of detailed evidence, which you are never going to look at again. It is quite distressing to see some bright people putting those kinds of things in place . . . If these trends continue I will certainly not be here in the future.
>
> *(Trevor)*

Trevor thus indicates that the GCF is a superficial allusion to meritocracy. One only has to scratch the surface to uncover reality. In his view, this is a system which is inherently 'subjective', but which power elites within the firm are unwilling to label as such; rather they position the system as objective, consistent and fair, evidencing this through a 'huge infrastructure' allowing the process face validity. The result is that rather than acting as a guardian of fairness and equity within the firm the GCF is subverted to represent a veil for inequity; enabling 'old patterns of behavior to go unchallenged and unchecked as before'. In Trevor's view, the basic idea of the GCF is fundamentally flawed. As he says, it is designed for a world 'that has already gone away from us', the idea that there is an objective measure of merit or performance is a fallacy and supporting it with '14 pages of evidence' does not mean that the process is any more useful. As he says, 'it is quite distressing to see bright people putting those kinds of things in place', his point being that the system clearly doesn't work, everyone knows that it doesn't work and yet there is an expectation of all involved to 'collude' and act as if it does, leading to extensive time spent on 'worthless' activities; time that could be more productively spent.

While the challengers had some motivation to change the system, the rejecters saw little possibility to do so. The system has had huge investment in terms of both money and time and there is clear organizational need for the system to be deemed a success. In this context, Trevor sees his only option as being to remove himself from the organization, as he says 'if these trends continue, I will certainly not be here in the future'.

Discussion and Conclusions

The previous discussion indicates that organizing expertise based on meritocratic principles, while a well-established and cherished ideal, is more difficult to realize in practice. Three ways of dealing with this discrepancy between ideals and practices by experts in organizations were identified— conformists, challengers and rejecters.

The *conformists* approach to bringing ideals and practices closer together is about—more or less cynically—fitting the GCF practices within a meritocratic framework. Founded in an individualistic 'career' discourse that emphasizes career advancement as a core meaning of work, the conformist reframes the meaning of 'merit' as being about succeeding in the GCF, 'ticking the right boxes', rather than delivering value to clients—or economic surplus to owners. Hereby, the broader meritocratic ideals—that those working hardest to create the most 'value' (for client or firm) will be rewarded—are deserted. The concept of 'merit' is redefined from excelling in value creation for the client or firm to excelling in the GCF. Through this redefinition of the work performed, the gap between ideals and practices is narrowed as the GCF provides an internally consistent and transparent practice for who should be rewarded.

The *challengers* pursue a different strategy toward stronger alignment between ideals and practices. The challengers are strongly committed to the meritocratic ideal and therefore the observation that the performance management practices of the GCF do not live up to its intentions is perceived as deeply troubling. The GCF doesn't reward the 'best' performers. In relation to this disconnect we see either an active or passive challenging of the GCF practices. The active-challenging seeks to 'fix' the disconnect between the meritocratic ideal and the GCF practices by moving the practices closer to the ideal. Thus we see Jenny raising her head above the parapet to challenge the process; to appeal her own grading. The more passive-challenging position is illustrated by Jackie. Though recognizing that the allocation of assignments to gain GCF appropriate experience is 'grossly unfair' and that gaining such experience is 'competitive' she is unclear of how she will respond. Moving toward more of a conformist position may be one possible response as she feels there is limited room to alter key practices.

The *rejecters*, finally, approach the discrepancy by questioning the realism of the meritocratic ideal as reflected in the GCF. This approach is anchored in what may be called a commercial or pragmatic discourse, in which 'value creation' is in focus. For rejecters, a more simple, subjective and in parts non-meritocratic performance management system has worked fine in the past, and it is implicitly questioned whether performance management practices in a business like management consulting can ever become entirely objective and transparent. Against this background, the GCF is pictured as a time consuming and costly way of 'adding a veneer of objectivity' over a process that is (and partly needs to be) subjective. Instead, the rejecters observe that by implementing a highly formalized system such as the GCF, room for 'conformists' is created which is seen as a threat toward value creation, and thus the basic foundation of the firm. However, rejecters are the least confident in their ability to increase the alignment by any changes in the organizational system. The rejecters express strong awareness of the financial and ideological investments made in the system. This distancing from the GCF system also implies a distancing from the organization which in the extreme case was manifest in an intention to leave.

All these three approaches involve actual or aspired changes of organizational systems and behaviors in order to increase the alignment between organizational systems and their intentions and organizational practices and can thus be characterized as examples of resistance toward these (Fleming & Spicer, 2003; Kärreman & Alvesson, 2009). These efforts toward resistance are however visible to different extents and their potential for success varies. The most overt form of resistance is observed from the active challengers, who engage in efforts to change the practices of the GCF in order to make them more aligned with claimed meritocratic ideals. By engaging in, for example, an appeal they hope to be able to change the practices, although their optimism to actually succeed with such changes seems limited.

Similarly, the rejecters have a clear target of resistance in the GCF system (rather than its practices), which is believed to be overly complex, bureaucratic and unfit to achieve either business or meritocratic intentions. However, the rejecters show low confidence in their ability to actually succeed in changing the system and instead indicate an exit strategy of resistance (Hirschman, 1970), which is noteworthy as they are the ones most concerned with the value creation of the firm and thus its long-term survival.

The conformists, finally, may at first glance be perceived as non-resisting, as they seem to uncritically adapt to the GCF. However, at a closer look, their collusion with a system that fails to deliver on its claimed meritocratic ideal is also a form of subtle resistance. Conformers evidence their understanding that processes of staff management and client satisfaction do not work as they should and more or less cynically use this understanding to support their own career projects. The GCF in their view becomes a facilitative process in this regard; they are in little doubt that seniors in the firm must be aware of these spaces between rhetoric and reality and the fact that they choose to ignore them and reward those exploiting them, must mean that these too are desired behaviors. Thus, efficient and effective 'ticking of the boxes' though unstated, may indeed be what constitutes merit and those willing to 'play the game', by working the system as it is rather than lamenting how it should be, are the winners in the process and valued members of the firm. That this subject position undermines the professional discourses of client service and key meritocratic principles of objectivity, reward for hard work and fairness

(Farber & Sherry, 1995; Anderson-Gough, Grey & Robson, 2000) seems relatively untroubling to conformists. It could thus be argued that the conformists 'kidnap' the system for their individual career purpose, well aware that this might have negative effects on the organization.

The current study thus indicates that the HRM practices in claimed meritocracies can, and to a large extent are openly questioned as they fail to deliver on their claimed meritocratic ideals. However, we also claim that even in the cases where HR practices pass seemingly unchallenged, their enactment implies a profound form of challenging targeted at the very foundation of the meritocratic ideal—that promotion goes to those with the most merit and thus most able to create value for the organization. The conformists in this study—more or less consciously—substitute value creation for the organization or client with adherence to the performance criteria formulated in the GCF, thus acting against meritocratic intentions. This is related to the resistance strategy 'believing too much' discussed by Fleming & Spicer (2003), which is not necessarily explicitly aimed at undermining efforts of (cultural) control. However, the consequences of taking corporate rules and policies too seriously (such as in the collective bargaining strategy 'work to rule') are subtle forms of resistance that are hard to deal with by management because organizational members are adhering to the prescribed practices.

Paradoxically, we thus find that those acting contrary to the espoused principles of meritocracy (in our study the conformists) seem to be rewarded and those seeking to behave in accordance with these same principles and ensure systems and processes that deliver meritocracy are the ones penalized. This indicates that the organization of expertise within firms according to the principles of meritocracy, because of the difficulties of objectively specifying and assessing key aspects of expertise, may have profound unintended consequences that reward a kind of behavior that challenges the experts' value creation both for the client as well as for the firm employing them.

References

Anderson-Gough, F., Grey, C. & Robson, K. (2000). In the name of the client: The service ethic in two professional services firms. *Human Relations, 53*(9), 1151–1174.

Basit, T. (2003). Manual or electronic? The role of coding in qualitative data analysis. *Educational Research, 45*(2), 143–154.

Brennan, J. & Naidoo, R. (2008). Higher education and the achievement (and/or prevention) of equity and social justice. *Higher Education, 56*(3), 287–302.

Brink, van den M. & Benschop, Y. (2012). Gender practices in the construction of academic excellence: Sheep with five legs. *Organization, 19*(4), 507–524.

Castilla, E. J. (2008). Gender, race and meritocracy in organizational careers. *American Journal of Sociology, 113*, 1479–1526.

Elvira, M. M. & Graham, M. E. (2002). Not just a formality: Pay system and formalization and sex-related earnings effects. *Organization Science, 13*, 601–617.

Farber, D. A. & Sherry, S. (1995). Is the radical critique of merit anti-semitic? *California Law Review, 83*(3), 853–884.

Fleming, P. & Spicer, A. (2003). Working at a cynical distance: Implications for power, subjectivity and resistance. *Organization, 10*(1), 157–179.

Heneman, R. L. & Werner, J. M. (2006). *Merit Pay: Linking Pay to Performance in a Changing World* (2nd edition). Greenwich, CT: Information Age.

Hirschman, A. O. (1970). *Exit, Voice and Loyalty: Responses to Decline in Firms, Organizations and States.* Cambridge, MA: Harvard University Press.

Kärreman, D. & Alvesson, M. (2009). Resisting resistance: Counter-resistance, consent and compliance in a consultancy firm. *Human Relations, 62*(8), 1115–1144.

Kluegel, J. R. & Smith, E. R. (1986). *Beliefs about Inequality: American's Views of What Is and What Ought to Be.* New York: de Gruyter.

Knights, D. & Richards, W. (2003). Sex discrimination in UK academia. *Gender, Work and Organization, 10*(2), 213–238.

Ladd, E. C. (1994). *The American Ideology.* Storrs, CT: Roper Center for Public Opinion Research.

Ladd, E. C. & Bowman, K. H. (1998). *Attitudes toward Economic Inequality.* Washington, DC: EI Press.

McNamee, S. J. & Miller, R. K. Jr. (2004). *The Meritocracy Myth.* Lanham, MD: Rowman and Littlefield.

Roithmayr, D. (1997). Deconstructing the distinction between bias and merit. *California Law Review, 85*(5), 1449–1507.

Scully, M. A. (1997). Meritocracy. In Freeman, R. E. & Werhane, P. H. (eds.), *Blackwell Encyclopaedic Dictionary of Business Ethics.* Oxford: Blackwell Publishers, 413–414.

Scully, M. A. (2002). Confronting errors in the meritocracy. *Organization, 9*(3), 396–401.

Sommerlad, H. (2011). Minorities, merit and misrecognition in the globalized profession. *Fordham Law Review, 80*, 2481–2512.

Thornton, M. (2007). 'Otherness' on the bench: How merit is gendered. *Sydney Law Review, 29*(3), 391–414.

Tomei, M. (2003). Discrimination and equality at work: A review of the concepts. *International Labour Review, 142*(4), 401–418.

Van Buren, H. J. III. (2002). Earning Your Place in Society: Is Workplace Merit an Operative Social Contract? Unpublished Paper, University of New Mexico.

Williams, P. J. (1991). *The Alchemy of Race and Rights.* Cambridge, MA: Harvard University Press.

Young, M. (1990). *Justice and the Politics of Difference.* Princeton, NJ: Princeton University Press.

Young, M. (1994). *The Rise of the Meritocracy* (originally published in 1958). New Brunswick, NJ: Transaction.

14 Leading Those Who Know Best

Ingalill Holmberg and Mats Tyrstrup

Is leadership needed in activities that require the efforts of experts? Experts in a particular area are distinguished from non-experts by the fact that they are largely responsible for planning and managing their own efforts as well as by the fact that they are usually responsible for evaluating these efforts (Maister, 1993). This is true, for example, when physicians make diagnoses and provide treatment, when attorneys counsel clients, when teachers evaluate students, or when management consultants advise organizations.

For some time researchers in the field of leadership have generally agreed that leadership, which is context-dependent and situation-dependent, is a broad term and may have different meanings in different situations (Yukl, 1989). One such situation is the special type of leadership required by companies and other organizations that employ experts. Therefore the relevant question in the analysis of leadership by such entities is the following: How does leadership function effectively in companies and organizations in which the work of experts contributes to the value creation processes?

One common conception of leadership refers to the leader's deliberate efforts to influence events and developments among followers. Such leadership can be exercised in various ways, with varying degrees of success. Leadership can also be exercised at different levels and, consequently, in situations of varying complexity. We also think leadership is not limited to situations with only a few followers—for example, in groups where certain people influence events and developments.

Our interest in this chapter is not leadership at the group level. We are instead interested in the key leadership issue when organizations employ experts, and, as a result, contradictions arise between different logics and perspectives (professional and managerial). While we recognize other leadership issues exist when experts work in organizations, our focus is the interaction between the formal leadership (i.e., management) and the leadership the experts claim to exercise.

Our intention is to examine how this key leadership issue in the expert-driven organization influences organizational management. An important starting point for our discussion is the recognition that expertise, and thus the work of experts, is itself somewhat ambiguous. For example, opinions differ on the requirements of eldercare, on the design of beautiful architecture, on the framework for effective pedagogy, or on successful courtroom strategy. Even in medical care, where we expect to find definitive treatment diagnoses and agreed-on treatment methods, opinions differ. Complicating the problem is that expertise, because of its emphasis on specialization, is accountable for a certain amount of tunnel vision that limits the expression of differences in opinions, creates contradictions, and even results in conflicts.

In terms of value creation in an expert-driven organization, a key task for management therefore is to ensure that the expertise increases, or combines with, the organization's knowledge and competences in ways that help the organization meet its objectives (Holmberg & Tyrstrup, 2002). However, at the same time, it must be recognized that legitimate spheres of status and power exist in organizations that control and influence their specific activities (Brunsson, 1985). These two realities, with their potential for conflict, are at the very heart of how we understand leadership in knowledge-intensive activities where experts and non-experts work side by side.

We use case studies of two organizations—a government agency (hereafter, the Agency) and an emergency care clinic (hereafter, the Clinic) to illustrate how context influences leadership. Both organizations employ experts who work with operational activities, and managers who work with strategic issues. Both organizations have ambitious agendas for policy and procedural changes. With such changes underway, the experts' contribution comes into focus at the same time as it creates obstacles to progress. A struggle developed in both organizations over who had the power to identify, define, and solve problems. Because the logic of the experts' professionalism and the logic of the managers' managerialism oppose one another, the conditions for a struggle over loyalties and values were clearly in place.

The Agency in the first case study is planning a major organizational change in which the overall objective is to create an evidence-based evaluation system that treats various activities under its authority equally. A consequence of this change, when flexibility in dealing with activities decreases, is that the experts may find their professional independence and status under threat.

Managers at the Clinic (at a relatively large hospital) in the second case study are planning to broaden the concept of expertise to include greater patient-medical staff interaction. A consequence of this change, which the experts actively oppose, is that the experts seem to prioritize their professional identity and status over the Clinic's goals.

We summarize the facts of these two cases separately, followed by our commentaries on the relationship between leadership, which is the responsibility of management, and value creation, which is the aim of the experts' work. In the subsequent discussion we generalize on the conditions and terms of leadership in organizations that employ experts in the expectation that their expertise can create value for stakeholders.

Case Study 1: The Agency

The Agency has its central office in Stockholm and regional units in most major Swedish cities. The Agency makes decisions for certain matters that, to simplify the explanation, fall into two main categories. The first category involves relatively simple cases requiring routine decisions. In principle these cases deal with matters that fall under the applicable regulatory framework and require the Agency to reject or grant a request/application. Because little discussion in such cases is required, the decisions are relatively straightforward and easily reached.

The second category involves more complicated cases that require more complex decision-making. In such instances, because the Agency may disagree with the advice and opinions of the experts, it has to craft arguments that support its decisions, some of which contradict that of the experts. Or, the Agency may require input from various parties who have a stake or interest in the decisions. A further complexity is that some experts may represent these parties.

The Agency also makes decisions in the second category of cases that require compliance with specific conditions. For example, the Agency may require the completion of particular actions or of specific changes. Such cases, which are typically very complex, therefore require that the Agency's staff have relevant experience and competence. Because multiple parties may be involved—individuals, companies, public organizations or other agencies—there may be many statements and claims requiring extensions of time for their preparation, analysis, and processing. This situation may also occur in cases that have not yet reached the appeals stage or the judicial review stage.

The Agency has found that quite different methods and approaches are used in various and rather normal situations. As a result, the Agency's general director and its deputy director have observed inefficiency problems in operations. After many years of relatively decentralized organization at the Agency, in which the central office simply acted as the regulator, it was proposed to adopt a significantly more centralized organizational structure. The Agency's management welcomed the proposal, which was presented in the context of a government review. The regional units were far less supportive of the proposal; some of them were decidedly unenthusiastic about the proposal.

Following the reorganization, the Agency's central office received explicit authority in various areas. The general director and the deputy director then established a number of new functions at the central level. Among other things, they created two new horizontal units: one for operational issues and one for developmental issues. The intention was that these new units would give management the needed tools to control the Agency's work and streamline its operations.

As expected, the regional units were strongly opposed to the reorganization in general and to the key proposals in particular. Their objection was that central management was acting very severely in enlarging its authority and that the internal political processes were complicated and energy and time consuming. Eventually, however, the reorganization took place. A number of executives from the regional units throughout the country were offered positions at the central office. Some executives accepted the new positions while others left the Agency.

New staff functions with specific responsibilities were created at the introduction of the reorganization. The regional units engaged in a tug of war with central management, leading to a lengthy and difficult process in which a wide range of proposals was discussed. Many possible solutions were suggested related to work methods, responsibilities, and procedures. The discussions were often heated and divisive. A complicating factor was that the regional units had always worked quite independently. Thus it was difficult for the regional units to make compromises, accept trade-offs, and agree to limitations on their authority. There were no easy solutions.

The Agency's underlying philosophy is to conduct its operations based on the so-called principle of equal treatment. This principle means that everyone who deals with the Agency should receive the same treatment regardless of geographic location in Sweden. Situation-specific variations are therefore subordinate to this overarching concept of equal treatment. Yet, at the same time, the Agency's staff must make decisions using case-specific information. Such information is often atypical and not easily generalizable. Therefore people working in the regional units generally think the Agency's central management does not fully understand the regional operating conditions. Many of these people doubt that the centralized organizational structure will mean greater efficiency and more equal treatment of citizens.

Nevertheless, after the formal change in the regulations the Agency acquired the authority to make nationwide decisions. The Agency soon made extensive use of this new authority. For example, the Agency adopted a so-called call center solution in which a centrally located office deals with telephone requests, thereby replacing the need for regional contacts. Another example of the Agency's use of its increased authority is its creation of a central IT department that serves all regional units in the country.

The debate on how authority at the Agency is to be allocated is intense. As is typical of such extensive organizational changes, it appears that the Agency's new management structure solves some problems even as it creates others. These new problems are not unique or even particularly remarkable, especially in expert-driven organizations where complexity and variation are more the rule than the exception. The fundamental question is whether the Agency has the expertise needed to handle its many diverse cases. This is a question central management must address.

Commentary on the Agency

As this description of the Agency reveals, the Agency's extensive reorganization, aimed at meeting public demands and expectations for equal treatment of citizens, is very controversial. The background for the reorganization was the revelation from several sources that variations in how the regional units applied the rules threatened citizens' confidence in the Agency and its activities. A government review also revealed that centralization of the operations among the Agency's units could produce significant efficiency gains.

The principle of equality means in practice that personnel-specific and situation-specific conditions are subordinate to the requirement that "the same" decisions must be made in all instances. A guarantee exists therefore that uniform work policies and procedures will apply to all citizens throughout the country. As the Agency was previously highly decentralized, with significant independence permitted to experts who dealt with various issues, the transition to a centralized management structure resulted in many conflicts between the experts at the regional units and the staff members at the central office.

These Agency staff members debated whether the experts at the regional units, who work closely with the regional activities, should make practice and procedural decisions or whether people from the central office should make these decisions. For the Agency's more routine activities it seems reasonable to standardize regulatory practices and procedures. A problem arises, however, with individual situations that are very complex. In such situations, when both internal and external experts are involved, how are optimal decisions made? Many people even question whether it is possible to follow standardized practices and procedures in such situations. Specifically, how it is possible to determine if the same evaluations (and decisions) are made for similar situations? In fact, how do we determine which cases are similar?

These are questions that relate to central themes in this book: the definition of expert knowledge, the decisions around when and how to use such knowledge, and the effect of its use. In short, what are the consequences of more comprehensive standardization of expertise?

When a new management structure transformed the Agency's practices and procedures—when the idea of centralization, so to speak, took root—this transformation downgraded the expertise in the regional units. Concurrently, actors at the central office acquired more power as the experts at the regional units lost power. In effect, as the role of the regional expert diminished, the regions risked the loss of this professional judgment. With the centralization of the Agency's activities, the new experts are the interpreters of regulations and the policy makers. The former view of efficiency—that rules should be adapted as necessary to individual situations—is no longer applicable. Instead, the goal is to adopt a "one size fits all" approach that can achieve greater operational efficiency and ensure greater equality of treatment (as narrowly construed).

When the assumption that the regional experts could achieve the same results, despite their use of different methods, was first challenged, the groundwork was laid for a fundamental reconsideration of how expertise is used and how rules are applied. At that point, methodology rather than results was in focus. With the standardization of practices and procedures, the Agency could ensure equal handling of all citizens, regardless of where they lived. Moreover, with a different understanding of operational efficiency and of what constitutes legitimacy in the opinion of the general public, a policy shift occurred that ultimately redefined expertise at the Agency.

From a leadership perspective, it is observable that a centralized management structure replaced a decentralized management structure at the Agency. Agency-wide rules, backed by rigid rule enforcement, replaced the regional experts' individual and independent evaluations that were based on their extensive experience and knowledge. Furthermore, impersonal central directives and guidelines replaced regional leadership that had been characterized by cooperation and collegiality.

Case Study 2: The Clinic

The Clinic employs about 120 people including physicians and nurses as well as administrators and other support staff. The Clinic's operations manager is a woman (to date, the position has always been held by a female nurse) who is assisted by two department managers.

In addition to its regular staff members, the Clinic also employs a number of people who are borrowed from other units. Because the work schedules are very flexible, these people to a large extent can arrange their work hours as needed as long as they meet their monthly work obligation. They are very independent and self-motivating and have wide-ranging experience suitable for the emergency care the Clinic provides.

Some years ago, and for unknown reasons, the Clinic experienced a significant personnel turnover. Around 30 people, mostly nurses, left the Clinic and sought employment at other clinics or with different employers. After a fairly intense recruitment effort the Clinic was once again reasonably staffed although more than a third of the staff members were newly hired. Thereafter staff turnover has remained at a normal level. With the expansion of its activities, the Clinic has also employed another 30 staff members.

Although the Clinic's work culture is properly characterized as professional, the Clinic has a certain reputation for staff opposition to management. Some of the Clinic's staff members, particularly those who have a specialist expertise or those who are temporarily employed at the Clinic, challenge managerial authority. There are many reasons for this opposition.

Because work schedules vary greatly, a degree of anonymity exists among the staff members. With the Clinic's many, impromptu changes in organization and scheduling, people typically work in various, often temporary, groups. The formation of group cohesion and support in such scenarios is unlikely. When people come and go at irregular times, depending on the need for certain expertise and on the service requirements, employer commitment is also doubtful. Moreover, employment at the Clinic is only a small fraction of some staff members' total employment. Such people tend to derive their professional identity from their expertise rather than from their employment at the Clinic.

The Clinic's managers, in particular the operations manager, want to provide good medical care as well as create a trusting environment for their patients. Patients should have confidence in the Clinic's staff and their activities. They need to feel the Clinic is responsive to their needs and wishes.

The Clinic's managers think they take a democratic approach to the work (with agreed-upon decisions); they listen to the staff members and reverse decisions when reasonable to do so. However, the managers still encounter difficulties in gaining support and respect for the measures and plans they propose for the Clinic. Often the gap between decisions and actions is large. Many staff members seem to make more or less deliberate misinterpretations of what management has advised, decided or done. They also ask questions of the operations manager that might be more appropriately addressed to their own managers.

On the whole, the Clinic functions well in medical terms except for some fairly routine problems that are typical in emergency care. It is really only in patient reception/interaction that the Clinic's managers express concern about the quality of care provided. Patients mainly complain about staff incompetence and disrespect in this area. As one way to improve this situation, the operations manager has tried to develop better and closer relationships with various staff members. In order to identify problems and discontent at early stages, she has given them more managerial responsibilities and used them as sounding boards and spokespeople for the others. However, because the response to this initiative has not been especially positive, there has been little change in the work environment or work performance.

The Clinic's staff members place a high value on their professionalism in providing emergency care. They approve the medical measures used to make internal evaluations of different personnel categories and to determine the relative status of the personnel in the medical hierarchy. The staff members' mantra is that it is important "to be where it happens, when it happens" if they are to make vital contributions and to experience some sense of "glamour" in their work.

The reward the Clinic can provide the staff members (in addition to their salaries and normal work benefits) is limited essentially to offering them a responsibility other than a purely medical responsibility. From time to time, the Clinic has offered more managerial responsibility to various staff members. However, with little positive response from the staff members, the Clinic has not pursued the idea. In fact, the staff members who took on such responsibility found the Clinic's work culture was a barrier to innovation and development; they eventually returned to their professional duties.

Commentary on the Clinic

As this description of the Clinic reveals, the managers' roles, as expected, are relatively limited as far as the daily, operational activities are concerned. The logic of medical science guides the organization and performance of these activities. For example, the work is divided among the various medical specialties and the expert professions, such as physicians and nurses. They make the medical decisions when patients arrive at the Clinic.

From a medical viewpoint, the Clinic cannot be criticized for the care it provides patients. However, the Clinic's managers have one ambition that is rather extraordinary in terms of emergency care in particular as well as in health care in general. The Clinic strives to provide a trusting environment for both its patients and its staff members. Moreover, the managers are disappointed that patients complain about their reception and handling at the Clinic outside the sphere of medical care.

Staff members and managers have frequently discussed the level of service and general trust at the Clinic. The unfortunate outcome of these discussions is that the medical professionals (i.e., the experts) think they are being criticized. This does not change the fact that some patients still think the Clinic is lacking as far as patient hospitality is concerned. The managers think this complaint is an issue for the experts, but the experts do not think a friendly, welcoming attitude is a required skill set of their professions. Some experts even remarked that the patients' complaints were peripheral issues; the important issue was the quality of the medical care. One expert stated, "An emergency clinic is, after all, an emergency clinic and not a spa hotel". Nevertheless, questions arise: What attention other than medical care should be provided to patients? And who should provide this attention?

The Clinic case raises a number of interesting issues related to leadership. One issue concerns how the medical experts relate to their profession and to their employer. A significant interest of the experts who work full-time at the Clinic is the interaction between patients and staff. However, for experts who work part-time at the Clinic, as one of several jobs, their interest is primarily the practice of their medical profession. Professional identity for the latter group is significantly stronger and more important than organizational affiliation. This prioritization of professionalism obviously diminishes management's possibilities for introducing new work perspectives at the Clinic, in particular, holistic health care that falls outside the perimeter of traditional medical care.

Another interesting leadership issue concerns the negative response of the staff members to management's initiatives and proposals. One explanation for this response may relate to the operation manager's gender and profession. As a female nurse in a management position, does she lack the authority a male physician in the position might command? This opposition to the managerial initiatives and proposals at the Clinic suggests that the consensus (albeit implicit rather than explicit) is that medical experts, the majority of whom are men, are more qualified to make medical decisions as well as to manage operational activities.

However, when the medical experts are involved in solving the Clinic's various problems, the Clinic's fundamental managerial approach seems unchanged. While the status of a profession establishes the legitimacy to make medical decisions, the status seems also to establish their authority to deal with non-medical, management issues. Professionals, who claim the right to a certain level of autonomy in organizational situations, also claim the right to define the management issues they think are strategically important. An unresolved dilemma then arises when medical experts reject their managerial roles even as they oppose the initiatives and proposals management structure assigns to administrative personnel.

Discussion

Professionalism and Managerialism as Opposites

To begin this discussion, the focus is on a key observation from both cases: experts and their expertise are suitable subjects for intense, even argumentative discussion.

Experts who are not allowed to use their expertise (whatever the reason) understandably have difficulty gaining others' support for their methods and others' confidence in their problem-solving ability. People can quickly lose trust in experts when new methods are introduced and accepted in activities in which the experts claim superior knowledge and experience. Such situations occur, for example, with structural power shifts in organizations when new experts appear with different value-creating processes (Bourdieu, 1998). In other words, expertise is a social construct; it emerges and acquires visibility in the interactions among different actors (Berger & Luckmann, 1966).

Although this issue of interaction is especially evident in the Clinic case study, it also appears in the Agency case study. The interactions in the relationships between the staff categories and between the staff members and the managers establish which work loyalties are prioritized, which work methods are selected, and which work attitudes are adopted. Furthermore, these interactions establish the expectations of functional leadership.

We find examples in both case studies of how new ways of defining efficiency and competence pose challenges to daily, operational activities. On the one hand, the experts with managerial responsibilities defend their professionalism and the right to act independently. On the other hand, the administrative managers establish new strategic goals such as providing equal treatment of citizens at the Agency and a trusting environment at the Clinic. In both case studies, management's intention is to change behavioral routines and ultimately to change the organizations' core values.

A struggle has developed in both cases concerning who has the power to identify, define, and solve problems as well as who has the power to decide on the objectives of the various measures and activities. For the experts in both case studies, maintaining their professional identity is a significant concern. They think their status as professionals gives them the authority to make independent evaluations of what needs to be done and how it should be done. In contrast, the administrative managers set overarching policy goals that focus on the citizen/patient and the achievement of internal and external efficiencies.

Trying to specify the expertise required in activities can thus easily turn into protracted negotiations about the nature and purpose of those activities. When two logics based on different values—professionalism and managerialism—oppose each other, the conflict reveals where the experts' loyalties lie. At the Clinic, in particular, this conflict appears in the expression of two fundamental, although somewhat irreconcilable, differences in perspectives—both of which have relevance and value. In general, experts in organizations view the shift from their purely professional perspective to a perspective that prioritizes managerial efficiency as the de-professionalization of citizen/patient services.

Evetts (2011) describes this development as a shift from "occupational [traditional] professionalism" to "organizational professionalism". Such a shift favors managerialism with its evidence-based standardization, systematic evaluations, and follow-ups over the collegial and mutual trust arrangements characteristic of professionalism (see Svensson, 2006; Leicht et al., 2009). Organizational professionalism is often described as 'new' as opposed to traditional professionalism and makes control over the nature of experts and expertise the main responsibility of the organization and its management and control systems (see Chapter 1, see also Choi, Holmberg, Löwstedt & Brommels, 2011). Given this interpretation of the competing logics, experts and managers in an organizational context may easily find themselves on a collision course.

Professionalism and Managerialism as Substitutes and Complements

However, another interpretation of the competing logics may be that they can substitute for each other or complement each other. Because of their knowledge and experience, especially with respect to the traditional professions, experts have wide-ranging capabilities for making independent evaluations of what needs to be done, what methods and approaches are preferable, and how the work should be planned and implemented. A significant portion of what we may call traditional labor management is not relevant in expert-driven activities. Experts in such activities often consult colleagues rather than managers when they seek advice or assistance. In these situations experts require no managerial oversight or instruction.

Thus oversight and instruction are inherent in the practice of expertise. The expert has the ability to analyze problems and thus the right to determine appropriate solutions. The administrative manager's role is to approve the expert's task, to provide the needed resources, and to ensure that the expert generally follows organizational guidelines.

Administrative managers make various other evaluations and trade-offs such as those that concern issues that lie on, or beyond, the perimeter of the expertise that experts bring to organizational activities. Such issues include, for instance, a more comprehensive division of labor allocation and actions that improve/strengthen experts' skills. At the Agency, a policy of equal treatment replaced the policy of individual adaptation. This change had implications for the overall allocation of the staff members' roles at the central office and the experts' roles at the regional units. At the Clinic, the medical experts favored professionalism over managerialism, even in issues normally viewed as typical management issues. We conclude that the medical experts were the victors in this struggle on how the work was defined and whether the hospitality treatment of patients was, or was not, a quality criterion for the organization.

Activities that rely on experts have their foundations in at least two main logics, often several logics. The content and forms of these logics constantly clash when they are discussed. Experts in organizations are typically said to exhibit strong commitment to their profession and reluctance to submit to managerial supervision and control. If one of the two logics dominates— whether managerialism or professionalism—a risk exists that the activity competence in a broad sense will be downgraded. This risk exists quite apart from the diversion of staff members' attention and energy away from innovation and continuous improvement issues toward internal political processes. Experts must exert the greater influence in certain situations, and managers in others.

One well-documented issue in current research and in theoretical/practical discussions is how health care should be organized and managed in the future (Porter & Olmsted Teisberg, 2006; Choi & Brommels, 2009; Choi et al., 2011). In addressing this issue, the blending of professionalism with managerialism has paved the way for a discussion about hybrid professionals (Blomgren & Waks, 2015) and hybrid organizations (Choi et al., 2011). Hybrid professionals are those professionals who have recognized expertise and competence in a particular domain as well as an authoritative claim to policy-relevant knowledge in another domain. The experts at the Clinic acted with that authority. Hybrid professionals are also described as actors who have a "plural expert status" in a particular (epistemic) culture (Knorr Cetina, 1999). Hybrid organizations are defined as organizations in which different logics co-exist and can substitute for or complement each other (Holmberg & Tyrstrup, 2002; Choi et al., 2011).

Leadership that Balances Different Perspectives and Logics

Experts in organizations create value using the expertise they have developed and maintained by gradually increasing and deepening the professional knowledge that is the basis of quality work in everyday life. Value creation, which also includes processes that ensure the effectiveness of activities, is the goal of organizations as they seek to capture new trends and to satisfy divergent interests (here referred to as managerialism). Thus, the main leadership challenge for organizations that employ experts is to integrate their views and professional knowledge with other competing perspectives. This challenge requires coordinating experts' work with others through interaction and cooperation.

Our analysis of the experts' work in organizations and of the leadership required to manage such work leads us to our first conclusion that organizations have a constant need to balance multiple perspectives and logics. Achieving this delicate balance requires a kind of framework for the organization's various policies, procedures, routines, activities, roles and responsibilities.

To be clear, we are not advocating the principle of harmonization with its support structures of uniformity and standardization. Rather, we see the integration of experts in organizations—in the context of the acceptance of diverse interests, opinions and competences—as a way to promote expertise within bounds. Effective leadership must integrate the various expert roles into the organization so that experts are encouraged (and supported) to contribute more than just their special skills and knowledge.

This kind of leadership is clearly distinguished from traditional administrative leadership in which the primary task in the organization is to allocate and assign responsibility for work tasks. When friction, divergent interests and conflicts arise in value-creating activities, the role of modern administrative leadership is to focus on the interaction and cooperation that promote the coordination of efforts and create the conditions needed for individual/joint evaluations. Such leadership does not necessarily mean that people must "see the same reality"; it is enough that they understand how their efforts link to the others' efforts and that they refrain from actively opposing others' initiatives (Weick, 1969).

When peoples' concepts of reality differ from others' concepts of reality, a kind of "structural hole" (Burt, 2004) appears—a gap in the understanding between people. According to Holmberg & Tyrstrup (2002), organizational gaps can result in lost opportunities and failures of various kinds. Such gaps are created, maintained, and changed in and by everyday work experiences (Tyrstrup & Holmberg, 2007) in the interactive relationships between people in the workplace, over time (Döös, 2003).

Our two case studies (the Agency and the Clinic) reveal how such organizational gaps can arise in the division and management of work in organizations when the professionalism of experts meets the managerialism of managers. Thus the two case studies lead us to our second conclusion that leadership in expert-driven organizations must be able to manage these organizational (and psychological) gaps. Through dialogue and discussion, managers can work to bridge the gaps between experts and non-experts in transparent and coordinated settings (real or virtual). Therefore, effective leadership in expert-driven organizations derives its main strength from impromptu searches for solutions to various problems (Tyrstrup, 2006; Holmberg & Tyrstrup, 2010).

Another leadership conception (which has not attracted much attention) is events-driven leadership. This conception is far from the typical, popular image found in business magazines in which the leader is presented as the powerful, charismatic executive in total control (Collins, 2001; Badaracco, 2002). Event-driven leadership does not emphasize managerialism and evidence-based standardization as "the new solution" (see the earlier discussion on professionalism and managerialism as opposites). Rather, event-driven leadership may originate in the professions' expertise and values as well as in managers' goals and values. In this conception of leadership, when events define and control leadership efforts, the question becomes whether the logic of professionalism or the logic of managerialism should be prioritized

Our ambition in this chapter has been to examine leadership in organizations that rely heavily on the knowledge and competence of their internal experts (and sometimes their external experts). A distinguishing characteristic of such organizations is the fundamental, possibly inevitable, tension between the experts' need for independence and status and the managers' need for control and efficiency. In addition, managers often have the added pressure of having to meet the demands of external stakeholders. Resolution of this tension requires patience and sensitivity and the willingness to make compromises; it is a high-wire act that requires skill and experience in balancing expertise, procedures, and policies.

Our two cases (the Agency and the Clinic) illustrate the scenario when organizations rely on experts for the conduct of their activities. Managing people—the people "who know best"—can be quite tricky, especially when such people propose (and often stubbornly support) new ways of working that managers find too costly, too complex, and/or too inequitable. In the ensuing struggle to identify, define, and solve problems, when various actors attempt "to create their version of order", the potential to develop new forms of expertise arises (cf. Brunsson, 1985). However, the opposite result is also possible: the attempt to create order may lead to failure such that management weakens or even ends activities or programs.

In our evaluation of leadership in expert-driven organizations we find the potential for balancing the different perspectives and logics we have described. Stated differently, leadership's main role in such organizations is to encourage compromise through discussion among, and interaction with, the opposing actors. In striking a balance between "occupational professionalism" and "organizational professionalism", organizations can find creative solutions to daily work issues and problems that allow them to achieve their goals and fulfill their missions.

References

Badaracco, J. (2002). *Leading Quietly.* Boston: Harvard Business School Press.

Berger, P. L. & Luckmann, T. (1966). *The Social Construction of Reality: A Treatise in the Sociology of Knowledge.* Garden City, NY: Anchor Books.

Blomgren, M. & Waks, C. (2015). Coping with contradictions: Hybrid professionals managing institutional complexity. *Journal of Professions and Organizations,* 2(1), 78–102.

Bourdieu, P. (1998). *Practical Reason: On the Theory of Action.* Stanford: Stanford University Press.

Brunsson, N. (1985). *The Irrational Organization: Irrationality as a Basis for Organizational Action and Change.* Chichester: Wiley Co.

Burt, R. (2004). Structural holes and good ideas. *The American Journal of Sociology,* 110(2), 349–399.

Choi, S. & Brommels, M. (2009). Logics of pre-merger decision-making processes: The case of Karolinska University Hospital. *Journal of Health Organization & Management,* 23(2), 240–254.

Choi, S., Holmberg, I., Löwstedt, J. & Brommels, M. (2011). Executive management in radical change: The case of the Karolinska University Hospital merger. *Scandinavian Journal of Management,* 27(1), 11–23.

Collins, J. (2001). *Good to Great: Why Some Companies Make the Leap and Others Don't.* London: Random House Business.

Döös, M. (2003). Arbetsplatsens relationik—Om långsamt kunskapande och kompetenta relationer [Workplace relations—On the slow creation of knowledge and competent relationships]. *Arbetslivsinstitutets Arbetslivsrapport,* 2003:12.

Evetts, J. (2011). A new professionalism? Challenges and opportunities. *Current Sociology,* 59(4), 406–422.

Holmberg, I. & Tyrstrup, M. (2002). Ledarskapets olika skepnader [Leadership's different guises]. In Danielsson, A. & Holmberg, I. (eds.), *Ledarskapets olika skepnader—exemplet Hallandsås.* Lund: Studentlitteratur, 185–199.

Holmberg, I. & Tyrstrup, M. (2010). Well then—What now? An everyday approach to managerial leadership. *Leadership,* 6(4), 353–372.

Knorr Cetina, K. (1999). *Epistemic Cultures.* Boston: Harvard University Press.

Leicht, K. T., Walter, T., Sainsaulieu, I., & Davies, S. (2009). New public management and new professionalism across nations and contexts. *Current sociology,* 57(4), 581–605.

Maister, D. (1993). *Managing the Professional Service Firm.* New York: Free Press Paperbacks.

Porter, M. E. & Olmsted Teisberg, E. (2006). *The Redefining of Health Care—Creating Value-Based Competition on Results.* Boston: Harvard Business School Press.

Svensson, L. G. (2006). New professionalism, trust and competence: Some conceptual remarks and empirical data. *Current Sociology,* 54(4), 579–593.

Tyrstrup, M. (2006). *On the Brink of Failure: The Art of Impromptu Action in Everyday Leadership.* Lund: Studentlitteratur.

Tyrstrup, M. & Holmberg, I. (2007). Vardagsarbetet och arbetsplatsen som forum för innovationer—Motsättning eller möjlighet? [Everyday Work and the Workspace as a Forum for Innovation—Opposition or Opportunity?] *CASL Research Paper Series,* 2007/3. Stockholm: Centre for Advanced Studies of Leadership.

Weick, K. (1969). *The Social Psychology of Organizing.* New York: McGraw-Hill.

Yukl, G. (1989). Managerial leadership: A review of theory and research. *Journal of Management,* 15(2), 251–289.

15 Organizing in the Contemporary Expert Society—Organizers, Organizing Attempts and Emerging Orders

Staffan Furusten and Andreas Werr

The main thrust of this volume has been the challenges that the contemporary expert society creates for its incumbents in terms of the need to create some kind of order among an increasing amount of more or less self-claimed experts. How do actors navigate among these experts and how do they create order among them? The foregoing chapters have provided a number of different examples of such organizing attempts aiming at (but mostly only partially succeeding in) creating order. In this final chapter, we pull together some of the lessons learned across these organizing attempts taking place on different arenas for organizing.

In Chapter 1, we developed a tentative framework for understanding the organization of the contemporary expert society. This identified three arenas on which this organizing took place—the field of expertise, the market exchange and the expert organization—and four dimensions of the organization of expertise—the (1) organizers, that undertake (2) different organizing attempts that (3) create experts and (4) expertise of different character. In the following, we will use the rich material provided in the previous chapters to fill this framework with content.

Three Arenas on Which Expertise Is Organized

We argue that the organizing of the contemporary expert society takes places on a number of different arenas. The studies in the current volume have broadly dealt with organizing on the expert field where field actors meet to demarcate new fields of expertise and order existing fields, the market exchange where buyers and sellers engage in organizing attempts to create sufficient certainty to close deals and finally on the organizational arena where experts and their managers engage in organizing attempts to reduce the ambiguity regarding employees' expertise.

We explored organizing at the *field of expertise arena* through studies of existing and emerging fields. Our investigation of organizing in existing fields of expertise took us to the management consulting industry (Chapter 2) where conflicting organizing attempts by different actors such as industry associations and large consulting firms were observed. As a contrast we also took us into the world of certification experts (Chapter 3) where more concerted organizing attempts on the filed level could be observed. To also get some images of fields under construction, we included studies of the organizing attempts in emerging fields of expertise. We covered this in three different examples—the establishment of the stock analyst as a key expert in the financial system where networking was a key activity (Chapter 4), the emergence of dedicated CSR-consultants where the productification of services offered on the market showed to be central ordering activities (Chapter 5), and the establishment of marketing consultants where specialization of different expert roles was seen as central in shaping order (Chapter 6). The organizing attempts of productification and specialization in these cases highlight the importance of negotiations between market actors as mechanisms for order creation on fields of expertise. Finally, we looked into the reorganization of expertise in terms of the establishment of counter-expertise in established fields (Chapter 7).

A second arena where the organization of expertise is salient is *the market exchange* on which buyers and suppliers need to reduce ambiguity enough to strike a deal regarding a specific supplier's expertise. The market arena is investigated in two chapters, both focusing on consulting services. In Chapter 8, we investigated how buyers of consulting services create order among potential suppliers either by emphasizing increasing transparency and applying well-defined judgment criteria to experts, or by accepting the opaque, complex and local nature of the expertise and relying on a trust-based, pragmatic and local organization of offered expertise. This second strategy is elaborated in more detail in Chapter 9 where improvisation as a way of handling local and opaque claims of trust was discussed.

Organizations represent the third arena on which we study the organization of expertise where different occupational groups (especially managers and expert employees) are involved in attempts to organize expertise within the organization. We investigated this in four chapters. One study reported on the organizing attempts undertaken by recruiters in order to motivate their expertise (Chapter 10). A second chapter focused on different expert occupations' expressions of expertise and consequential construction of occupational identity (Chapter 11). This was followed by a chapter (Chapter 12) focusing on the development environments for experts. Chapter 13 discussed the organizing attempts undertaken by managers to order the expertise of employees based on meritocracy and performance management. Finally, in Chapter 14, we studied how leadership may be a way of dealing with conflicting orders in organizations where experts are employed and where they base their performance on established professional standards while the management is emphasizing contradictory organizational goals.

Four Dimensions of Organizing Expertise

After the brief overview of the organizing of expertise on the different arenas in focus here, we will now turn to a more systematic discussion of the organizing of expertise in the different chapters. We will do this based on the framework developed in Chapter 1, identifying four dimensions of organizing expertise—organizers, organizing attempts and the expert and expertise these attempts create (see Table 15.1 for an overview).

Organizers

What kinds of actors are involved in organizing the contemporary expert society? The different examples discussed in the foregoing chapters identify a number of different actors such as professional associations, certification and accreditation bodies, individual experts, expert organizations, managers, buyers and recruiters. Not all types of organizers are present in all expert communities, but seen from a macro perspective, where we view the contemporary expert society as a phenomenon of our time, these actor categories are all examples of organizers. The different types of organizers identified when exploring expert fields such as management consulting, eco-auditing, corporate social responsibility, marketing, investment banking, recruiting, PR and communication consulting, and law do therefore not represent a complete list of all types of organizers populating the expert society. We see them instead as typical types of organizers of the contemporary expert society.

A closer look at these organizers indicates that these may be categorized into six generic categories—professional associations, expert organizations, auditors, the experts themselves, buyers and managers (Table 15.2).

Not surprisingly, *Professional associations* are key organizers in the contemporary expert society. In line with a professional logic (e.g., Larson, 1977) they, as claimed representatives of a certain category of experts, in our case management consultants, take upon themselves to create order in the field of expertise—generally with an espoused purpose of guaranteeing an ignorant client a service with a specified quality. In the current case, however, they were less successful because an alternative category of organizers—large consulting organizations—refused to support these efforts. Instead, their established brands had become an alternative guarantee of expertise thus exploiting organizational professionalism (McKenna, 2006) as an alternative organizing logic.

A second category of organizers are thus the *organizations* that deliver expert services. In line with the earlier reasoning, they share an interest in creating sufficient order to enable smooth market transactions. However, their idea of order on an expert field is more about establishing themselves as trustworthy suppliers than about creating a transparent field in which buyers may chose freely among easily comparable suppliers.

Table 15.1 Observed organizers, organizing attempts and resulting experts and expertise

	Chapter	Organizers	Organizing attempts	The organized expert	The organized expertise
Field organizing	2	Professional association Consulting organizations Individual consultants	Establishment of professional certification Active exclusion	Generally validated expert Organizationally validated expert	Transparent and standardized Opaque and organizationally standardized
	3	Certification bodies Accreditation bodies	Accreditation	Generally validated expert	Transparent and standardized
Field emergence	4	Analysts	Networking with other actors in the financial field	Recognizable experts	Relatively transparent expertise
	5	Consultants	Creation of products	Hirable specialists	Different versions of defined and commodified expertise
	6	Marketing managers and consultants	Specialization	Global specialists	Narrow expertise
	7	Professionals	Knowledge combination, formulation of explicit actionable alternative (productification), coalition building	The "moral" global expert	Transparent and eclectic; Pragmatic and useful
Market	8	Buyers of expertise	Transparent service specification Reliance on relationships	Carrier of well-defined expertise Relationship oriented specialists	Objectively assessed Opaque and local
	9	Providers of expertise	Establishing local relevance	Carrier of "useful" expertise	Pragmatic and local

Organization				
10	Recruiters	Formalization Gut feeling	Carrier of well-defined attributes Locally appropriate	Objectively assessed Opaque and local
11	Experts	Identity work	Carrier of appropriate self	Socially conform
12	Management	Hierarchical meritocracy Authorization of the fittest	Carrier of well-defined attributes Entrepreneurial performer	Objectively assessed Opaque and local
13	Management	Meritocracy Subjective selection	Carrier of well-defined attributes Subjectively appropriate	Objectively assessed Opaque and local
14	Management Experts	Managerialism "Professionalism"	Loyal organizational citizen Loyal professionals	Organizationally decided Professionally defined

Table 15.2 Organizers of the expert society

Organizer	Examples
Professional associations	Swedish association of management consultants
Expert organizations	Large consulting firms
Auditors	Certification and accreditation bodies (e.g., European Accreditation, Accreditation Services International)
Experts/professionals	Management consultants, stock analysts, recruitment experts, lawyers, accountants, economists
Buyers	Purchasers and users of management consulting services
Managers	Consulting managers, hospital manager

Auditors are a third category of actors similar to professional organizations in their ambitions to organize expertise on a field in a clear and transparent way. They, however, differ from these former in that their drivers are typically commercial, whereas the professional organizations are assumed to be primarily driven by professional interests (Abbott, 1988). As Tamm Hallström shows in Chapter 3, they may still be very effective organizers. In the field of eco-auditing certifying and accrediting, auditors create rules necessary for all to follow with ambitions of acting in the role of eco-auditor. In this case, there was no competing category of organizers challenging their ambitions for dominance. Still, within the category there can very well be auditors and auditing organizations that compete with each other in offering services for certification and accreditation. We also saw how actors within the same category of organizers can divide their efforts into actions tied together in chains of actions, or action nets (Czarniawska, 2013), where some actors can act as standardizers producing standards, others hook on and act in the role of certifiers offering services to organizations that demand the standard and pay for implementation services and certification, while yet other actors act as accreditors of the certifiers or meta accreditors of the accreditors in order to guarantee that the order decided by the standard producer is followed (Chapter 3). Thus, by specializing skills and services and building and maintaining interfaces between these specialized areas of expertise, and networks of interlinked activities, organizers contribute to the organization of particular expert communities.

The *experts* themselves are a fourth group of actors engaged in the organization of expertise. In comparison to the former groups of organizers, their organizing, however, also takes place on a micro level, ingrained with day-to-day work of establishing and maintaining their status as experts among clients and colleagues. In their daily work as experts selling and delivering their expertise, they enact both the boundaries between fields of expertise as well as the structures within these fields. Hereby, the experts contribute to a reduction of ambiguity both for themselves as well as for the potential buyers and clients of their services (Chapter 9). However, as illustrated in Chapter 7, professionals may also engage in challenging the established field order by engaging in the establishment of counter-expertise—i.e. different ways of view and approaching certain challenges. A fifth category of organizers is *buyers* of expert services in organizations. In a similar way as the experts, they have a need and interest in organizing expertise on the local level. For buyers, this need is directly related to their task of selecting a suitable expert from a potentially large number of possible providers of expertise. As was demonstrated in Chapter 8, buyers differed in relation to the scope of their organizing attempts. While some had a rather local outlook and thus narrow scope, focusing on the organization of expertise in their immediate closeness (e.g., focusing on those suppliers they had worked with before) others had a broader scope aiming a structuring expertise in a more universal way (e.g., through explicit and well-specified criteria). When making decisions on what experts to hire and what they expect them to do, buyers also contribute to organizing the interfaces between different fields of expertise. This is clearly illustrated in emerging fields such as expertise in marketing (Chapter 6) and CSR (Chapter 5), where there are ongoing negotiations between the suppliers and the buyers about what kind of expertise different actors hold. Rademaker et al. show in Chapter 6 that marketing managers in buying organizations are not considering experts from advertising agencies or media agencies as holders of more sophisticated expertise than internal marketing managers. Consequently, the power of buyers to define when someone is given the role as an expert is high.

A sixth kind of organizers, finally, are *managers* of expert organizations. A large number of the decisions they make on a daily basis are in one way or another related to organizing expertise. Strategic choices on what services to offer and how to organize the firm as well as operational decisions about who to recruit, who to reward and promote or who to staff on what project all affect the organization of expertise (see Chapters 12 and 13). Moreover, in complex expert organizations, where different types of expertise are colliding, such as in organizations in the health-care sector where the logics of professionalism and managerialism induce conflicting interests and assumptions of appropriate actions to take, leadership exercised by managers can be a core organizing power. This is discussed in detail in Chapter 14.

Previous research has to a large extent emphasized the professionals themselves and the professional organizations that represent them as the organizers of expertise, enrolling different additional actors (such as the state) in their efforts to establish and protect their expertise (Abbott, 1988). In more recent years, the organization employing experts has been identified as an additional actor involved in the reduction of uncertainty regarding expertise. Through standardization and administrative surveillance processes, organizations have been found to play an increasingly important role in organizing the contemporary expert society (Evetts, 2011). The current discussion, however, indicates that the actors involved in organizing the contemporary expert society are more diverse than formal professionals and the organizations employing them. While these are important actors, additional actors are identified, including independent auditors and accreditors as well as the buyers of expert services.

In contrast to previous research, that has mostly focused on the isolated organizing attempts of one type of actors, the current study also demonstrates that the organization of the expert society takes place in a force-field of different actors, that may pursue different interests. While, for example, the purchasing agents are driven by a desire to increase the transparency and comparability of expertise, the suppliers and users of this expertise are driven by a desire to facilitate trustful and smooth collaboration.

Organizing Attempts

The earlier categories of organizers are engaged in a number of different organizing attempts illustrated in the different chapters (see Table 15.3 for a summary). A closer look at these different organizing attempts shows that there seem to be two rather different approaches. One type of organizing attempt is based on an understanding of expertise as a globally definable and organizable entity. This kind of organizing has been the focus of previous efforts to conceptualize the organization of the expert society, such as the research focusing on the dynamics of the professions (Larson, 1977; Abbott, 1988; MacDonald, 1995; Freidson, 2001/2007). A second type of organizing attempts is based on an understanding of expertise as a rather local and contextual phenomenon. This kind of organizing attempts has, however, been much less discussed in previous research.

Table 15.3 Different organizing attempts

Organizing attempts based on an understanding of expertise as global	Organizing attempts based on an understanding of expertise as local
Auditing/certification/ accreditation	Networking, coalition building
Standardization for systematic procurement	Establishing of local relevance
Specialization	Trust
Productification	Gut feeling/ subjective selection
Classic professionalism	Identity work
Formalization	Business negotiations and deals
Knowledge combination	
Meritocracy	

Organizing Attempts Based on an Understanding of
Expertise as Global

Previous research has to a large extent focused on organizing attempts founded in an understanding of expertise as possible to define and assess in a universal and global way. In the different chapters, we find a number of different attempts made by different organizers to establish some form of transparent, global and universal order among experts. On the field level, we have seen examples of attempts to install certification and accreditation for actors fulfilling certain requirements (Chapter 3). A similar type of attempt is reflected in classical professionalism in which experts that formally meet requirements for professional conduct and attributes in terms of background will be identified as experts while those who do not meet such prerequisites are formally excluded from the professional community (Chapters 2 and 9). Such organizing attempts build on a universal logic and are supposed to make experts in a field part of one global expert community. If these attempts are successful it also means that only experts that meet these qualifications are members of the community, and those that are excluded from membership are not able to act in the expert role. That these qualifications are under constant negotiation is illustrated by the example of establishing counter-expertise in Chapter 7.

This strive for a transparent, objective and potentially universal way of organizing expertise can also be observed on the market arena where formalized and systematic procurement procedures are increasingly introduced (Chapter 8). The essence of these procedures is to define expertise in such a way that suitable suppliers can be easily identified and compared in a transparent and objective way. Hereby, competition is meant to be facilitated which in turn is believed to create lower prices and increased quality (Axelsson & Wynstra, 2002). By building on such procedures, buyers reify and manifest general and assumed transparent formal procedures for defining what needs of expert services their organizations have and what an expert should look like in order to be hired. If many organizations employ the same standard, such as in the case of public organizations that have to follow national and EU acts for public procurement when they make deals, global standardization may be the outcome.

Such efforts toward increasing the transparency of expertise could also be observed among providers in terms of their efforts to "productify" their expertise. This means that they struggle to package their services into tangible and actionable formats. As a consequence, they also strive for specialization of expert work into identifiable packages of expertise and expert services. This contributes to the creation of typologies and informal standardization in the sense that market structures emerge where categories of experts providing specific types of expert services become established over time. The cases of corporate social responsibility (Chapter 5), marketing (Chapter 6) and the establishment of counter-expertise in copyright law and financial reporting (Chapter 7) illustrate such organizing attempts.

Similar organizing attempts aiming at a transparent and explicit definition of expertise can also be found on the organizational level, where we find efforts to introduce meritocratic organizational principles that aim to clearly structure expertise of the organization's employees. In the same way in which a certification is aimed at unambiguously legitimizing an expert on a field of expertise, the meritocratic career system aims at unambiguously defining what is required of experts on different levels of the organizational career ladder.

Organizing Attempts Based on an Understanding of Expertise as Local

While the aforementioned organizing attempts are well-described in the literature under labels such as professionalism, commercialism and meritocracy, the second set of organizing attempts, building on a more local and opaque understanding of expertise, are less well discussed. Where they have been identified, they have typically been discussed as deviations from a desirable norm (e.g., "maverick buying" where local "pre-modern" criteria or expertise are prioritized before "modern" and global criteria (Giddens, 1990) or the meritocracy critique, where it has been shown that meritocracies generally fall short of their ideal (e.g., Brint, 1994; Grey, 1998).

This second set of organizing attempts builds on a rather different logic. Instead of aiming at a transparent and potentially global organization of experts, the ambition of these organizing attempts is more limited. As expertise is seen as a temporal and local accomplishment, focus is put on experts in the local context, and the experience of that expertise in interaction. Organizing attempts based on such an understanding of expertise thus mainly take place on the market and organizational arena rather than the field of expertise, although, as illustrated in Chapter 7, the establishment of a counter-expertise in an established field of expertise is dependent on the experts' ability to build coalitions with central stakeholders.

On the market exchange arena, it is illustrated how organizing attempts involve building and maintaining relationships and networks in order to build confidence that particular expert service providers are likely to be seen as appropriate suppliers of locally relevant expertise (e.g., Chapters 2, 8 and 9). The ultimate definition of a close and trustful relationship between experts and their clients is when actions from both sides can be taken based on what they both experience as gut feeling. Here, trust is the main organizing mechanism.

Buyers' efforts to build and establish relations in order to establish settings where they know who to trust for different expertise contributes to organizing, both in the local setting, seen from an organizational point of view, but also in more general field perspectives because trust building and procedures for that are institutionalized among both experts and buyers. Different experts' struggle to cultivate their respective identities as trustworthy representatives of a field of expertise (Chapter 11) further illustrate the importance of local organizing attempts.

On the organizational arena, several organizing attempts by managers are founded in an understating of expertise as local. In Chapter 12 we, for example, identified the Expert House as a common development and career context of expertise that to a large extent was based on a complex and opaque judgment of experts' ability in a local context. Furthermore, Chapter 13 illustrates how this mode of organizing expertise is also present in a claimed meritocracy, where it for some employees clashed with the claimed norms of the meritocracy.

An important role for organizations in organizing expertise is thus to select and develop the individuals they define as suitable for acting in the role of experts. Recruiters as a kind of expert have been discussed in this context in Chapter 10. These have gradually emerged into a recognizable expert community with an own expert culture. Although it still is not completely formalized, those working in the role tend to have similar backgrounds in terms of education in HRM related subjects and there are now also international standards for recruiters. Still, in making their judgments, the local context was shown to play an important role, limiting the applicability of the global standards.

This illustrates that the organizing of the contemporary expert society takes place based on two fundamentally different understandings of expertise. While previous research has mainly focused on the organizing attempts based on an understanding of expertise as global, the earlier discussion indicates that organizing attempts based on an understanding of expertise as local are at least as common and important. A number of these organizing attempts have been identified and discussed. In contrast with previous research, we do not see these as anomalies, or failures of the more global organizing attempts. Instead, we view them as alternatives, often enacted in parallel with organizing attempts based on a global logic of expertise.

Characteristics of the Organized Expert and Expertise

Given the different assumptions about the expert and her expertise underlying the two kinds of organizing attempts, these attempts produce rather different experts and expertise. Organizing attempts based on an understanding of expertise as global create generally validated experts holding transparent and standardized expertise while organizing attempts based on an understanding of expertise as local create a local and temporally validated expert holding complex, multidimensional but also opaque expertise.

The Global Expert

Attempts to organize expertise in an objective and transparent way can be observed on all arenas for organizing. On the field of expertise we have the certification and accreditation initiatives, on the market level the trend toward professional buying involving the evaluation of experts in relation to clearly specified criteria and finally, on the organizational level we observed the meritocracy clearly organizing experts and their expertise in relation to formal and transparent criteria. In common for all these attempts is that they enact an expert that is globally and objectively validated in the sense that she carries well-defined general attributes for professionalism and generally defined expertise, such as required education and documented experience. The generally approved expert represents a number of traits that are highly valued in contemporary society, such as transparent expertise, based on well-documented general and global standards. Their expertise is defined by professional associations, in prerequisites for certification, in explicit evaluation criteria on the market or in an explicit performance management and career system. This means that it is supposed to be possible to be objectively assessed for being a holder of a particular expertise. Any dimensions of expertise that are not specifically defined are deemed as irrelevant in the context and potentially problematic as they would obscure the transparency and objectivity of the organizing attempts.

The Local Expert

Organizing attempts based on an understanding of expertise as local and temporal produce an expert with rather different characteristics and expertise. Instead of being generally and globally validated they tend to be organizationally or intersubjectively validated. Thus, they are not authorized as experts because they live up to generally defined standards and are formally authorized or certified as global specialists, but because a particular organization or individual, either the organization where they are employed or organizations that hire them, or both, validate them as hirable specialists, which, as the different cases illustrate, is often based on a more opaque and holistic assessment of expertise. This means that they can be seen as carriers of what is locally established as relevant expertise in the interaction between two actors. What they do must be recognized as locally relevant and appropriate and the expertise they promote as useful. This means that one important skill they need to develop is to improvise in the sense that they are ready and prepared to adapt their performance to peculiarities in every new situation. This makes them somewhat of entrepreneurial performers.

The expertise assumed to be carried by this kind of local experts is more opaque and multifaceted and thus also less widely legitimate. Rather than being defined by a number of explicit criteria, it is about a holistic judgment of the client/manager in a specific situation of the experts' potential to create value in that situation. This judgment is often based on first-hand observations from interaction. The outcome of organizing attempts at this local level is either the establishment of trust or the failure to do so. If trust is established, the expert is validated.

Characteristics of the Achieved Order—Contested Organizing Attempts

Previously, we identified two logics for organizing attempts, each enacting a different kind of experts and expertise. So far, we have discussed them separately, but looking at the different chapters we can in most cases observe their co-existence. This suggests that rather than being based on one or the other logic, the organization of expertise in contemporary society seems to involve the interplay of organizing attempts based in opposing logics, in many cases creating challenges for both the experts and those organizing them.

One way to conceptualize the organizing going on is in terms of different and parallel organizing spirals (Czarniawska, 2013) emerging through organizing attempts creating reactions, that fuel further reactions, etc. Local organizing attempts thus initiate organizing spirals that evolve in parallel with other locally induced organizing spirals and, as discuss earlier, we often find organizing spirals based on opposing logics.

Examples of such organizing spirals can be found on all arenas. On the field arena, we can observe both examples of organizing spirals based on a global understanding of expertise as well as spirals based on a more local understanding. An example of the former is the work by e.g., professional associations to define explicit criteria for being an expert in a specific domain—which triggers the development of education programs that develop experts toward these requirements and make buyers demand a certain proof from the experts that they live up to these requirements. An example of the latter organizing spiral are the big management consulting firms actively resisting the establishment of global, transparent standards for management consulting. Instead they initiate an alternative organizing spiral where expertise is legitimized by their global brands. Here, management consulting expertise is safeguarded by the less transparent recruitment and quality assurance mechanisms of the consulting firm. This, in turn, induces buyers to rely on reputation and trust in a specific consulting organization in a purchasing situation.

Similar parallel organizing spirals can be found on the market arena. One organizing spiral is initiated by managers in need of consulting services. Driven by a desire to purchase consulting services that will "solve their problem", they apply a local definition of expertise and thus use their personal experience of different suppliers as a key means of organizing. This is reciprocated by the management consultants, which put strong efforts into building and maintaining positive personal relationships with potential clients. In parallel we have seen that purchasing professionals pursue a different organizing spiral based on a global understanding of expertise. By defining explicit and transparent requirements for expertise, they induce an adaptation among experts to present their expertise in the required and comparable terms and thus enable a purchasing process based on competition and objective evaluation rather than trust. While these organizing spirals may unfold in parallel, they are not independent of each other. In the earlier example the relationship is mainly one of contestation, where the organizing attempts based on a local understanding of expertise by its opponents are seen as problematic because of their local and opaque nature while the organizing attempts based on a global understanding of expertise by its opponents are perceived as a threat toward the expertise to be purchased as they fail to take into account the complex interplay of different skills and competencies required to create value in the specific local context.

Parallel organizing spirals based on different logics are finally also observed on the organizational arena, where we observe an increasingly strong ideal of the global expert that managers as well as the experts themselves strive to adhere to but also struggle with. As illustrated in Chapter 13, the ideal of the meritocracy as an organizing principle with its understanding of expertise as explicit and easily assessable is a strong one (as also illustrated by the Career Factory model discussed in Chapter 12) which is, however, difficult to realize in practice where organizing spirals based on more opaque and complex assessments of expertise are pursued in parallel. Also on the organizational arena we can observe how the parallel organizing spirals contest each other, creating frustration among the experts themselves. Depending on the position, this frustration is about either a perceived inability to capture the complex skill set of a successful consultant in a fair way in the performance management system designed based on an understanding of expertise as global or about the inability to the managers/experts to adhere to the principles of the meritocracy.

When organizing spirals based in different understandings of expertise evolve in parallel, tensions are thus common. In the aforementioned case, for example, managers, confronted with the purchasing agents' organizing attempts may feel restricted in their ability to hire the consultants they feel may provide them with the best services, while the purchasing professionals, confronted with the managers' organizing spiral may feel that the organization's resources are wasted as a transparent assessment and comparison of expertise is lacking. Moreover, the attempts by the experts to earn legitimacy for their business models and safe guard their organizational interests may clash with the needs the buyers have as well as the attempts by professional associations and professional purchasers to establish global standards. Against this background, we thus characterize the overall order of the contemporary expert society as a contested order (see Figure 15.1 for an illustration).

The parallel existence of organizing attempts based on a global view of expertise and such attempts based on a local understanding of expertise have long been acknowledged in the sociology of professions. For example, key to the professional logic is both a well-defined body of knowledge reflecting a global view of expertise but also the judgment of to what extent this has been acquired, which is based on a more local understanding of expertise and only

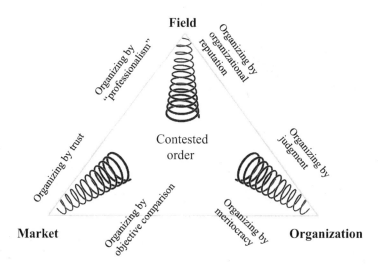

Figure 15.1 Parallel organizing spirals based on different.

possible for the professionals themselves to judge (Larson, 1977; Abbott, 1988; Freidson, 2001/2007). In these, more traditional cases, the relationship between the two organizing logics is however complementary. The contested relationship between organizing spirals based on different organizing logics, we would thus like to suggest, is a key feature of the contemporary expert society. Examples that have been discussed in the different chapters include the contestation of traditionally trust-based organizing mechanisms on the market arena by organizing mechanisms based on objective comparison and the contestation of judgment-based organizing mechanism by meritocratic organizing principles on the organizational arena.

While a detailed investigation into the drivers that create the identified features of the contemporary expert society is beyond the scope of the current chapter, we would like to suggest a possible explanation to the observed pattern. As discussed in the first chapter, the contemporary expert society contains a majority of experts that lack the basic features of "professionals" i.e. a basic organization on the field level that provides a universal guarantee of basic expertise. When such a transparent organization on the field arena is lacking, it might be argued that this lack is compensated by organizing attempts following a global logic on the market and organizational arenas thus fueling contested organizing spirals. Paradoxically, it may thus be argued that a global order on the field arena enables uncontested local organizing spirals on the market and organization arenas.

In summary, our investigation into actors' organizing of the contemporary expert society shows that there is no dominating organizing logic in the sense that there are certain organizers that, based on their attempts to organize a field of expertise, also control it. Rather, we see a co-existence of different organizing attempts, based on different understandings of expertise. In Chapter 1, we discussed professionalism as the dominating theory for how we tend to think about the organization of experts, where we, based on Freidson's (2001/2007) argument that this theory is a pipe-dream, made the point that professionalism in its classical pure form is not a representative theory for how expertise is organized in practice. Our discussion of the achieved order of the contemporary expert society supports this view. Attempts are made to implement an order of professionalism, but there are also other attempts made on the different arenas based on similar and different organizing logics. In line with the constructivist perspective taken here, focusing on organizing as an ongoing and local process, we cannot identify one organization of the contemporary expert society. Rather, order is an ongoing, local accomplishment achieved in the context of contested organizing spirals.

In a way, this is in line with what Grey (1998), Freidson (2001/2007) and others pointed out in their criticism of theories of professionalism as being based on ideological stands rather than empirical observations of the practice of professionals. They argue that professionals provide their services as employed in organizations that compete with other service providers on markets. Thus, according to them and observed in the studies included in this book, in practice the logic of organization, markets and professionalism are interlinked. Brante (2014) argues that it is rare that studies of professions theorize on such relations. Studies of hybrid professionalism give some contribution to explain how different logics are blended in organizing practice for professionals based on observations of medical doctors. So far, however, the focus has been on how professionals tend to blend in the logics of managerialism in their work, and that this tendency causes institutional change to the organization of work for professionals (e.g., Blomgren & Waks, 2015; Nordegraaf, 2015). Leaning on Freidson (2001/2007) and others, however, we claim that the observations in this volume indicate that the interplay of organizing logics is more fundamental in the construction of contemporary expertise. As discussed earlier, the different arenas of the organization and market do not represent a single organizing logic but rather different, contested logics with which organizers need to deal with and struggle. The consequences of these struggles are the focus of the final section of this chapter.

The Rise of an Expert Society Based on Ignorance

While the earlier discussion depicts the organization of the expert society as an ongoing process fueled by multiple and often contesting organizing spirals, our empirical illustrations also indicate an increasing prevalence and influence from organizing attempts based on an understanding of expertise as global. This development toward an increasing focus on transparent and non-ambiguous organizing attempts based on an understanding of expertise as global is an expression of intensified attempts from various stakeholders to organize the expert society by clarifying the borderlines between experts and non-experts in various fields in more transparent and universal ways.

What then may be the consequences of this development? One way of looking at it is that the system that gives someone legitimacy to assume and act in the expert role is becoming more sophisticated and transparent. Another way to look at it is that the individual expert gets a more regulated and limited space in which she/he can solve difficult problems. An interpretation of this may be that organizing attempts in the contemporary expert society lead to increased and decreased professionalism at the same time, all depending on what view of expertise—local or global—we apply. Without building his arguments on any particular studies, Giddens (1990) outlined a similar scenario long before the movement toward global, transparent, comparable and objective acknowledgment of expertise really took off. He argues that the pre-modern facework commitments at local levels stand against the modern global faceless abstract system. In his terms, society's movement toward modernity is a movement from trust in persons to trust in systems.

If we adhere to the view that expertise are "global", the organization of the expert society toward more general and objectively verifiable expertise means increased professionalism in an abstract faceless sense, as the system that gives legitimacy to act as an expert has more general validity. Thus, all experts in a field will be evaluated based on the same neutral criteria without interference of individual and subjective assessments. This means that more stable and mobile knowledge requirements are the base for making somebody an expert and the person who can be called an expert has expertise that is valid in more than one place, and it is possible to check the competence level of each expert against an established standard. Expertise becomes something transparent, possible to judge for those not part of the in-group, as there are clear criteria for when somebody is an expert and when somebody is not. In Giddens (1990) terms, this represents a typical system of modern orders.

There are obvious advantages with such a system. It guarantees objective and fair treatment of different expert candidates. How well they perform in relation to a global system of expertise standards makes them comparable. The one who scores best, tops the ranking lists, stands out as the best in class. It is a powerful way to distinguish experts from non-experts or the better from the worse experts because it is difficult to oppose the idea that, for example the choice of consultants should be based on systematic consideration of several different suppliers that are compared according to a few specified criteria in order to identify the best possible expertise at the best possible price.

Furthermore, this type of organizing expertise makes it simpler to distribute and demand accountability on both a general and local level. Only if we can clearly establish the difference between a good expert and a non-expert, can we make the expert accountable if she/he has not done a good job.

If we instead adhere to the view that expertise as local, manifested in experts' ability to handle and solve complex, unique problems on the basis of a complex, hard-to-define, versatile and tacit knowledge base, the increasing dominance of organizing attempts based on a view of expertise as "global" will have some more doubtful consequences. In this case, they may limit the expert's space to improvise in the specific situation and the local expertise, which is the base for this work, will be devalued. From an understanding of expertise as local, conforming to a well-defined knowledge base is not the only thing that makes somebody an expert; it is instead the ability to use this expertise to find a solution to a specific problem, and this ability is harder to describe (Schön, 1983). If we use the medical professional as an example, we do not only want our doctor to possess generally accepted expert knowledge, but we also want her/him to be able to solve difficult non-predefined problems. We want our doctor to be able to improvise in such situations with her/his knowledge and experience as reference, not as a taken-for-granted game plan that needs to be followed no matter what. Most of us do not want to be treated by someone whose walls are filled with formal diplomas but whose quality and skills are doubted by people with professional insight and local experience. Thus, completely replacing local assessment of experts with global faceless and abstract ones is not automatically a guarantee for the qualification of the best suited for the job.

In the classical expert society, local trust in the expert, based on local and professional assessments, had a tighter relation to the global logic of professionalism with local trust building and the professional system having a complementary relation, as discussed earlier. Along with increasing pressures toward global transparency and general and comparable systems for justification of expertise and experts—typical for the contemporary expert society—potential experts can no longer rely on their formal status as authorized professionals. They must continuously convince various organizers on the field, the market and the organizational arenas of the quality of their ability to handle complex challenges. As shown in the chapters of this book, this requires a great number of elusive and diffuse competencies, which are rarely included in more formal specifications of expertise. Examples of such competencies are compliance, accessibility, relevance, differentiation, certain attitudes, an ability to dress and behave professionally, an ability to cooperate, be collegial and create and maintain a supportive social climate, etc. The consequences of organizational initiatives in the expert society based on general and local knowledge perspectives have been summarized in Table 15.4.

The table shows that the ambitions to formalize expertise and organize experts on a general level, in line with the traditional meaning of professionalism, can be seen as a step toward professionalization. If we regard expertise as a local phenomenon, then the aspirations toward formalization and organization of expertise will paradoxically be a step toward

Table 15.4 The consequences of organizing attempts based on a view of knowledge as global and transparent—both professionalization and de-professionalization.

Consequences of organizing attempts based on a view of expertise as global and transparent—as seen from a global perspective on expertise	Consequences of organizing attempts based on a view of expertise as global and transparent as seen from a local perspective on expertise
Better specified limits of expertise	*Formal and general systems of expertise replace local assessment of expertise based on trust*
Convergence of various local expert systems; possibility to accumulate and diffuse expertise over time and space	*Focus on measurable and explicit manifestations of expertise at the expense of quiet and qualitative dimensions of expertise*
Standardized systems for the legitimization of expertise	*Documented expertise is prioritized at the cost of improvising solutions for local problems*
Transparency	*Adherence to procedures is given priority over local, innovative solutions to problems*
Increased possibilities to check and hold experts responsible	*Increased possibilities for professionals to rescind personal accountability and instead transfer it to "systems" and "procedures"*
Professionalization	*De-professionalization*

de-professionalization, as the focus on development of expertise is deflected from the expert's ability to solve everyday problems to instead fulfill formal requirements of expertise. This parallel development means severe restrictions on the professional person to act in her/his role as expert and handle complex situations by improvisation.

It is against this background that we may address the question how the organization of the contemporary expert society, characterized by a contested order, affects the character and nature of the contemporary expert and her expertise. Giddens expressed the risks with such scenarios (1990, pp. 108–109):

> The primacy of place in pre-modern settings has been largely destroyed by disembedding and time-space distanciation. Place has become phantasmagoric because the structures by means of which it is constituted are no longer locally organized. The local and the global, in other words, have become inextricably intertwined. Feelings of close attachment to or identification with places still persist. But these are themselves disembedded: they do not just express locally based practices and involvements but are shot through with much more distant influences.

Our discussion earlier, where formal systems make it more difficult for experts to adjust to the specific conditions of each local situation, and devalue and disqualify a lot of expertise, which cannot be contained in formal representations of expertise, shows that the effects may be not all positive. When organizing spirals based on an understanding of expertise as global gain increasing influence we can often observe a shift in the goals of the experts. It becomes more important for the recruiter to use the right recruitment model rather than finding the right person for the job; for the purchasing department to choose the consultant that best fits the sourcing criteria rather than the one that has the best knowledge and ability to solve the specific local problem; or to promote the expert who best lives up to the formal performance management system rather than the one who best solves the customer's problems.

The organization of the contemporary expert society may thus promote ignorance rather than expertise as far as local, everyday problem solving is concerned, if it does not at the same time leave space for and reward the expert's ability to improvise in order to find new solutions to local problems, and leave room and appreciation for expertise that cannot easily be included and specified in formal definitions of expertise. Without this openness the organizing attempts where those based on an understanding of expertise as global gain influence, risk making an important part of expertise—the part which makes it possible to solve complex problems in complex every-day life—invisible. If this is absent, ignorance of the problems based in reality will win, i.e. the problems that the experts with their knowledge were hired to solve. The organization of the contemporary expert society may then be described as promoting ignorance. If this is the case, there is a risk that the least controversial and challenging solution will win, where the affirmation of what already has been discovered, the already trodden paths, are rewarded, but where challenges and aspirations to discover new things, but also to further develop what has already been discovered, will be discouraged.

If we are convinced modernists, it means that continued specialization, standardization, certification and formal and global meritocratization is the only way forward in organizing fields of expertise. Society needs qualified experts to tackle present and future challenges such as increased globaliza-tion, migration and climate change. However, if organizing spirals solely based on a modern order risk to qualify ignorant experts, maybe it is time to revisit the way we tend to assess experts in contemporary society. We have shown that some core competences needed to carry out expert work are opaque and can only be assessed locally by people qualified to do it. If this is a "pre-modern" order of qualifying experts, and if pre-modernity is the order to provide society with experts qualified to do their job, maybe it is time to think of progress in less modernistic terms and as something that should be based on knowledge, not ignorance.

References

Abbott, A. (1988). *The System of Professions*. Chicago: University of Chicago Press.

Axelsson, B. & Wynstra, F. (2002). *Buying Business Services*. Chichester: Wiley.

Blomgren, M. & Waks, C. (2015). Coping with contradictions: Hybrid professionals managing institutional complexity. *Journal of Professions and Organization*, 2(1), 78–102.

Brint, S. (1994). *In an Age of Experts*. Princeton, NJ: Princeton University Press.

Czarniawska, B. (2013). Organizations as obstacles to organizing. In Robishaud, D. & Cooren, F. (eds.), *Organization and Organizing: Materiality, Agency and Discourse*. New York: Routledge, 3–22.

Evetts, J. (2011). A new professionalism? Challenges and opportunities. *Current Sociology*, 59(4), 406–422.

Freidson, E. (2001/2007). *Professionalism, the Third Logic: On the Practice of Knowledge*. Chicago: University of Chicago Press.

Giddens, A. (1990). *The Consequences of Modernity*. Stanford: Stanford University Press.

Grey, C. (1998). On being a professional in a 'Big Six' firm. *Accounting, Organization and Society*, 23(5/6), 569–587.

Larson, M. S. (1977). *The Rise of Professionalism*. Berkeley: University of California Press.

Macdonald, K. (1995). *The Sociology of the Professions*. London: Sage.

McKenna, C. D. (2006). *The World's Newest Profession. Management Consulting in the Twentieth Century*. Cambridge: Cambridge University Press.

Nordegraaf, M. (2015). Hybrid professionalism and beyond: New forms of public professionalism in changing organizational and societal contexts. *Journal of Professions and Organizations*, 2(2), 187–206.

Schön, D. (1983). *The Reflective Practitioner: How Professionals Think in Action*. New York: Basic Books.

Index